Twayne's United States Authors Series

EDITOR OF THIS VOLUME

David J. Nordloh

Indiana University, Bloomington

William Jennings Bryan

William Jennings Bryan

WILLIAM JENNINGS BRYAN

By DAVID D. ANDERSON
Michigan State University

TWAYNE PUBLISHERS
A DIVISION OF G. K. HALL & CO. BOSTON

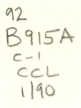
Copyright © 1981 by G. K. Hall Co.

Published in 1981 by Twayne Publishers,
A Division of G. K. Hall & Co.
All Rights Reserved

Printed on permanent/durable acid-free paper and bound
in the United States of America

Library of Congress Cataloging in Publication Data

Anderson, David D.
William Jennings Bryan.

(Twayne's United States authors series ; TUSAS 415)
Bibliography
Includes index.
1. Bryan, William Jennings, 1860–1925—Literary art.
2. Statesmen—United States—Biography.
I. Title. II. Series.
E664.B87A83   818'.409   81-1227
ISBN 0–8057–7294–4   AACR2

To
Marilyn J. Atlas,
friend, colleague, collaborator

Contents

About the Author

David D. Anderson's long interest in American literary and intellectual history and criticism has produced seventeen books, including five for Twayne, *Louis Bromfield, Brand Whitlock, Abraham Lincoln, Robert Ingersoll,* and *Woodrow Wilson,* and hundreds of articles, essays, and short stories in the *Yale Review, Mark Twain Journal, The Personalist,* and many other journals. He is currently editor of the *University College Quarterly* and *MidAmerica,* the yearbook of the Society for the Study of Midwestern Literature, which he founded in 1971.

Recipient of many awards, including the Distinguished Faculty Award from Michigan State University, where he is Professor of American Thought and Language, and the Distinguished Alumnus Award from Bowling Green State University, he was Fulbright Professor of American Literature at the University of Karachi, Pakistan, and he has lectured throughout Europe, Asia, and Australia. He is currently at work on a photobiography of Sherwood Anderson and a cultural history of the Midwest.

Preface

Few American historical figures and no prominent presidential candidates, successful or not, have been victimized by stereotypical interpretations as completely as has William Jennings Bryan. In the popular American mind his memory is dominated by two contradictory images: that of "the Boy Orator of the Platte," the youthful figure who captured the Democratic party and the party's nomination in the presidential election year of 1896, and that of the decrepit old man dominated by obsolete ideas who was thrown into confusion by the new rationalism of Clarence Darrow in the Scopes trial of 1925. Since the success of stage and film versions of what was known as "the Great Monkey Trial," the latter image has largely predominated.

All stereotypes have within them the germ of truth, and these two are not exceptions. Bryan did dominate the Democratic Convention of 1896, and he did capture his party's nomination; twenty-nine years later he was humiliated by Darrow at Dayton, Tennessee. But beyond this germ of truth, the stereotyped memory of Bryan ignores other facts that are equally dramatic and more pertinent in constructing a valid interpretation of a man whose ideas and whose eloquence in expressing those ideas were largely responsible for laying the foundations of American liberalism for our time.

However, the drama of the popular stereotype of Bryan is also Bryan's tragedy; the Scopes trial, in laying bare a fundamental lack of profundity in Bryan, particularly in the last decade of his life, has deprived him of the recognition that should be his. More than any other American political figure he provided the transition between American idealism of pre-Civil War America—that of Jefferson, Jackson, Emerson, and Thoreau—and that of an industrial America in the twentieth century, the America of Theodore Roosevelt, Woodrow Wilson, Franklin Delano Roosevelt, and of the New Frontier and Great Society as they attempted to point the way toward the twenty-first century. Bryan, like his early nineteenth-century predecessors and his twentieth-century successors, was firmly convinced that the American ideal could be made real, that it could be made so through concerted human effort; and he was determined to devote his strength and talent to that end.

Bryan's idealistic vision and his realistic determination were very much in the American tradition, in spite of the epithets applied to him by his political enemies. Neither a socialist nor an anarchist, he was instead motivated by two parallel ideological movements that gave much intellectual substance to his day and ours: the political egalitarianism of Jacksonian democracy and the moral egalitarianism of frontier evangelical fundamentalism. For Bryan, Jefferson's concept of the open society and the natural aristocracy were irrevocably modified by the frontier egalitarianism and Jacksonian deification of the common people so that his political ideology was based on the conviction that advancement in American society should be open to all. For Bryan, as for Jackson, the proper role for government was to create such a society; progress toward it should be rapid and dynamic so that continued expansion would create opportunity for all. In such a society, Bryan was convinced, all human beings would find within themselves the ability and virtue to advance, and until that society became a reality, the few in power would be able to frustrate those without it.

Bryan's concept of the nature of the common people was thoroughly imbued, too, with the philosophic view, largely inherited from Emerson and his contemporaries, that the common people—in fact, all human beings—were naturally good, and that when evil resulted from human actions, it did so because society had encouraged it through its own shortcomings. The logic that resulted was, for Bryan, inescapable: if one were to perfect humankind, one must first perfect society, and to him society was identical with the politico-economic system. His entire life, personal as well as political, was devoted to changing that structure.

Like virtually all reformers Bryan was a moralist, and his visionary perfect society would have as its foundation a perfect moral order. But Bryan's moral convictions were not the result of the impact of philosophical principles; they were derived instead from the evangelical Protestantism of the frontier, and all his life he was convinced that human beings could save themselves. But they could only do so if they were willing to acknowledge their own inclinations to evil and to expunge them. For the common people this evil was manifested in the common sins of early America, those of drunkenness, violence, and greed, all of which he condemned all his life.

But Bryan's world was infinitely more complex than the world of

Jackson, of Emerson, or of the frontier revivalists. In his own lifetime the Civil War had been fought and the slaves had been freed, but the price paid had been higher than anyone had expected: agriculture went into a decline from which it was not to recover completely during his active political life, and a new industrial oligarchy began an ascendancy that was to rule national life for the same period. The nation had become a world power, and he was to see it become an empire, the strongest in the world.

The weapons with which Bryan was to do battle with the complex forces that had come to dominate the country, to degrade the common people, and to refuse them their dignity were the principles and talent of his youth. He was neither an economist nor a philosopher, and he neither pretended nor wanted to be either. Instead he was driven by a motive that his political enemies—and many of his friends—could neither understand nor perceive. He was determined to persuade the nation that the principles upon which the country had built its independence, those phrased by Jefferson more than a century before, were neither mere rhetoric nor an abstract ideal but a valid, workable way of political, social, and economic life. Thus, at the core of what many of his contemporaries saw as radicalism was, instead, a conservatism that, in effect, spanned the national existence. Those who, even yet, remember Bryan in terms of the contradictory images of the young Bryan of 1896 and the aged Bryan of 1925 still refuse to see or understand the consistency of this inherent conservatism, not drastically different in either his political or his moral convictions, but a personal and political continuum.

Bryan's greatest talent, his most potent tool, and perhaps the source of personal faith and satisfaction was not, however, ideology or philosophy but language—in the words that, he was convinced, would move and save the nation. His faith in the power of words to convince Americans that they must reform their institutions and save themselves was manifested most clearly in the gift of oratory that he had perfected long before teleprompters and public address systems, ghostwriters and television, were available to contribute to the illusion of personal communication. Bryan's gift enabled him to speak to masses and reach individuals, a gift that, in spite of the primitive recordings of his voice still in existence, is impossible to recreate today. But Bryan's faith in language extended beyond the immediate, and the more than twenty-eight volumes of his works, the countless individual speeches published or reprinted, and the twenty-two-year files of *The Commoner,* published from 1901 to 1923, speak in his voice to friend and enemy alike.

Such a written record is greater than that of most professed writers of his time and ours, and it will be the basis of this study. In it I will examine Bryan not as political figure, but as writer and thinker, two important dimensions of the man that are all too frequently overlooked or minimized in the many political studies that have appeared in the past three quarters of a century.

Studying such a man as a writer—in effect, studying the record of an active political career of more than thirty years—cannot, of course, be accomplished through conventional literary critical or analytical techniques; Bryan's writings are, in a sense, his political and intellectual autobiography, and they will be treated as such in this study. It will not be a conventional biography of his life or career; excellent studies of both already exist. It will, insofar as the distinction is possible, be a critical biography, examining what he wrote in the effort to determine what he thought, how he expressed his thoughts, and the effectiveness with which he did so.

Such a study demands a variety of critical approaches—biographical, analytical, linguistic, textual, and psychological—and this study will employ those approaches whenever necessary in the effort to understand the man and his work. The result, I hope, will be a chapter in American literary and intellectual history too long unwritten and, at the same time, an illumination of the work and mind of a man whose tragedy it was to be a generation ahead of his time, a man who has thus far suffered the fate of the ideological and active pioneer.

DAVID D. ANDERSON

Michigan State University

Acknowledgments

For the many kinds of assistance that made this study possible, I am deeply grateful to the staffs of the Michigan State University Library, the Library of the State of Michigan, the University of Michigan Library, and the University of Iowa Library; to William Thomas and William McCann for their helpful comments; to Toni Santone for her skillful, critical typing; and as always to Pat for so many things.

Chronology

1860	William Jennings Bryan born 19 March in Salem, Illinois, the fourth child of Silas and Mariah Jennings Bryan.
1860–1870	Educated at home by his parents.
1870–1875	Attends "Old College" school in Salem.
1875–1877	Attends Whipple Academy in Jacksonville, Illinois.
1877–1881	Attends Illinois College in Jacksonville, Illinois.
1881–1883	Attends Union College of Law in Chicago. Works in law office of former Senator Lyman Trumbull. Becomes active Democrat.
1883	4 July, establishes practice in Jacksonville, Illinois.
1884	1 October, marries Mary Baird. Serves as president of the YMCA. Speaks widely for Democratic candidates. Seeks federal appointment unsuccessfully.
1885	30 September, daughter Ruth born.
1887	1 October, moves to Lincoln, Nebraska. Establishes law firm with Adolphus Talbot.
1888	Becomes active Democrat in staunchly Republican city and state. Attends Democratic national convention in St. Louis; supports Cleveland.
1889	24 June, son William born.
1890	Unsuccessfully seeks a publisher for a book on the tariff. Elected to Congress from Nebraska's First Congressional District.
1891	Stumps Ohio against McKinley.
1891–1893	Served in Congress. First major speech on tariff, 16 March 1892. Becomes principal silver supporter, opposing Cleveland.
1892	Renominated and reelected narrowly in gerrymandered district, with Populist support. Unsuccessfully seeks election to U.S. Senate by legislature.

1894   Seeks fusion of Populists and Democrats for 1896 presidential election. Fails in bid for U.S. Senate. Edits *Omaha World-Herald* to 1896.

1896   "Cross of Gold" speech in platform debate at Republican National Convention. Nominated for the presidency. Defeated by McKinley. *The First Battle* published.

1899   *Republic or Empire, The Philippine Question.*

1900   Nominated for president by Democrats and Populists. Defeated. *The Second Battle.*

1901   Founds *The Commoner.*

1901–
1904   Progressivism usurps many of his issues. Supports Alton B. Parker after his nomination. Democrats defeated.

1905–
1906   Attacks Roosevelt. Travels around the world. *British Rule in India* and *Letters to a Chinese Official*. Seeks public ownership of railroads.

1907–
1908   Lectures and travels widely. In Panic of 1907 advocates control of banks. Nominated for president by Democrats on first ballot. *The Old World and Its Ways, Under Other Flags*, and *Guaranteed Banks*. Resigns as managing editor of *The Commoner*. Worst electoral defeat.

1909–
1912   *The Prince of Peace, The Speeches of William Jennings Bryan, A Tale of Two Conventions, The Forces That Make for Peace*. Supports Wilson. Wilson elected by fewer popular votes than Bryan received in 1908. Bryan appointed secretary of state.

1914   Campaigns for Democrats. *The Making of a Man, Man, The Value of an Ideal, The Royal Art, The People's Law*. Seeks restraint and promised neutrality after outbreak of war.

1915   *Christ and His Companions*. Resigns over Wilson's strong reply to German response. *Two Addresses.*

1916   *Prohibition, Temperance.*

1917   Issues "An Appeal for Peace to the American People." Ceases pacifist action after declaration of war. *Heart to Heart Appeals, Address, America and the European War, World Peace, The First Commandment.*

1919   Supports League of Nations, seeks unsuccessfully to compromise with Lodge.

1920   Without a major issue, denied candidacy for presidency. Attempts unsuccessfully to keep League out of convention and campaign. Nominated for presidency by Prohibition party, declined. Votes for Cox but does not campaign.

1921   Attempts to convince Harding to accept League; supports disarmament. Seeks appointment to Paris Peace Conference.

1922–   Supports profarm legislation. *In His Image, Famous Fig-*
1924   *ures of the Old Testament, Orthodox Christianity Versus Modernism, Seven Questions in Dispute,* "The Menace of Darwinism." Eulogizes Harding as common man.

1924   Ailing, appeared to be presidential candidate. Supports William G. McAdoo. Charles Bryan nominated for vice-president. Campaigns for John W. Davis in West.

1925   Ill, begins preparing for 1928 election. Opposes Clarence Darrow in Scopes trial. Died 26 July. Buried in Arlington National Cemetery. *The Memoirs of William Jennings Bryan* completed by Mary Bryan.

CHAPTER 1

Origins

THE year 1860, in which William Jennings Bryan was born, was the denouement of a decade that had moved as surely as Greek tragedy. It began with a compromise that was unacceptable to abolitionist or Southerner as it admitted California to the ranks of free states and provided a federally enforced fugitive slave law. The decade passed quickly through the border war in Kansas, another attempted compromise in the Kansas-Nebraska Act, the Dred Scott decision, Harper's Ferry, and John Brown's execution; it saw the passing of Henry Clay, Daniel Webster, and John C. Calhoun, and it concluded with the election to the presidency of Lincoln, an unknown Westerner at the decade's beginning, and with, finally, the tragedy of secession. The decade saw the two major political parties in chaos and a new party born.

The year 1860 was also, for all practical purposes, the end of a period of reform, of social and economic change and expansion, that had begun with the accession of Thomas Jefferson to the presidency at the beginning of the century, thus launching the American democratic tradition and smashing for all time the concept of a limited, controlled American republic. The period between Jefferson and Lincoln brought American expansion west of the Appalachians to the Rockies and the Pacific Coast, making America a continental nation; it had seen the successful prosecution of two foreign wars and the primacy of the common people as what became known as Jacksonian democracy dominated the political life of the nation, wresting economic control from the hands of the few and giving the franchise and a measure of dignity to the many; it had seen a new, rude, energetic American psyche emerge; and it had become convinced of a peculiarly American destiny.

An American philosophy had emerged, giving a rationale and direction to the nation as Emerson taught Americans about their intrinsic worth, their share of the Godhead, and their potential for perfection. A new American theology gave Americans the opportunity to choose or reject salvation. Earnest groups of people, determined to realize the American potential for perfection, set out to make it so; they saw pacifism, temperance, care for the helpless, the reformation of offenders, and the freeing of slaves as achievable goals, and they determined to make them part of the American reality.

By 1850 the impetus toward creation of a potentially perfect society had largely become fused into one overriding issue, the abolition of slavery, an attempt resisted strongly by those who, in eighteenth-century fashion, insisted that property and individual rights were transcendent. As the 1850s began, the debate was still largely political and philosophical; as the decade proceeded, it became evident that the issue could not be resolved by political, economic, or constitutional means, and through the person of the single-minded John Brown, it became evident that the final resolution would come about by force. The nation, Lincoln had already observed, could not endure half slave and half free.

I   *Family Background*

On 19 March of the year of the American denouement, William Jennings Bryan was born in the Illinois prairie town of Salem.[1] Illinois in 1860 was a microcosm of the America of that year. The home state of Senator Stephen Douglas, who was then attempting to marshal his Democratic party and his tremendous personal and political energy to defuse the imminent explosion that threatened to destroy the nation, it was also the home state of Abraham Lincoln, a prairie lawyer on the verge of capturing the leadership of the new, antislavery Republican party. That party had not yet found an identity or program, and Lincoln was determined to give it both, at the same time saving the life of the nation.

The family into which Bryan was born was staunchly Democratic in the tradition that had descended from Jefferson and Jackson and which to Illinois Democrats was personified in Stephen Douglas. Silas Bryan was a young lawyer who had followed the democratic path to a modest success and had become active in the affairs of his party, and his wife Mariah had risen with him. By 1860, the Old Northwest of which Illinois was a part had already become the Midwest, but the frontier of the Old West had been as much a part of Silas and Mariah's background and experience as the new, stable

Midwest represented their circumstances at the time of the birth of William, their fourth child.

Silas Bryan was the descendant of Scotch-Irish immigrants who had immigrated to America in the mid-seventeenth century, settling in what was then the West—the eastern slopes of the Blue Ridge—and the family was always to look west for its fortune. Silas's grandfather fought in the Revolution, and after Silas was born in Winchester, Virginia, in 1822, his father moved west, to Point Pleasant in what was to become West Virginia, where Silas remembered the excitement and pleasure of Jackson's election to the presidency in 1828. Jackson was a Westerner, the champion of the common people, and the Hero of New Orleans, and Silas was to remain Jackson's disciple all his life.

Orphaned at twelve, Silas walked West while still in his teens, joining his brother William near Troy, Missouri, where he worked as a farmhand. Like Lincoln at about the same age, Silas determined on a career in law, and he attended McKendree College, a Baptist school in Lebanon, Illionois, one of the countless denominational institutions that flourished, however briefly, on the frontier. There he studied the classics diligently, became fond of oratory, and, after a bout with pneumonia, acquired the devout fundamental religious faith that was to direct his life.

After reading law, he moved to Salem, Illinois, where he became active in local Democratic politics. Elected county superintendent of schools, in 1852 he married Mariah Jennings, a former pupil and a devout Methodist who was a talented musician. Shortly after their marriage, Silas was elected to the Illinois state senate, where he spent the rest of that critical decade in which the political fabric of the nation seemed to disintegrate. In 1860 he was defeated for reelection, and later that year he was elected judge of the state circuit court. Judicial restraint did not mean to Silas restraint in propagating either his fundamentalist beliefs or his Democratic faith as he traveled the Illinois circuit; indeed, to Silas and to young William, as he later remembered, the law, religious devotion, and Democratic fervor seemed not merely complimentary but fused into a single comprehensive way of life.

During the first ten years of his life William remained at home, educated largely by his mother and, in court recesses, by his father. As the family fortunes improved, Silas built a substantial farm home outside of Salem. There William's education consisted of classic literature, recitation, and the activities of a typical Midwestern farm boy in the immediate post-Civil War years. Two of William's most vivid memories were hunting with his father after molding the bullets in the kitchen at dawn, and his father's pleasure at William's recitation of Silas's favorite poem, William Cullen Bryant's "To a Waterfowl," replete with the didactic morality that to the Bryan family was a basic test of literary merit. That verse remained William's favorite poem for the rest of his life.

Family dinner was at noon, and when Silas was there it was marked by biblical reading and discussion. The family went to bed at night only after further reading and discussion. With Mariah at the parlor piano, the family often sang hymns and sentimental songs of the day. But Sundays were limited to church and to hymns and the Bible. William never questioned the value of the culture he acquired at home, and the memory of the family's closeness and devotion remained with him as the ideal he would like to see become real for all Americans everywhere. From his father he learned, too, that the Democratic party, with its concern for the common people, was the instrument by which that ideal might become real.

His home life was strict, and in his *Memoirs* he recalled that he "sometimes considered the boys more fortunate who were given more liberty,"[2] but there is no evidence to suggest that he was ever disobedient or wayward. Silas was a nonsmoker and strong advocate of temperance, and William never tasted either tobacco or alcohol; before he was twelve he signed pledges to abstain from both, and those pledges were never violated. Silas hated swearing, and William never in his life, even among politicians and in the heat of political warfare, was profane. His character and his faith were permanently fixed in the first decade of his life.

II   Formal Education

At ten William was sent to school in Salem, to what was known as the "Old College" because it had once housed a girls' school. There he spent five years of diligent application to the McGuffey readers, the McGuffey and Webster spellers, and rote recitation of geography and arithmetic; at home he recited as diligently to his mother.

Perhaps his only independent decision in those years involved religious preference. Raised as both a Baptist and a Methodist, attending the former on Sunday morning and the latter in the afternoon, at fourteen, at a religious revival, he became a Presbyterian, a decision that never wavered. But denominational distinctions were minor in the rural Midwest still close to its frontier origins, particularly because each of the three faiths stressed fundamentalism, evangelicalism, and individual responsibility, and apparently his defection caused no alarm at home.

In 1872 Silas became Democratic candidate for the United States Congress and William accompanied him on many of his campaign trips through the district. Although Silas was defeated, a defeat he accepted gracefully because his Democratic faith could not question the wisdom of the electorate, the experience whetted William's interest in politics, and he announced that his ambition was "to be a lawyer and to go to Congress." The experience also taught him a great deal about the way in which defeat should be accepted. The people were not only the final authority; they were the ultimate wisdom.

At fifteen William left the "Old College" and was enrolled at Whipple Academy, an adjunct of Illinois College in Jacksonville. Admitted as a middle student, he spent two years at the academy and four at the Jacksonville college, living during the entire period with an old family friend and distant relative, Dr. Hiram K. Jones, and his wife.

Bryan's six years in Jacksonville gave him important new perspectives and provided new experiences, all building on the moral and political foundations established at home in Salem, those years reinforcing those foundations rather than altering them in any way. Dr. Jones and his wife provided firm, kindly guidance, but they provided, too, greater intellectual stimulation than Bryan had known before and more profound insights into the nature of human beings and their potential. Dr. Jones was a Transcendentalist; a friend of Emerson and Bronson Alcott, he had taught at the Concord School of Philosophy; he had read widely in the English and German romantics; and he delighted in discussing science and philosophy. Bryan later recalled that the Jones family profoundly influenced his "ideals and ideas."

At the academy Bryan pursued a rigorous classical curriculum: Latin, Greek, rhetoric, and mathematics, and with the other students he was allowed to participate in the literary or, more properly, debate and speaking societies in the college. He joined Sigma Pi, and he spoke at every opportunity. During his first year he entered the annual declamation contest. Failing, however, to place, he determined to improve. When he entered again the following year he expected to win, but, speaking on the topic "The Palmetto and the Pine," he placed third. Disappointed, he worked at his delivery, particularly his diction, even at one point emulating Demosthenes by practicing with pebbles in his mouth.

Although his record at the academy was apparently undistinguished, he was well prepared for work at the college. Relationships between the schools and curricula were close, and he continued his classic studies: Latin for three years, Greek for four, mathematics through trigonometry, rhetoric, and a year of German. His science courses included physics, chemistry, geology, and astronomy, and—innovatively for the time—in his senior year he studied economics, political science, and American history as well as the traditional principles of Christianity.

Although he recalled that he enjoyed the logic inherent in mathematics, his best performance and perhaps his most valuable study for the future was the rhetoric curriculum. Classic in nature, it stressed composition and logic as well as public speaking. It was taught by Professor S.S. Hamill, to whom Bryan credited much of the training that permitted him to make the most of his natural gifts. A regular speaker at college events, he continued the development that had begun at Whipple, in his first year winning second prize in the annual contest. Representing Jacksonville in a contest at Galesburg, he was runner-up in the standings, and in his senior year he placed second in a contest at Monmouth, although reports of the occasion insisted that he should have been first.

In retrospect, the substance of Bryan's collegiate speeches was much less significant than the skill that he had learned to employ effectively. Invariably idealistic, his speeches exhorted their listeners to do the right thing because it was right, a principle that he was not to neglect in later years, even when it might have been politically more expedient to do so. His delivery, however, according to contemporary accounts, was masterly; his presence was calm, confident, and controlled; his enunciation and modulation were firm and clear; his manner and gestures were natural; his voice was resonant and powerful. These techniques, the product of practice as well as natural talent, were as important in undergraduate exercises as they were to be on the political stump. College students, like their elders, are quick to spot artificiality or theatricality, and they found neither in Bryan.

In the classroom Bryan discovered two books that he remembered as profoundly influential and to which he returned on occasion later in life. These were George Bancroft's *History of the United States* and Alexis de Tocqueville's *Democracy in America*. The former not only reinforced his Democratic faith in Andrew Jackson and in the common people, but, together with de Tocqueville, provided philosophical substance and perspective that his political education had thus far neglected. The latter work, more than any other, made clear to him the eternal enmity between democracy, equality, and liberty on the one hand and political privilege on the other.

Continuing his preoccupation with Democratic politics during his years in Jacksonville, Bryan attended the party's national convention in St. Louis in 1876, watching as Samuel J. Tilden was nominated for what was to be the tragic, contested centennial election, and in 1880 he resolved to campaign actively for Winfield Scott Hancock for the presidency. In that campaign he was apparently asked to make his first political speech (although a family tradition insists that he had earlier spoken on behalf of his father's campaign for Congress). But Bryan's audience did not materialize, and he did not speak.

Two important personal events characterized his years at college in Jacksonville. The first was his meeting with eighteen-year-old Mary Baird, who was to become his wife five years later, and the second was the death of his father. Mary was attending Jacksonville Female Academy; Bryan, at nineteen, met her at a social function and fell completely in love. Apparently she was not as stricken at first, but Bryan immediately embarked on a sustained courtship that strained and on several occasions broke the proprieties of Midwestern Victorian convention. Although Bryan attempted to assume full blame for the transgressions, the principal of the academy suspended Mary for the remainder of the year. They exchanged rings and letters, and upon Mary's return to Jacksonville in the fall, they determined to be married as soon as Bryan could support a wife. That Thanksgiving, Bryan met Mary's father, and in scrupulous attention to the proprieties, asked for Mary's hand in marriage. Bryan charmed Mr. Baird and won his consent.

In the spring of 1880 Silas Bryan came to Jacksonville to secure treatment from Dr. Jones for his recurring diabetes and to meet Mary, with careful attention to the proprieties, at tea at the Joneses. But the day before the meeting he suffered a stroke, and he died the next day without meeting the woman who was to prove such a significant asset to William's career.

Other experiences during Bryan's college years were also of

personal importance. At one point, torn by the discussions of
evolution among the undergraduates and at Dr. Jones's house as
well, he underwent a period of troubled faith, perhaps even a crisis.
Reconciliation of the story of creation in Genesis with the implications of Darwinism proved impossible, and he apparently found
himself attracted to the latter, at least for a time. He wrote to Robert
Ingersoll in the search for clarification, but he received only a brief
reply from a secretary. Years later he recalled the episode, attribut-
ing his doubts to the adolescent tendency to become overconfident
of one's intellectual powers. But he put the doubts aside, became a
devout member of the Jacksonville Presbyterian Church, and never
again questioned the literal truth of God's word.

Perhaps less emotionally trying but of unquestioned importance
in his later attitude toward blacks as members of the commonality
of the human race was the general attitude of liberalism that
prevailed at the college. Founded by New Englanders, it had a long
tradition of abolitionist and Negro advancement sympathies; its
president at one time had been Edward Beecher, son of Lyman
Beecher and a friend of Elijah P. Lovejoy. After witnessing Lovejoy's murder and the destruction of his press, Beecher impressed
upon the college a firm dedication to freedom of speech and the
press and to black advancement. Although Bryan had heard little of
slavery, abolition, or black rights in his traditional Democratic
home, he never wavered in his search for black support or his
dedication to black rights, at times at the expense of alienating some
of his fellow Democrats.

III   *Valedictory Address*

Bryan ended his college career at the head of his class. As
valedictorian, he spoke on "Character," an address that in many
ways defined his concept of the nature of human life, of society, and
even of the universe as he saw it at twenty-one and as he was to
believe it to be all his life. His moral upbringing, his transcendental
attitude toward human beings, and his political and social convictions all taught him that life was characterized by a struggle
between the forces of good and evil, and that much of that struggle
took place within the individual. "Character," then, was the ability
to accept eternal principles, to live by them, and to choose alternate
courses of action on their bases. The struggle, he concluded, was
eternal, but must be waged with strength, wisdom, and virtue.

In beginning his valedictory, Bryan sets the tone and defines the theme with a technique that he was to use many times in the future, particularly on the Chautauqua circuit: he introduces an analogy, seemingly unrelated at first, which permits him to move quickly to the substance of the lecture:

> It is said of the ermine that it will suffer capture rather than allow pollution to touch its glossy coat, but take away that coat and the animal is worthless.
>
> We have ermines in higher life—those who love display. The desire to seem, rather than to be, is one of the faults which our age, as well as other ages, must deplore.
>
> Appearance too often takes the place of reality—the stamp of the coin is there, and the glitter of the gold, but, after all, it is but a worthless wash. Sham is carried into every department of life, and we are being corrupted by show and surface. We are too apt to judge people by what they have, rather than by what they are; we have too few Hamlets who are bold enough to proclaim, "I know not 'seems.' "
>
> The counterfeit, however, only proves the value of the coin, and, altho reputation may in some degree be taking the place of character, yet the latter has lost none of its worth, and, now, as of old, is a priceless gem, whenever found. . . .[3]

After setting forth his basic premise, as he was to do consistently on other occasions, Bryan then marshalls evidence, pro and con, to amplify and support his point, expressed in terms that he was to adapt to other moral issues as well as political and economic controversies in the future. To Bryan, the basic problem involves penetrating the appearance of language and life and finding the reality beyond them. Perhaps reflecting his passing attraction for Darwinism a short time before, he defines a general and not uncommon experience:

> Have you not listened to those whose eloquence dazzled, whose pretended earnestness enkindled in you an enthusiasm equal to their own, and yet, have you not felt that behind all this there was lurking a monster that repelled the admiration which their genius attracted? . . . That something is want of character, or, to speak more truly, the possession of bad character, and it shows itself alike in nations and individuals. (S, 2:374)

Bryan then cites examples of persuasiveness combined with lack of character: Eschines, who attracted listeners, but was simply "the hireling of Philip"; Napoleon, whose thousands of followers failed to see that "Talent, genius, power, these he had—character he had none." And without naming them, he describes those (though clearly he has men like George Washington and Abraham Lincoln in mind) who "formed a character whose foundations were laid broad and deep in the purest truths of morality—a character which stood unshaken amid the terrors of war and the tranquility of peace: a character which allowed neither cowardice upon the battlefield nor tyranny in the presidential chair" (S, 2:376).

But for Bryan, character, good or bad, is neither fixed nor the result of a decision made by some whimsical fate. True to his democratic principles, he identifies it as a matter of individual choice, conscious effort, and a determination to grow:

> But if each day we gather some new truths, plant ourselves more firmly upon principles which are eternal, guard every thought and action, that it may be pure, and conform our lives more nearly to that Perfect Model, we shall form a character that will be a fit background on which to paint the noblest deeds and the grandest intellectual and moral achievements; a character that cannot be concealed, but which will bring success in this life and form the best preparation for that which is beyond. (S, 2:377)

The "Perfect Model" is, of course, Christ, and Bryan would use the analogy again in the future; for him Christ was a model against which human achievement, including his own, must always be measured, and the results, he was and would remain convinced, would always be evident:

> Character is the entity, the individuality, of the person, shining from every window of the soul, either as a beam of purity, or as a clouded ray that betrays the impurity within. The contest between light and darkness, right and wrong, goes on; day by day, hour by hour, moment by moment, our characters are being formed, and this is the all-important question, which comes to us in accents ever growing fainter as we journey from the cradle to the grave, "Shall those characters be good or bad?" (S, 2:378)

Bryan's ending is conventional for the circumstances: tributes to the faculty for developing "character not less than intellect"; a farewell to his classmates that refuses to be final; an invocation of the message of "the poet"; and a "last, long, lingering look" at "Halls of learning, fond Alma Mater," before the movement into the future.

Bryan's valedictory message has much in common with the

thousands of similar speeches that have marked commencement
ceremonies the country over, before and since. But for Bryan it was
neither an exercise in oratory nor a mark of a stage of development
of a young, reasonably bright graduate from a provincial college. It
was a statement of faith that was to provide the philosophical
foundations of his every decision and pronouncement for the rest of
his life.

It is possible to criticize the oration from many perspectives,
particularly that of the more sophisticated age of a century later: it
is simplistic, sophomoric, naive; it betrays no recognition of the
complexity of people, issues, or choices; it accepts without question
moral maxims of the age. But it was and remains a clear insight into
Bryan's world view as it was to be reflected in the great issues that
he faced and judged for the rest of his life. There is a choice on
every issue, he maintained, a choice between right and wrong, good
and evil. The moral person is obligated to make a choice on moral
principles and then to support it, no matter what the cost.

Upon his graduation, Bryan planned to go to the Union College
of Law in Chicago, secure his diploma after completing the two-
year curriculum, and then go into practice so that he and Mary
might be married. His father's ambition for William had been
considerably grander: he would go to Oxford University in England
for a year, and Silas had been fattening thirty steers so that they
might be sold to finance William's education abroad. But at Silas's
death it was discovered that he had signed a $15,000 note for a
friend who defaulted payment. The family made good the debt at
the expense of William's Oxford fund, and it even became doubtful
that he could enter law school if his younger brother Russell were to
go to college. But Russell died in August 1880, and the family had
sufficient money to allow William to go to Chicago on an extremely
meager budget.

IV   The Law and the City

The Union College of Law, sponsored jointly by Northwestern
University and the old University of Chicago, was a small institution
housed in a four-room suite on Dearborn Street. Its limited curriculum emphasized torts, pleadings, criminal law, patents, contracts,
equity, and jurisprudence. Bryan worked hard and received good
grades, particularly enjoying the Socratic dialogues examining specific cases in the classroom as well as his work in constitutional law.

He participated in debates and enjoyed public speaking in the school's literary society.

As in Jacksonville, experiences outside the classroom were perhaps as significant to his development as those inside. His debates and declamations focused on such topics as the tariff, prohibition, imperialism, and women's suffrage, and in them he emphasized many positions that were to be his for the rest of his life. He learned, too, about the nature of city life and city politics, noting much the same political and economic privation suffered by the city worker that he had seen on the farm; and he recognized the source of those abuses in exploitation, corruption, and indifference.

Most important was his experience as a part-time law clerk in the office of Lyman Trumbull, an old family friend and former United States senator who had broken with the Democrats over slavery, supported Lincoln, and won election as a Republican. In the Senate he drafted the Thirteenth Amendment, but again put principle over party in voting against the impeachment of Andrew Johnson at the expense of his security in office. In political eclipse, he fought the growing economic power of business and taught Bryan much about the exploitation of workers by the great corporations and trusts, which Bryan witnessed at firsthand in the car shops in nearby Pullman. These shops were later to be the scene of one of the country's greatest and most tragic strikes, during which Bryan was to support the workers and their union.

Bryan learned, too, much of the practical nature of party politics in Chicago. The industrialists and the bankers were invariably Republicans, and the party served them well. But the Democrats, the opposition party, were no better, and in Cook County the ruling Democratic machine under Mayor Carter Harrison was particularly corrupt. Perhaps the seeds of his determination to reform his party in his image and of his lifelong opposition to Eastern "Gold" Democrats were planted in Chicago. Certainly his experience there had much to do with his future break with President Cleveland, his party's only president since James Buchanan.

The Chicago years were exciting, stimulating, and intellectually profitable, but Bryan and Mary were torn by the enforced separation, and as his graduation neared they planned to marry as soon as he established a practice. Intrigued by the idea of moving West, where he might grow with a new country, he visited Troy and Kansas City, Missouri, in the summer of 1882; but the former was too small and settled and the latter too large, with little opportunity for an inexperienced young lawyer to establish himself. After consulting with Mary, with his mother, and with Dr. Jones, he decided to return to Jacksonville. There his friends would open doors for him, and in a stable, orderly community he would become a success. At the time, that meant earning $500 a year, the amount he had set as a minimum for marriage.

CHAPTER 2

Politics or the Law?

O N 4 July 1883, Bryan hung his shingle in Jacksonville, literally
nailing a sign that read "W. J. Bryan, Lawyer" to the door of
his new office. Largely through the influence of Dr. Jones and on
the basis of his excellent reputation from the college in Jacksonville,
he had become a member of an established firm, Brown, Kirby, and
Russell. Although he was well thought of in the firm, his position as
the newest, youngest lawyer meant that he was literally as well as
metaphorically peripheral.

Bryan's office was on the first floor of the firm's building; its main
office was on the second. But he managed to greet most of the firm's
visitors, and apparently some of the business—largely the collection
of debts—remained on the first floor. His first month's fees totaled
$9.60. But in November, together with another lawyer, he took his
first case, of assault, to court and made his first speech to a jury.
Although he admitted his fright, he apparently did well.

But he remained dissatisfied in Jacksonville and dreamed of going
west, at one point briefly considering joining his friend and law
school classmate Henry Trumbull in Albuquerque, New Mexico.
But his practice, primarily collections, improved, in one case paying
him $200, and he settled down to what appeared to be a career in
the petty litigation of a small Midwestern town. In 1884 he acquired
the degree of master of arts from Jacksonville by giving a speech on
"The American Citizen." That summer he managed to attend the
Democratic National Convention in Chicago.

He and Mary decided to marry in the fall, and he borrowed
money against his expected inheritance from his mother and from
Dr. Jones to build a house. On 1 October 1884 the couple were wed
in her parent's home in nearby Perry, and after a honeymoon in St.
Louis, both went back to their premarital residences until the new
house was completed in November.

In 1884 Bryan earned $700, in 1885, $1,000, and in 1885, nearly $1,500 through a variety of means, including continued debt collection, selling real estate and books, and acting as a rental agent. But even the birth of his first child, Ruth, on 30 September 1885, did not satisfy him with his lot. His heart was in politics and the West.

Nor was Mary satisfied in her role as housekeeper, mother, and wife of a small-town lawyer. While she began to take courses at Jacksonville College, a rather daring act in the town, Bryan studied the issues that concerned him—railroad control, the tariff, and economic problems—and continued to serve the local Democratic party faithfully, speaking at every opportunity and enjoying himself tremendously. He also supported the temperance cause in the town with enthusiasm. In both cases he saw himself aligned with the forces of good in the battle against evil.

Early in 1887, however, he felt that four years in Jacksonville were enough; not only had he not been nominated for local or county office, but even if he had, the predominant Republicans would have continued to win, as they had consistently for twenty years. With Grover Cleveland's accession to the White House, Bryan sought federal appointment, first as assistant district attorney for Southern Illinois, and then to any suitable position in Washington; he was ignored in both cases.

I The West

It was evident to Bryan that the frontier dynamism that permitted the political mobility he longed for had left Illinois far behind, and again he sought the opportunity to move, first, unsuccessfully, to Minneapolis. Then in the summer of 1887 came a stroke of good fortune. He was asked to go to Kansas to collect interest overdue on notes held by Jacksonville College, and he combined the trip with an inspection of property in Iowa owned by his father-in-law. As part of the journey he visited a law school classmate, Adolphus Talbot, in Lincoln, Nebraska, for a long weekend.

Apparently it was the busiest of weekends. Not only did he and Talbot dream up an ideal partnership—Talbot a Republican and Bryan a Democrat—but the editor of a weekly paper offered him the opportunity to write a regular column. Nebraska was as solidly Republican as Illinois, but it was West and the frontier was still a reality. Bryan returned to Jacksonville with Nebraska fever.

Mary's reaction to Bryan's enthusiasm was typical of that which was to prevail until his death nearly forty years later: "If you think that a change is for the best, I am willing to go," she told him, and he began immediately to make plans. He was to go to Lincoln, arrange for temporary housing until a house could be built, and begin his practice with Talbot. He arranged his travel so that he would arrive in Lincoln on 1 October 1887, his third wedding anniversary and a date he was later to use as often as possible for beginning a new enterprise. In Lincoln he found that a new law practice there was not decidedly different from his experience in Jacksonville; Talbot's practice, other than his sporadic work for local interests of the Union Pacific Railroad, was small, and Bryan's was smaller. Between his arrival and his return to Jacksonville in December to sell the house there, he earned $82.25, and he slept on a cot in his office to minimize expenses.

But Bryan's unfailing optimism was justified. On his return to Lincoln, supported by a loan from his father-in-law, he contracted for a house to be completed by June; he and Talbot, the law firm of Talbot and Bryan, engaged a suite of offices, and the practice began to develop, largely, at first the trivia of debt collection that had disillusioned him in Jacksonville, but increasingly the legal work inherent in constructing an orderly society in what had so recently been the frontier. Still, although Bryan's cases were occasionally exciting—appearances before the State Supreme Court, constitutional issues, and jury trials—the firm remained one among many small firms of young lawyers seeking to grow with the country. In Nebraska, Bryan knew, the race would go to the competent, and he was confident of his abilities; nevertheless, he earned only $800 during 1888.

Early in June the Bryans, together with Mary's parents, who had decided to live with them in Nebraska, moved into the new house in Lincoln, and both Bryan and Mary began to take part in the life of the community. Together they became active in the Presbyterian Church and in its Sunday School; Mary was instrumental in founding Sorosis, a discussion group for women; and Bryan was a founder of the Round Table, a similar group for men. Although both groups stressed that discussions would focus upon philosophy, religion, literature, science, and politics, it appears that politics soon became the primary topic in both. In addition, Bryan became active in the YMCA, often lecturing there as well as in nearby churches on moral and religious topics, and he joined local chapters of virtually every civic group in Lincoln: the Chamber of Commerce, Rotary, Elks, Moose, Masons, Odd Fellows, Knights of Pythias, and others. Although many of his memberships must have been little more than nominal, he regarded their ideals with much enthusiasm, and he was frequently called upon to speak upon brotherhood and service, to him the greatest ends of a civilized society.

II *Political Apprenticeship*

He was equally active in Democratic politics. Although Nebraska was more solidly Republican than Illinois, boasting a record of almost continuous Republican electoral victories since statehood in 1867 and without the tradition of a Stephen Douglas to give the Democrats hope or heart, Bryan found a small, active, but split party, both factions of which were eager to welcome the young, talented, energetic newcomer to their cause. Whereas in Illinois he had been one among many young aspirants to political influence in the Democratic party, in Nebraska he found what he had been seeking: a party that needed him.

His first important contact was with J. Sterling Morton, acknowledged as the leading Democrat in the state and destined to play an important part in Bryan's rise to influence. Morton, formerly publisher of the *Nebraska City News*, was wealthy; he was a noted agronomist and founder of Arbor Day; and he was conservative—sharing, however, Bryan's abhorrence of the protective tariff. Morton welcomed the young Bryan to his imposing home to observe Arbor Day and to discuss his future in the politics of the state.

Impressed, as was Morton with him, Bryan allied himself with the Morton wing of the party, the so-called "Slaughterhouse Democrats," in what was to prove an important decision. Although the other wing, the "Packinghouse Democrats," led by Dr. George L. Miller, was close to the Cleveland administration, enjoying for their labors the bulk of Nebraska's share of political patronage, Morton's faction was firmly in control of the party within the state. He had been the party's unsuccessful nominee for the governorship in 1880, 1882, and 1884, and the consensus of the political leadership in both factions was that any nomination for office was his for the asking.

Although there is no contemporary evidence to suggest it, Bryan must have been aware that both factions were conservative, and that in a state dominated by agriculture, with the bulk of the electorate small farmers, neither faction was interested in reform. The Nebraska farmers suffered from isolation, poor communications, and hard work, as did farmers everywhere, but their lot epitomized too the problems of overproduction and tight money that had intensified since the Civil War and particularly since the Panic of 1873. They had become the victims of an economic system that few of them could understand or articulate and none could control. Nevertheless, the problems were familiar to Bryan, and he must have seen the indifference of the party leadership to them at once. Tariff reform, the farmers acknowledged, was essential, but so too was reform in other areas: overextended land holdings, high interest rates, decreasing prices for corn and other commodities, high railroad rates. The Burlington, the Northwestern, and the Union Pacific railroads dominated the economy of the state and the leadership of both parties, thus effectively denying the rural electorate a voice and a means of redress.

This year 1888 was characterized by continuous political success for Bryan. In April, as a delegate to the Lancaster County convention, he supported Morton's successful bid for control, and as a result he was elected a delegate to the state convention. There, in a speech firmly rooted in the traditional Democratic ground of the tariff, he impressed both factions of the party. Not only did it meet Morton's wholehearted approval, but his effectiveness became evident to the party at large, and he later remembered it as a major indication that his ambition for power and prestige might be achieved, largely "thru the power of speech" that he had cultivated so carefully. Indeed, the speech may have been more important in determining Bryan's future than the "Cross of Gold" speech is reputed to be in Bryan folklore. The young orator was, according to one perceptive account, "rocked in a cradle of hickory"; he became "Bryan the Invincible"[1] to sympathetic newsmen. At Morton's insistence he was offered the nomination for lieutenant governor or for attorney general, both of which he refused, publicly because he could not afford to run, but more importantly, because he knew that defeat would be inevitable. Never, in spite of frequent insistence from Nebraska Democrats, was he to be a candidate for state office.

With Morton the nominee for Congress in the first district for the third time, Bryan, at Morton's request, spoke throughout the district, largely on the tariff, for Morton and for Cleveland's reelection. Important to his future, he spoke to and for the farmer. The protective tariff, it was clear to Bryan and increasingly clear to his audience, was robbing the farmers in order to enrich the industrialists, and it could not continue. Accounts of the speeches, written by Bryan himself, were featured in the *Omaha Daily World Herald*, and he was rapidly becoming the best known young Democrat in the state.

That fall, while on legal business in Chadron in northwestern Nebraska, he learned, almost mystically, of the power inherent in his voice, his delivery, and his ideas. Attending a rally at nearby Gordon with Chadron friends, he offered to speak when the featured speaker did not arrive. One friend, James C. Dahlman, described the event: "We had never heard such oratory before in northwestern Nebraska. For two hours, Mr. Bryan held that crowd enthralled. When he closed, because he had to catch a train, the crowd yelled for him to continue. I believe they would have listened all night." [2]

After reaching home at dawn, Bryan awakened Mary, and, sitting on the edge of the bed, told her, ". . . I have had a strange experience. Last night I found that I have power over the audience. I could move them as I chose. I have more than usual power as a speaker. I know it. God grant that I may use it wisely." [3] Humbled and excited, he began to pray.

As was foreseen, Morton was defeated in the election, but Bryan was disappointed at Cleveland's loss in the electoral college. Further, although Morton had recommended Bryan for membership on the state railroad commission, he was rejected by the Republican-controlled legislature. Even so, perhaps inspired by his own oratorical success, Bryan wrote to his party's lame-duck president, suggesting that Cleveland move to Nebraska and run again in 1892: "As a Western man with friends you have in the East, we can elect you. Why not come to Omaha or Lincoln." [4] There is no record of a reply.

It may have been at this time that Bryan told his wife that in 1890 he could not only win the nomination for Congress in the first district but that he could go on to win the election. Mary was skeptical; not only was he still a newcomer to a state where the nomination had always gone to an estabished politician, but election of a Democrat in the district was impossible. She advised him to wait until he could afford the luxury of such indulgence.

Nevertheless, it is evident that Bryan began to think in terms of 1890 almost immediately after the campaign of 1888, perhaps even during that long train ride from Chadron back to Lincoln, and his actions between the election of 1888 and the spring of 1890 were without question those of an active candidate. Although he returned to his neglected law practice, augmented by increased work as a result of his new prominence, and he and Mary continued their active social and intellectual life, Bryan began to talk of his possible candidacy with Democratic leaders as early as the spring of 1889. During the interlude Mary completed her law studies and was admitted to the Nebraska bar; William Jennings Bryan, Jr., was born on 24 June 1889; and Bryan continued his study of the tariff problem, at one point unsuccessfully soliciting a New York publisher for a contract to write a book on the subject.

His political prominence moved further toward the accession of power when Morton, in charge of the platform committee for the state convention, asked Bryan to assist in writing the tariff, prohibition, and pension planks, in each case focusing primarily on correcting state abuses through special legislation. The tariff plank was easily agreed upon: the protective tariff was condemned as detrimental to agriculture in the state. But Morton and Bryan disagreed on the prohibition plank. Although both were prohibitionists, Morton favored a strong prohibition plank, but Bryan, aware of the possibility that it might offend Democratic voters, did not, suggesting instead a compromise on the issue, as he was to do again in the future. The platform was well received, and Bryan spoke eloquently in its favor. However, the Republicans swept the state in the fall, except for Douglas County in the first district, and Democratic promises were unimportant.

Although Bryan devoted much of his time and energy to legal and family affairs during 1889, at some time during the year, certainly no later than just after the fall campaign and perhaps as early as the spring of that year, he had made up his mind to become an active candidate for the congressional nomination. He was twenty-nine years old, married, with a growing family; he was personable, honest, and willing to work; he was a devout church member, a prohibitionist but not a fanatic, and an effective campaigner. His eloquence had already become almost legendary in the district, the state, and increasingly the region. He was sound on the tariff, he worked well with the party leadership, and he was popular with farmers. As 1890 began, it was evident that, with increased rural unrest, a new, fresh, popular candidate might be able to succeed where Morton and others failed. In February party leaders formally but secretly offered him the nomination.

At twenty-nine Bryan's intellectual and philosophic convictions were firmly rooted in the political and religious traditions of his youth, and they were to remain fixed for the rest of his life.

Philosophically he was a Jeffersonian, believing firmly in the tenets of an open society, education, and the democratic process as the means by which individual and collective progress could be made toward a perfect American society; he believed, too, that government was a convenience, designed to aid the individual and the nation in that progress, and he believed in the fundamental equality and wisdom of human beings. He believed in fair, open competition in a society that permitted and encouraged it, and he believed that in such a society, preferably agricultural, natural, virtuous leaders would emerge. His ideology and his personal convictions were clearly of the eighteenth century, and they would not change.

But by temperament he was most clearly a man of the nineteenth century, nurtured on the practical, often pragmatic doctrines of the frontier. He believed in Jefferson's political philosophy, but he knew, too, like Jackson, that only concerted action could make that ideal a reality. He knew that political systems, however idealistically conceived, were imperfect institutions and that if people were to be free to pursue their happiness and fulfillment, the institutions must first be improved, just as he believed in the perfectability of the institutions people had created and of which they had lost full control.

By instinct he was a reformer, primarily of political institutions but also of individuals, yet personally and temperamentally he abhorred revolution. Change, if it were to occur, would only be acceptable to him as an expression of the popular will. As the nominating convention of 1890 approached, he had made himself clear on two major issues, the tariff and prohibition, both of which suggest the basis upon which his political judgments would rest throughout his career. The protective tariff was, he was convinced, class legislation passed for the benefit of an industrial minority at the expense of the majority, and it was morally wrong, to be opposed regardless of political cost. Conversely, the prohibition issue was a matter of personal rather than political morality; it demanded education rather than legislation. Only much later, when the popular will indicated its desirability, did he support prohibition by legislation. To the end of his life, he attempted to distinguish between political and personal morality and to conduct his life and his campaigns accordingly. Never did he advocate breaking the law, however often he advocated its change.

There was much that Bryan had yet to learn, and he devoted a good deal of time to self-education during the months before the convention of 1890, as he was to do in relatively quiet moments in the future. He had not yet expressed himself clearly on other pressing issues: the trusts, the railroads, currency reform, and others, all of which were issues becoming increasingly important. His vision was Western and rural rather than national, as was much of the impulse that provided the impetus toward political reform in the late nineteenth century; but he was to learn a great deal about the East and the cities—learn, indeed that the gulf between them was narrower than he thought. He was insular, he was convinced of a peculiar American destiny, and he had not yet come to grips with the greater issues of peace and war that were to prove painful to the party and the nation in the future.

But by 1890 Bryan had prepared himself for a political career more completely than most of his generation; he knew that the times required change, and he felt that he was equipped to determine its course. The passing of the geographic frontier demanded a new economic, political, and social frontier, and he believed that he knew the direction in which it could be found. He was to be called a revolutionary, a radical, a socialist, and worse, but in 1890 he was and he remained a conservative who sought to return in reality to an older ideal, a course of action from which he never faltered.

CHAPTER 3

To Congress and Beyond

ON 30 July 1890, William Jennings Bryan received his party's nomination for Congress in the first district, and in November he was elected for a two-year term in the Fifty-second Congress, to take office the following fall. Although he had been offered the nomination as early as February 1890, he had then accepted only conditionally; at the time his path to the nomination in the months prior to the convention was as uncertain as the path to his election.

Within the party Morton could have had the nomination again had he chosen to claim it, and Charles W. Brown of Omaha was put forward by an active faction. But Morton chose not to run. Bryan wrote to Brown to ask him his plans, making a statement in the letter that was to be repeated many times in the future: "I have told [my supporters] that the interest of the party is above the interest of anyone."[1] Brown pledged his support to Bryan, but even so it seemed evident to most Nebraskans well before the election that Bryan would have the opportunity to suffer defeat at the hands of the incumbent Republican, William J. Connell, a strong supporter of the protective tariff.

Of immediate danger to Bryan's hopes was the changing political structure in Nebraska, resulting from what has come to be called the Populist revolt, a movement that he was to learn to use to his own advantage. Its origins were in the farmers' movements that began in the 1870s, particularly the Grangers, essentially local and state action groups, and the Farmers' Alliance organizations which moved toward concerted political action. Rural activism began in Nebraska and throughout the agricultural South and West in the late 1880s, and by 1890 it had taken on the proportions of an economic-based third-party movement.

In Nebraska, as in other states of the agricultural West, the farmers' movements coincided with and were spurred on by the declining prices of corn and wheat on the world markets, a dramatic drop in land values, and the concurrent paradox of mortgages—some forty percent of farms in the West were mortgaged—for values that had been set at boom prices far beyond true worth. In Nebraska alone foreclosures annually were in the thousands, and farmers found it cheaper to burn corn for fuel and to slaughter hogs than to market them. In the late 1880s economic problems were compounded by drought, and in a short time the People's Independent party became a national reality as a party dedicated to serving and saving the farmer by seeking currency and tariff reform, railroad and bank control, and tax reform. In many respects a genuine people's movement, it drew together and gave voice and direction to the latent socialistic impulses of a growing number of disgruntled farmers and rural businessmen.

Many academic and theoretical explanations have been advanced for the farmer's plight: the transition from an agricultural to an industrial economy; overproduction on the farms and underconsumption elsewhere; a faulty distribution system; the growth of a world-wide economic and marketing system; the lack of adequate representation on the national level. All of these problems and more had contributed to the individual farmer's dilemma, but to him this was a personal struggle seen in personal terms against the rampant greed of the railroads, the bankers, and the trusts, and he demanded change and control through government action.

To Bryan, a farm boy who had cast his lot with the agricultural West, the problem was also personal, and he believed that it could be solved through government action. Yet the emergence of the Populists as he was to make his first attempt at public office threatened the future that he had marked out for himself. When the Nebraska Populists called a state convention for 29 July 1890 to organize the party and nominate a slate of candidates, Bryan knew that the probable result would be the split of reform votes and the return of Connell to the House. On the twenty–ninth, the Independents nominated a former senator and popular reformer, Charles H. Van Wyck, on a strong reform platform.

Bryan thus faced two problems: opposition to his nomination from conservative Democrats and the competition from a strong reform candidate for the votes of reform-minded Democrats, Republicans, and Independents. In the district convention, however, he had two advantages, his own popularity and his strategic position as author of the platform.

I   *The First Platform*

Bryan's platform was both a campaign document and a statement of principle, and it was liberal but not radical, appealing to the broad spectrum of dissatisfaction among Democrats, Republicans, and Independents alike. After a conventional opening tribute to democratic government and Democratic party tradition, he welcomed all those who believed in "free citizens, just laws, and economical government"[2] to join him; he castigated the Republican Fifty-first Congress for extravagance and tyranny; and he denounced the McKinley tariff for its ineffective protection of farm products while it drove up the price of manufactured goods.

Conversely, Bryan's platform contained specific reform planks directed toward remedying the economic and political abuses to which the farmers attributed their economic predicament. Of the tariff, he wrote: "We demand that wool, coal, lumber, sugar, salt, and iron ore be placed on the free lists; that the tariff on articles of necessary use be greatly reduced, and that articles of luxury be subjected to the heaviest duties. . . ."[3] Such a proposed program fell far short of the free-trade or revenue-only proposals of those who condemned the existence of tariffs, but it was designed to appeal to large segments of the electorate, Republicans and Independents as well as the conservative members of Bryan's own party.

Although the tariff occupied a prominent place in the platform, Bryan took the opportunity to demand constitutional change that would place even more power in the hands of the people. Less strongly phrased, these planks were no less clear:

> We favor an amendment to the federal Constitution which would take the election of the United States Senators from the state legislatures and place it in the hands of the people, where it belongs.
> We favor the Australian or some similar system of balloting which will assure to every citizen the right to cast his vote according to his judgement, free from corruption or intimidation.[4]

Three important planks addressed themselves to specific rural and Western complaints, the power of the trusts, the passage of land titles to nonresidents and nonsettlers, and the issue that had captured the minds and the imaginations of the West, that of currency reform. Of the trusts, Bryan wrote: "We are opposed to the 'trust' in all its forms, and favor vigorous measures for its prevention and suppression."

His statement on the land issue was equally forceful: "The public domain should be preserved for the actual settler and we demand the enactment of a law by Congress prohibiting the acquiring or holding of lands by non-resident aliens."[5]

The currency plank—with which Bryan was to be concerned throughout his career in Congress and his drive for the presidency and which continues to be most closely associated with him in the public mind—was perhaps the clearest indication of Bryan's determination to express the will of the people of his district and at the same time to usurp the principal plank of the Independents. But its place in the platform and its phraseology suggest that to Bryan at the time it was only one of many issues rather than the dominant concern that it was to become in 1896: "We demand the free coinage of silver on equal terms with gold and denounce the effort of the Republican party to serve the interests of Wall Street against the rights of the people."[6]

Just as there are significant inclusions in the program, particularly the currency plank, there are significant omissions. Not only did Bryan ignore the cries of the Independents for public ownership of the railroads and the telegraph systems, a demand to which he was to turn more than a decade later, but it omits the temperance issue to which he was to devote much of his nonpolitical energy in later years. There is no suggestion of either a national or international vision. The platform, in spite of the forcefulness and simplicity of its demands, was essentially a moderate document on which Bryan could comfortably stand, but it was too radical to suit the conservatives in his own party who threatened to prevent his nomination, just as it was too conservative for some Independents, who were determined that their party should not be absorbed by the Democrats.

In the light of later events, the proposal for free and unlimited coinage of silver has received a good deal of attention. Not only was it Bryan's first major public statement on what was becoming known as the "silver issue," but in retrospect it is evident that Bryan had little idea of the possible detrimental effects of such a proposal, and the evidence suggests that he knew he did not at the time. In *The First Battle* (1896) he makes clear his own recognition of his fiscal innocence:

I wrote the plank and it expressed my views at the time. . . . When I spoke upon the silver question at all it was only briefly and the argument made was, in substance, that we needed more money rather than less and that the use of both metals for standard money would give more money than the use of one alone.

After the election I determined to make a thorough study of the money question. . . . [7]

In the convention Bryan demonstrated his growing political skill. Traditionally, nominations were made and then the platform adopted, but Bryan introduced the platform first, conservative opposition was overcome, and the platform, which he knew no conservative could stand upon, was adopted. His nomination on the first formal ballot was anticlimax, and it was quickly made unanimous.

Bryan's acceptance foreshadowed the emphasis of his future campaigns; he considered himself embarked upon a battle that was not merely political but moral as he represented the forces of good locked in combat with evil. He would "meet in joint debate, in every county in my district, the champion of high taxes, whoever he may be, and I shall go forth to the conflict as David went to meet the giant of the Philistines, not relying upon my own strength, but trusting to the righteousness of my cause. . . ."[8] Furthermore, he concluded, again foreshadowing his campaigns of the future,

I will visit you in your homes. I will call upon you on your farms and help make hay while the sun shines, and I shall expect you to help me make votes all the time. . . .

If you will work as hard as I, your congressman elected from this district will bear the name which thirty years ago last March my parents gave to me. . . . [9]

Bryan began his campaign almost immediately, speaking forcefully at the state convention in August. He participated in the principal debate over the liquor question and accepted a plank which did not demand prohibition but instead proposed a bill calling for high license fees and local option. Later the Republicans were to insist that he had compromised principle in the attempt to lure wet votes, especially when he campaigned with James Boyd, a wet and the candidate for governor. Later, too, he was charged with selling out to the railroads when it was disclosed that he, in common with almost every other lawyer in the state, had a railroad pass. But Bryan had returned his pass immediately after his nomination.

Other charges were leveled, most of them in desperation as his lead became evident: that he was a "calamity howler"; that he frequented saloons while posing as a moralist; that he had made political deals; that he was antilabor and a member of the anti-Catholic (and generally Republican) A.P.A. All these charges and more were refuted easily, and Bryan did so when he felt them personally damaging enough to warrant attention. But the majority of them he ignored, chosing instead to concentrate on the chief issue, the tariff.

Bryan received unexpected assistance when Van Wyck, the Independent candidate, withdrew in September, leaving the campaign to an unknown and enhancing Bryan's image as a reformer. On the road, the Bryan campaign, in spite of limited funds, worked continuously; Boyd and Bryan clubs paraded in Lincoln and Omaha with brass bands; and Bryan spoke almost daily, sometimes as often as three times a day, more than eighty times on the tariff, advocating "reform" rather than the free-trade position to which he later came. The tariff had become the chief issue because Connell had voted with the Democrats on money issues in Congress and supported bimetalism, but he remained a strong supporter of the McKinley tariff. Consequently, Bryan took his campaign to the farmers, shaking hands, occasionally pitching hay, and talking at every opportunity. On one occasion, standing on a manure spreader, he began with, "Friends, this is the first time I ever spoke from a Republican platform"; he spoke simply but without condescension, one reporter pointing out that his speeches were so clear that "a child can understand the points and follow the argument."

The focal point of the campaign was a series of eleven debates in the first district patterned after the Lincoln-Douglas debates of an earlier era. Connell and Bryan were friends and there was no malice in their encounters, but Bryan's quick, lucid arguments made him the popular favorite as the series gave virtually every voter in the district the opportunity to hear and compare both candidates on the same platform. Mary Bryan later referred to the first debate, in which Bryan admitted to nervousness approaching nausea, as "marking an important epoch in Mr. Bryan's life." [10]

The series closed at Syracuse. It was marked by a touching exchange that delighted the audience. After his rousing conclusion Bryan handed Connell a copy of Gray's "Elegy in a Country Churchyard," and spoke in the manner that was to mark all his campaigns and rivalries:

We now bring to a close this series of debates which was arranged by our committees. I am glad that we have been able to conduct these discussions in a courteous and friendly manner. If I have, in any way, offended you in word or deed I offer apology and regret, and as freely forgive. I desire to present to you in remembrance of these pleasant meetings this little volume, because it contains "Gray's Elegy," in perusing which I trust you will find as much pleasure and profit as I have found. It is one of the most beautiful and touching tributes to humble life that literature contains. Grand in its sentiment and sublime in its simplicity, we may both find in it a solace in victory or defeat. If success should crown your efforts in this campaign, and it should be your lot "Th' applause of list'ning senates to command," and I am left

A youth to fortune and to fame unknown,

Forget not us who in the common walks of life perform our part, but in the hour of your triumph recall the verse:

Let not ambition mark their useful toil,
   Their homely joys and destiny obscure;
Nor grandeur hear, with distainful smile,
   The short and simple annals of the poor.

If, on the other hand, by the verdict of my countrymen, I shall be made your successor, let it not be said of you:

And melancholy marked him for her own,

But find sweet consolation in the thought:

Full many a gem of purest ray serene,
   The dark unfathomed caves of ocean bear;
Full many a flower was born to blush unseen,

But whether the plan of victory is given to you or to me, let us remember those of whom the poet says:

Far from the madding crowd's ignoble strife,
   Their sober wishes never learned to stray;
Along the cool sequester'd vale of life,
   They keep the noiseless tenor of their way.

These are the ones most likely to be forgotten by the government. When the poor and weak cry out for relief they, too, often hear no answer but "the echo of their cry," while the rich, the strong, the powerful are given an attentive ear. For this reason is class legislation dangerous and deadly. It takes from those least able to lose and gives to those who are least in need. The safety of our farmers and our laborers is not in special legislation, but in equal and just laws that bear alike on every man. The great masses of our people are interested, not in getting their hands into other people's pockets, but in keeping the hands of other people out of their pockets. Let me, in parting, express the hope that you and I may be instrumental in bringing our Government back to better laws which will give equal treatment without regard to creed or condition. I bid you a friendly farewell.[11]

(Gray's elegy remained one of Bryan's favorite, most frequently quoted poems; perhaps not coincidentally, it had played the same part in Abraham Lincoln's life and career.)

With a friendly response from Connell, Bryan's leading the audience in three cheers for "so able and gallant a defender of a lost cause," and the presentation to Bryan of a floral wreath on one side of which was inscribed "Truth" and on the other, "Eloquency," the campaign was effectively over.

For the Republicans the results were unexpected; although they retained all statewide offices except the governorship, they lost control of the legislature to the Independents, and lost all three congressional contests, to an Independent, a fusion Independent-Democrat, and a genuine Democrat, Bryan, in the first district. The official count gave Bryan 32,376 votes, Connell, 25,663, and Root, the Independent, 13,006. Although there were numerous accusations of fraud, the result was clear: Bryan had won an impressive victory.

Although he would not take office for nearly a year, Bryan took his status as Congressman-elect seriously. Almost immediately he withdrew from active law practice, retaining, however, a nominal relationship with the firm, and he began a concerted effort to educate himself on the issues with which he would have to deal in Congress. The currency issue, he knew, would be the most critical, and he began to study it systematically if innocently, recalling in *The First Battle* that

The first thing read was a little pamphlet issued by the Bimetal League and entitled "Silver in the Fifty-first Congress." Professor Laughlin's book on bimetalism was next read and afterwards, the "Report of the Royal Commission of England" and the works of Jevons, Bonamy Price, Cernuschi, De Laveleye, Chevelier, Jacobs and others. By this time the agitation upon the question had reached a point where people were dividing upon the subject and I was pained to find my opinion running contrary to the opinions of many with whom I have been politically intimate, but the more I investigated the question the deeper my convictions became.[12]

Bryan's interest in the money issue was not only honest and deeply felt, but it was perhaps inevitable. The money problem, or more properly, the lack of money, had been the most widely discussed issue among Midwestern farmers and townsmen since, in the years following the Civil War, Bryan had become aware that such issues existed. His father's unsuccessful campaign for Congress as a Democrat in 1872 had received substantial Greenback support. He knew that the depression of 1873, which adversely affected his family and friends, was the result of gold speculation, and he had heard that the lack of money in his youth was related to the withdrawal of greenbacks from circulation. As a young lawyer he experienced the difficulty of collecting debts from honest men, and he saw the rate of farm foreclosures rise dramatically as he stumped rural Nebraska. The need was obvious, and the supply of silver available in Nevada and Colorado was endless, according to those who presumably knew. The answer to the problem, it seemed to him and thousands of others, was to make it possible for those who needed money to have a chance to earn it, and while gold was securely locked in the banks of the East, silver was plentiful in the mountains of the West.

Bryan and his colleagues demanded a policy of inflation in an age dominated by those whose best interests, they were convinced, were served by deflation and stability. But in a more fundamental sense Bryan and his colleagues were the heirs of an older tradition rooted not only in the sectionalism of East versus West, but also in the demand for dynamic growth and expansion that had been the underlying faith of those who moved West since the beginning of the century. But where the Westerners of Jackson's time put their faith as well as money and mortgages in wildcat banks, Bryan and his colleagues believed in the tangible reality of silver.

Bryan's commitment to the cause of currency reform quickly became evident, and it began to give substance to the national attention he was receiving as a Democratic congressman–elect in a traditionally Republican state. As a delegate to the First Western States Commercial Congress in Kansas City in April 1891, he voted for free coinage of silver and introduced and secured the adoption of a resolution that was simple, clear, and popular:

Resolved: that it is the sense of this congress that all legal tender money of the United States should be made a full legal tender for all debts, public

and private, any condition in the contract notwithstanding; provided that
this should not affect contracts already in existence.[13]

In spite of the concession in the last phrase, Bryan's intent was clear,
and he concluded his supporting speech with a rhetorical flourish
that brought the delegates to their feet cheering: "We simply say to
the East, take your hands out of our pockets and keep them out."[14]

During 1891 his new prominence took him to Iowa to speak for
the reelection of Governor Horace Bois, a silver Democrat whom he
was to support for the presidential nomination in 1892 against
Grover Cleveland, and to Ohio to speak against William McKinley
at the invitation of Governor James Campbell. By the fall of 1891,
with his new national as well as regional prominence—The *St. Louis
Post-Dispatch* referred to him as an "emerging national symbol"—
Bryan felt secure enough to challenge the conservative Democratic
leadership in Nebraska, cutting his ties with his mentor Morton at
the same time. In the first display of the independence that was to
mark his congressional career, it quickly became known that he was
determined to reshape the Democratic party and direct its rededi-
cation to the well-being of the common people. As chairman of the
resolutions committee for the state convention in September, he
fought for a strong free-silver plank against the committee majority
and then introduced it as a minority report, speaking so strongly
that it was nearly adopted. Then, by way of compromise, the
convention passed Bryan's plank essentially unchanged. But the
break with Morton was permanent and Bryan, for the time at least,
was effectively the leader of the Nebraska party.

Later that fall, before his departure for Washington, Bryan made
his first attempt at what was to be a recurring effort to construct a
Democratic-Independent Populist party fusion. When the Democratic nomineee for State Supreme Court justice withdrew, Bryan
persuaded the Democrats to endorse the Independent nominee. But
the fusion candidate lost to the Republicans, and Bryan went off to
Washington to take up his seat, where he was unable to continue to
exploit the temporary arrangement in Nebraska.

II   *The Young Congressman*

Bryan's two terms in Congress—he was reelected by a narrower
margin in a Republican-gerrymandered district in 1892 in spite of
another failed attempt at fusion—were dominated by two issues,

silver and the tariff, and by a recurring battle with the antisilver forces of his own party, Cleveland Democrats nationally and at home. In a House at least nominally controlled by members of his own party by a substantial three to one majority, Bryan's new prominence won him a seat on the powerful Ways and Means Committee, a signal honor for a freshman congressman, and a voice in party caucuses. On 16 March 1892 he made his first major speech in the House.

The issue was the tariff, the province of the Ways and Means Committee, which was controlled by the reformers. Their initial strategy was to reduce tariffs on specific items, with Bryan to speak initially on the reduction of tariffs on wool and woolen items and binding twine and other farm items. Normally such a speech and topic are dull at best, with many congressmen finding excuses to absent themselves or wrestling with the impulse to sleep. But Bryan's reputation had preceded him to Washington, and as he began to speak, chairs filled, senators drifted over, and Mary sat proudly in the gallery.

Bryan began prosaically enough, examining first the logic of protective tariffs on wool and then on twine, and introducing his own logical and statistical analysis to support their abolition. Of the former he said,

I read in the address of Judge Lawrence, before the Ohio Wool-Grower's Association, that in his opinion the man in this country who raises sheep receives for his wool the foreign price of wool plus the duty upon wool. But there are many who disagree with him. Many sheep-raisers believe that the farmer does not receive the tariff duty upon wool which is imposed ostensibly for his benefit, and they point to the decline in the number of sheep and the price of wool under protection.

I care not, for the sake of the argument, which position is true. One of three conditions must exist at this time. We have imposed a tariff upon wool; we have given a compensatory duty, which is equivalent to that tariff, upon wool in all its manufactured forms. The manufacturer of wool must, if he buys foreign wool, pay this duty. Now, if the farmer gets no increased price for his wool because of protection, and the manufacturer deals honestly with the people and does not charge them anything extra, then the removal of this duty will still bring relief to the consumers of woolen goods by reducing the price of imported wool without affecting the price of the farmer's home-grown wool. . . .

It is also possible that the manufacturer in this country, having the advantage of the compensatory duties, does charge up to the people who buy woolen goods the amount of the tariff as if he paid it to the farmer, and yet he may not pay it to the farmer. In that case the passage of this bill will still more largely reduce the cost of goods to the consumer and not affect the farmer who raises sheep.

There may be a third condition. It may be that the manufacturer of woolen goods pays the duty upon imported wool and pays a like amount on home–grown wool and then charges to the consumer just exactly, under the compensatory duties, the amount which he has had to pay as a tariff upon foreign wool and as an additional price upon the home-grown wool. If that condition exists, then the operation of this bill will be to bring to the people of this country who consume woolen goods the reduction made by the bill. . . .

Now, those are the three conditions, one of which must exist. I do not care, my friends, for the sake of the argument, which condition exists. I am in favor of the bill. I am in favor of it, in the first place, because it makes a reduction in ad valorem rates; and in addition thereto, if the first condition supposed exists, reduces the price of woolen goods to the extent of the tariff paid on imported wool. This is only just, because such necessary articles as woolen goods should not be made so expensive as they are to the great masses of our people.

If the second condition exists, and the manufacturer is charging up against us as consumers that which he does not pay, I am still in favor of the bill, and in favor of taking away from him this unjust and unfair advantage.

If the third condition exists, and the manufacturer collects from us simply what he pays to the farmer who raises sheep, I am still in favor of this bill, because I do not believe we should make a manufacturer or any one else an agent to collect money from one man and pay it into the pocket of another man. So you can take any of these conditions you like, and you can frame any defense you please, but I am in favor of this bill from any standpoint and on any condition. . . .(S, 1:8–10)

To Bryan the issue was clear and simple, and the argument he made was equally clear and simple. That part of the speech, while sharply defined, bordered on dull, and Bryan went on to inject a bit of life into his remarks:

Out in Nebraska there was a time when we had almost one sheep for each man, woman, and child. We look back to it as the "mutton age" of Nebraska. But, alas, that happy day has passed! The number of sheep has continually decreased, until now, if every woman in the State named Mary insisted upon having a pet lamb at the same time, we would have to go out of the State to get enough lambs to go around. (S, 1:14)

From folklore, Bryan turned to classical and biblical antiquity to expand his metaphor:

You may go back into history, sacred or profane, as far as tradition runs, and you will find a record of the sheep. Homer tells how Ulysses escaped from the cave of the Cyclops by means of a sheep. We read in the Bible that when Isaac was about to be offered up, away back in the patriarchical days, a ram was found caught by the horns in a thicket, and offered in his stead; and further back than that, in the fourth chapter of Genesis, I think in the second verse—my Republican friends, of course, will remember—it is recorded of the second son of the first earthly pair, "Abel was a keeper of sheep." And from that day to this—

Mr. Simpson: I want to ask the gentlemen if we are to understand that this is the sacrifice you are offering up on the altar of protection.

Mr. Bryan: No, sir; we are only beginning an attack, which will be continued just as long as there is anything to remedy. But I was going to say, Mr. Chairman, that from that day to this the sheep has been the constant companion of man in all his travels, and it has differed from its modern owner the most in that it is recognized as the symbol of meekness. (*S*, 1:14–15)

Unwilling, however, to let his beginning—the attack against the wool tariff—rest without immediate reinforcement, Bryan turned to the protective tariff itself:

I have said that the purpose of the protective tariff is to transfer money from one man's pocket to another man's pocket. I want to show . . . that it is the only purpose a protective tariff can possibly have. Why do you impose a tariff? You impose it upon the theory that you cannot produce in this country the article which you protect as cheaply as it can be produced abroad; and you put the tariff upon that article in order that the price of the article may be so much increased that American manufacturers can afford to produce it. You mean that the man who buys that article shall pay into the public Treasury the tariff upon the article, and you expect that this, together with the price, will be sufficient to protect somebody else. . . .

I submit this proposition: Either a tariff is needed or it is not needed. If a tariff is needed, it is in order to add the price of the tariff to the price of the home article to enable the American manufacturer to compete with the foreign. If it is not needed, who is going to justify it? Now, which horn of the dilemma will you take? Will you say that this tariff is needed and used; or will you say it is not needed and ought to be abolished? . . .

You cannot in this way raise an "infant industry" without putting the burden somewhere. Whenever you see the Government by operation of law send a dollar singing down into one man's pocket, you must remember that the Government has brought it crying up out of some other man's pocket. (*S*, 1:40–42)

After yielding for a series of questions that were in essence debating points from Republican protectionists, in each of which Bryan, in complete control, refuted the arguments through his inflexible definition of the nature of the tariff, he turned again to homely metaphors to support his point at the expense of the protectionists—his farm background, the nature of true exchange, and the perennial old maid:

> They tell you that a tariff on wool is for the benefit of the farmer, and goes into his pocket, but that the tariff on manufactured products goes into the farmer's pocket, too, "and really hurts us, but we will stand it if we must." They are much like a certain maiden lady of uncertain age, who said, "This being the third time that my beau has called, he might make some affectionate demonstration;" and, summing up all her courage, she added "I have made up my mind that if he does I will bear it with fortitude." (S, 1:68)

With Bryan's time elapsed, a motion to adjourn was shouted down by cries of "Go ahead!" and he finished with an emotional and rhetorical flourish: an appeal to his listeners to consider both threats to small industries hurt by protection and the threat to the home itself. Then he created an image of the long lines of white crosses marking the graves of those who sought no special privilege, and ended with a vision of the future.

> If [the Democratic party] comes into power in all the departments of this government it will not destroy industry; it will not injure labor; but it will save to the men who produce the wealth of the country a larger portion of that wealth. It will bring prosperity and joy and happiness, not to a few, but to everyone without regard to station or condition. The day will come, Mr. Chairman—the day will come when those who annually gather about this Congress seeking to use the taxing power for private purposes will find their occupation gone, and the members of Congress will meet here to pass laws for the benefit of all the people. That day will come, and in that day, to use the language of another, "Democracy will be king! Long live the king." (S, 1:76-77)

This speech, described by Mary Bryan as "the second most important event in his career as a public speaker,"[15] lasted for three hours and four minutes. To H. A. Sommers of Kentucky it was a "great speech" of "about an hour and a half." Its effects were both immediate and long range. The House, the gallery, and the press burst into applause, and he was surrounded by congratulating Democrats and Republicans; Congressman Constantine Kilgore said that "This is the first time I ever left my seat to congratulate a member, but it is the first time I ever had such great cause to break the record"; to protectionist Julius Burrows, it was "the best tariff reform speech I have ever heard." Bryan, a first-term congressman faced with a difficult fight for reelection that fall, emerged as the principal spokesman for tariff reform in the House, a figure of national prominence, and a prophet of a new order in the South and West.

The speech was important to Bryan's future. It aided in determining the outcome of his strongly contested campaign for reelection in November, and it instigated the first mentions of his possible candidacy for the presidency in 1896. Immediate results, however, were mixed. Although the twine bill, for which he was responsible, passed by a substantial majority in the House, it was defeated in the Republican-controlled Senate. Nevertheless, more than a hundred thousand copies of the speech were circulated by members of Congress; hundreds of letters poured in, one correspondent commenting that "I don't rightfully know your age, but in case you are old enough to be President of the United States, I sure favor it." The *New York World* described it in glowing terms: "Today, almost with the effect of an ambuscade, the Democrats uncovered a ten-inch gun, and for . . . hours shelled the surprised enemy so effectively that the protectionist batteries . . . were silenced. . . . This speech has been a revolution. . . ." But it was not the speech Bryan had hoped to make on the silver issue.

Nevertheless, the speech was important for two reasons other than its effect on Bryan's career. It marked the maturity of Bryan's mastery of the speech form, and it reflects the completeness of his commitment to Jeffersonian democratic principles as the basis of his political philosophy. This conviction shaped his developing beliefs in other specific areas, including currency reform, imperialism, pacifism, and even prohibition.

Not only did Bryan's voice ring clearly in every corner of the House chamber as he moved into the aisle and then to the speaker's desk, Democrats, Populists, and some Republicans trailing him as if he were some Pied Piper of the prairie, but it was a speech designed carefully to appeal to the mind as well as the heart, and to use the latter appeal only as ancillary support for his primary appeal to reason. It was a well-researched speech, with careful statistical

analysis combined with equally precise examination of the inconsistencies of those who supported the tariff; and its organization was
designed to build from a low-keyed, frank opening through the
amassed evidence supporting that frankness to the final vision of a
greater future. Rooted in Bryan's interest in the debate as a means
of persuasion, the technique was honed on the political stump, and,
recognizing that the weight of such a speech must be alleviated at
times by humor, Bryan drew on his store of rustic metaphors and
illustrations, again using them carefully as much for reinforcement
and for delight of the partisan mind as for the necessary dramatic
relief. In so doing he pointed up as effectively as any political orator
has ever done the relationship between the microcosmic political
issue and the macrocosmic nature of the American dream, and in
clear, simple terms he asserted that achieving reality for the smaller
brought the larger closer to its own reality.

Jeffersonianism was to Bryan not merely an article of faith but a
means by which that faith might be made meaningful governmental
practice. Like Jefferson, Bryan believed that governments were
made by men to do for them what they could not do for themselves.
He believed too that government was essentially a social contract,
that the common people had, as he pointed out in this speech, kept
the contract, as the rows of crosses in Arlington gave testimony, but
that government in many instances had not. The protective tariff
was one such instance; the gold standard, unequal taxes, wars of
imperialism, and entangling foreign relations were others that he
was to point out in the future.

Bryan's ideas on the nature of the tariff were not new, but in the
speech he gave voice to the many objections against it that had been
raised, largely by his own party members, for more than half a
century, just as many of the same arguments would be raised by
others. But no one, before or since, has used those arguments in
such detail, nor has anyone expressed them more compellingly.

As a result of this speech, however, Bryan was to receive much
criticism from later scholars; he has been accused of a Western bias,
of a lack of understanding of the evolution of American society, of a
naive faith in the virtues of the agrarian way of life, of transmuting
political issues into the realm of morality, of lack of sympathy for
industrial workers, even of demagoguery. But none of these critics,
in this instance, at least, has accused him of ignorance of the facts or
the issues. Bryan had prepared carefully and presented effectively
the most compelling argument yet made against protection, an issue
still raised in American political debate.

While repercussions of the speech were still echoing in Congress and beyond, Bryan returned to Nebraska to find a split party, with Morton, an avowed gold Democrat, seeking the nomination for the governorship, the Independents, sensing success, in no mood for a fusion, and his own district gerrymandered by the Republican legislature, while on the horizon Grover Cleveland had announced his interest in a third nomination on a sound-money, tariff-reform platform. On 13 April, the day after he returned from Washington, Bryan began his fight in a narrow, hotly contested vote in the state convention, the results of which are still not clear. His addition to the platform of a statement that "We declare ourselves in favor of the free coinage of silver" was rejected. Stung by the opposition, he refused to support Cleveland's candidacy, instead declaring for Governor Bois of Iowa for the presidency, and with his followers, he dramatically left the convention.

In the first district, however, he was renominated by acclamation on a strong free-silver platform, and he stumped the district tirelessly, ignoring the candidacies of Morton and Cleveland. With Omaha, the seat of his urban strength, outside the new district, he based his campaign on agrarian unrest, but he found it necessary to seek financial support from out-of-state silver interests. Not only was this issue raised against him by the Republicans, but they brought William McKinley from Ohio to speak against him, as he had spoken against McKinley in Ohio in 1891. The results were in doubt to the end; even after eleven debates between Bryan and the Republican nominee, it was evident that Bryan had stirred more enthusiasm than pledged support or votes.

On the morning after election the results in Nebraska were almost clear: although Cleveland had won the presidency, Nebraska voted for Republican electors; Morton was overwhelmed for the governorship, and the Republicans captured three House seats, while two Populists were also elected. In the first district, however, the vote was so close that not for two days was it determined that Bryan had been reelected—by 140 votes. He had won over gerrymandering, and he had overcome Gold Democrat hostility and an influx of Eastern money and speakers; he had survived sustained personal attack and the strong political intrigues of the railroads. Bryan's victory was narrow, but it was impressive, and he remained Nebraska's only Democratic congressman and proven vote-getter.

The nature of his appeal was obvious, as it was to be for the rest of his career, whether on the political stump or the lecture platform. Not only had he tailored his campaign to the needs and hopes of his

Western rural constituency, but his personality, talents, and man-
nerisms had been formed by the values and attitudes of those same
people. His oratorical talent had been honed in a tradition steeped
in the drama of frontier politics and revivalism; it was eloquent and
exciting, flamboyant and sincere, serious and humorous, dynamic
and controlled. He was simple but forceful, one of them in his
openness, but cultured beyond them, as a leader should be.

Fundamentally, too, he shared their world view, as the twin
traditions of frontier politics and religion had taught them to see the
world: as a battleground between the forces of good and evil,
between those who earned their livings by the sweat of their brows
and those who lived in pampered luxury. Bryan was a man of faith
in the simple virtues that they shared, and yet he did not condemn
their simple vices: a teetotaler, he imposed his abstinence on no
one. He was an idealist and a visionary, but he was practical and
understood the value of necessary compromise and adaptation to
circumstances. He was, as Willa Cather observed, a man of the West
and his times, reflecting "all its newness and vigor, its magnitude
and monotony, its richness and lack of variety, its inflammability
and volubility, its strength and its crudeness, its high seriousness
and self-confidence, its egotism and its nobility." [16] He had found
the issue that would give substance to his dream.

CHAPTER 4

Silver!

EVEN as he prepared to return to Washington, secure until 4 March 1895, Bryan made a brief, unsuccessful attempt to gain election to the Senate, but, in a legislature divided among fifty-three Republicans, fifty-three Populists, and seventeen Democrats, he was pleased to throw his influence to the successful Populist candidate, demonstrating again, for those who would observe it, the value of fusion. The experience also reaffirmed his belief that Senators should be elected by popular vote, and he made more notes for the future.

In Washington, in the lame duck session of the Fifty-Second Congress and in the Fifty-third, Bryan determined that he would redirect the Democratic party, that he would make it the party of currency reform, even at the cost of permanent alienation from the Cleveland administration. Cleveland immediately showed his initial hostility by appointing Morton secretary of agriculture—without consulting Bryan, the only Democrat from Nebraska holding national office—and then giving Morton control over Nebraska patronage.

During the first months of the new Congress Bryan was caught up in two problems, the accelerating Panic of 1893 and the determination of the Cleveland administration to repeal the Sherman Silver Purchase Act of 1890. To Bryan, the threat to the act was largely responsible for the Panic. Conversely, Cleveland was convinced that the act itself had brought on the Panic by permitting the exchange of silver for gold at the Treasury, thus threatening the gold reserves that supported the gold standard. In his preliminary speeches Bryan portrayed a conspiracy of financiers, stretching from Wall Street to London, that was determined to demonetize silver and gather gold into their vaults. Cleveland, he was convinced, was their tool.

I   *Congressional Speech on Silver*

On 16 August 1893, Bryan rose in the House to mount the major attack of the silver forces against those of repeal. The scene was in many ways reminiscent of his speech on the tariff: public and press galleries were full, congressmen of three parties were in their seats, senators and outsiders lined the walls. Bryan paused momentarily, dramatically turned over the pages of his prepared speech, and began:

Mr. Speaker: I shall accomplish my full purpose if I am able to impress upon the members of the House the far-reaching consequences which may follow our action and quicken their appreciation of the grave responsibility which presses upon us. Historians tell us that the victory of Charles Martel at Tours determined the history of all Europe for centuries. It was a contest "between the Crescent and the Cross," and when, on that fateful day, the Frankish prince drove back the followers of Abderrabman he rescued the West from "the all-destroying grasp of Islam," and saved to Europe its Christian civilization. A greater than Tours is here! In my humble judgement the vote of this House on the subject under consideration may bring to the people of the West and South, to the people of the United States, and to all mankind, wealth or woe beyond the power of language to describe or imagination to conceive. (S, 1:78)

After recognizing the seriousness of the problem in terms of one of the great watersheds of human history, expressed in language and tone that emphasized his seriousness, Bryan turned at once to the attempt to refute criticism directed at the silver Democrats as disloyal to the administration. At the same time, using Cleveland's own words, he made it impossible for the president to demand loyalty:

Some outside of this hall have insisted that the President's recommendation imposes upon Democratic members an obligation, as it were, to carry out his wishes, and over-zealous friends have even suggested that opposition to his views might subject the hardy dissenter to administrative displeasure. They do the President great injustice who presume that he would forget for a moment the independence of the two branches of Congress. He would not be worthy of our admiration or even respect if he demanded a homage which would violate the primary principles of free representative government.

Let his own language rebuke those who would disregard their pledges to their own people in order to display a false fealty. In the message which he sent to Congress in December, 1885, he said, in words which may well be

our guide in the great crisis: "The zealous watchfulness of our constituen-
cies, great and small, supplements their suffrage, and before the tribunal
they establish every public servant should be judged." Among the many
grand truths exprest felicitously by the President during his public career
none show a truer conception of official duty or describe with more clearness
the body from which the member receives his authority and to which he
owes his responsibility. (*S,* 1:79)

Bryan's olive branch, it is evident, was held by a mailed fist, and,
although his tongue was evidently not in his cheek as he paid
exaggerated tribute to Cleveland's wisdom and sense of justice, he
immediately pointed out that Cleveland had made a similar recommendation in 1885, during his previous administration, only to see
it defeated by those responsible to their constituents. Again, in
exaggerated tribute, he commented, "Time has proven that the
members, reflecting the opinions of their people, were wiser than
the Executive, and he is doubtless grateful today they did not follow
his suggestion" (*S,* 1:81).
At this point it was evident that Bryan had made his formal
declaration of war against the Cleveland administration, tight
money, and the gold standard:

We hear much about a "stable currency" and an "honest dollar." It is a
significant fact that those who have spoken in favor of unconditional repeal
have for the most part avoided a discussion of the effect of an appreciating
standard. They take it for granted that a gold standard is not only an honest
standard, but the only stable standard. I denounce that child of ignorance
and avarice, the gold dollar under a universal gold standard, as the most
dishonest dollar which we could employ.
I stand upon the authority of every intelligent writer upon political
economy when I assert that there is not and never has been an honest
dollar. An honest dollar is a dollar absolutely stable in relation to all other
things. (*S,* 1:82–83)

The only possible effect of such a standard is, Bryan asserts, a
constantly appreciating dollar that will see mortgages foreclosed,
banks failing, laborers unemployed, all the trappings, in effect, of
the Panic surrounding them as the mad scramble for gold intensifies.
Furthermore,

I have only spoken of the immediate effects of the substitution of gold as
the world's only money of redemption. The worse remains to be told. If, as
in the resumption of specie payments in 1879, we could look forward to a

time when the construction would cease, the debtor might become a tenant upon his former estate and the home-owner assume the role of the homeless with the sweet assurance that his children or his children's children might live to enjoy the blessings of a "stable currency." But, sir, the hapless and hopeless producer of wealth goes forth into a night illuminated by no star; he embarks upon a sea whose farther shore no mariner may find; he travels in a desert where the ever-retreating mirage makes his disappointment a thousandfold more keen. Let the world once commit its fortunes to the use of gold alone and it must depend upon the annual increase of that metal to keep pace with the need for money. (S, 1:89)

Free government cannot long survive when the thousands enjoy the wealth of the country and the millions share its poverty in common. Even now you hear among the rich an occasionally exprest contempt for popular government, and among the poor a protest against legislation which makes them "toil that others may reap." I appeal to you to restore justice and bring back prosperity while yet a peaceable solution can be secured. We mourn the lot of unhappy Ireland, whose alien owners drain it of its home-created wealth; but we may reach a condition, if present tendencies continue, when her position at this time will be an object of envy, and some poet may write of our cities as Oliver Goldsmith did of the "Deserted Village." (S, 1:90–91)

It is clear that Bryan had done his homework, although his citations contribute to the conviction among his critics then and now that he had read very little about the issue other than the work of authors who agreed with him. Nevertheless, he went on to quote from an array of economists and politicians, conservative and liberal, who had addressed the issue: William Stanley Jevons, Sir Robert Giffin, George Joachim Goschen, James G. Blaine, John Sherman, and others. In the context of the debate, Bryan's use of arguments presented by the latter two was particularly effective, especially those of Sherman in the not dissimilar debates of 1869: "The contraction of the currency is a far more distressing operation than Senators suppose. . . . What prudent man would dare to build a house, a railroad, a factory, or a barn with this certain fact before him?" (S, 1:94).

Important in the speech are two issues which Bryan was to raise again in his "Cross of Gold" speech at the Democratic National Convention in 1896: the relationship between foreign money standards, particularly that of England, and the ratio of gold and silver coinage that he insisted was appropriate. Of the former, he said,

Shall we make our laws dependent upon England's action and thus allow her to legislate for us upon the most important of all questions? Shall we confess our inability to enact monetary laws? Are we an English colony or an independent people? If the use of gold alone is to make us slaves, let us use both metals and be free. If there be some living along the Eastern coast—better acquainted with the beauties of the Alps than with the grandeur of the Rockies, more accustomed to the sunny skies of Italy than to the invigorating breezes of the Mississippi Valley—who are not willing to trust their fortunes and their destinies to American citizens, let them learn that the people living between the Alleghanies to the Golden Gate are not afraid to cast their all upon the Republic and rise or fall with it. . . . I do not overestimate it when I say that out of twelve millions of voters, more than ten millions are waiting, anxiously waiting, for the signal that shall announce the financial independence of the United States. (S, 1:106–7)

The second point was less rhetorical and emotionally charged, suggesting a flexibility that Bryan was willing to explore and perhaps compromise, just as he had earlier retreated from his initial demand for the free and equal coinage of silver: "The principle of bimetalism does not stand upon any certain ratio, and may exist at 1 to 30 as well as 1 to 16. . . . we should select that one which will secure the greatest advantage to the public and cause the least injustice. The present ratio [16 to 1], in my judgement, should be adopted" (S, 1:107).

In his conclusion, addressed primarily to those of his own party who favored gold or who were undecided, he again invoked the memory and heritage of Jefferson and Jackson:

He was called a demagogue and his followers a mob, but the immortal Jefferson dared to follow the best promptings of his heart. He placed man above matter, humanity above property, and, spurning the bribes of wealth and power, pleaded the cause of the common people. It was this devotion to their interests which made his party invincible while he lived and will make his name revered while history endures. And what message comes to us from the Hermitage? When a crisis like the present arose and the national bank of his day sought to control the politics of the nation, God raised up an Andrew Jackson, who had the courage to grapple with that great enemy, and by overthrowing it, he made himself the idol of the people and reinstated the Democratic party in public confidence. What will the decision be today? The Democratic party has won the greatest success in its history. Standing upon this victory-crowned summit, will it turn its face to the rising or the setting sun? Will it choose blessings or curses, life or death—which? Which? (S, 1:144–45)

Just as his earlier speech had placed him in the front rank of the antitariff forces, this speech, in the words of the *Washington Post*—

not noted for its Western or Democratic sympathies—"roused the young Nebraskan to international renown. . . ."[1] Its effect in the White House was, however, predictable: Cleveland was furious, insisting, according to some accounts, that the Nebraska Gold Democrats, under Morton, discipline "that young upstart from Lincoln. . . ."[2]

The speech was again illustrative of Bryan at his best, intensely partisan but eloquent, ranging widely from the narrow specifics of the issue to its broader, fundamental implications, and ultimately to its place in the evolution of democratic reform in America. His appeals and his evidence were equally varied, from statistical to expert, often unexpected testimony, from the home and fireside to patriotism and morality. It was a speech that engendered strong reactions from supporters and opponents alike. Invariably, as in this case, Bryan concluded with a strong, rhetorical appeal; however, the demand for an answer to the question "Which?" was not merely a rhetorical device, but a skillful suggestion that his point had been made and proved, and that the need for action was immediate. Indeed, so carefully constructed was his conclusion that almost without exception his opponents, as deeply moved as his supporters, joined in the applause.

Nevertheless, the speech was a declaration of war, and response was almost immediate. From Western papers came comments that Bryan should indeed become the people's candidate for the presidency in 1896, and thousands of requests for copies of the speech came from the South and West, from politicians, silver miners, and citizens caught up in financial crises.

Conversely, the Morton faction in the Nebraska party determined to smash Bryan, and at the state convention in Omaha that fall they came close to doing it. Bryan's candidate for the chairmanship, Joseph E. Ong, was defeated; the Resolutions Committee, on which Bryan's supporters were outnumbered six to one, introduced a resolution supporting Cleveland and the repeal of the Sherman Act; it was accepted and the minority report shouted down. In a fiery speech, Bryan threw down the gauntlet: not only would he not support a Gold Democrat for the presidency in 1896, but, "If you represent the Democratic party in saying you are for the gold standard of Wall Street, I want to tell you if the Democratic party ratifies your action, I will go out and serve my party and my God under some other name than as a Democrat."[3]

In Congress, the Sherman Act was repealed that fall, resulting in a run on the Treasury and further depletion of gold reserves, thus intensifying the Panic rather than easing it as Cleveland had predicted. Bryan had lost the battle, he had lost control of the Democratic party in Nebraska, and it was evident that his political career was in jeopardy. Yet he knew that the silver cause was not only not dead, but that there were other reform issues, and he continued to build support for what he saw as a long war.

Even as repeal was a foregone conclusion, Bryan again attacked it in Congress, and then turned to another compelling issue, the income tax. That imposed during the Civil War had been repealed in 1870, and since then another such possibility was regarded with horror in financial circles. But to Bryan it was both a moral issue and a weapon against plutocracy, and he read widely, particularly of its use abroad, in preparation for what he knew would be another struggle. With brilliant foresight, he determined to attach an income tax rider to the tariff reform bill supported by Cleveland and almost certain of passage in the Congress. He proposed a graduated tax beginning on incomes of $2,500, anticipating that it would affect 50,000 to 80,000 persons, but he was more interested in establishing the principle than in setting a specific rate. The Cleveland forces opposed the tax, insisting that it was both unnecessary and a step on the road to socialism, and that it would drive development capital out of the country.

II   *Speech on the Income Tax*

Bryan rose to the challenge on 30 January 1894, speaking against Congressman Bourke Cochran of New York, Cleveland's eloquent spokesman in the House. Bryan's speech was brief but forceful as he disposed, point by point, of the attacks made on the tax and supplied his own evidence to demonstrate its fairness and its universality in Europe. First he turned to the major objections, that it was unnecessary and that it was hostile to corporations. To refute the former objection, he pointed out that the other members of the committee did not agree; to the latter objection, he addressed his concept of the role of corporations in the life of the nation:

The stockholder in a corporation limits his liability. When the statute creating the corporation is fully complied with the individual stockholder is secure, except to the extent fixed by the statute, whereas the entire property of the individual is ordinarily liable for his debts. . . . Corporations enjoy certain privileges and franchises. Some are given the right of eminent domain, while others . . . are given the right to use the streets of the city— a franchise which increases in value with each passing year. Corporations occupy the time and attention of our Federal courts and enjoy the protection of the Federal Government and as they do not ordinarily pay taxes the committee felt justified in proposing a light tax upon them. . . .

We are not hostile to corporations; we simply believe that these creatures of the law, these fictitious persons, have no higher or dearer rights than the persons of flesh and blood whom God created and placed upon his footstool. (S, 1:160)

Bryan traced then the role of the income tax in modern history: its precedent during and after the Civil War; its widespread use elsewhere—in England, two percent; in Prussia, four; in Austria, from eight to twenty percent; in Italy, thirteen; in the Netherlands, from two to three and a fifth; in Switzerland, from one to eight. The tax, he insisted, was neither new nor innovative, and the American proposal was modest.

That it was unconstitutional he denied, and cited prededents in law; that it was class legislation was untrue; as one rose, he became subject to it, and he hoped that more farmers would eventually pay; that it was unjust, he denied because it imposed true justice upon a system in which the poor had paid a higher rate of their incomes than the rich; that it was undemocratic he saw as absurd—the poor would be delighted to earn enough to pay; that it was "inquisitorial" was refuted by more stringent legislation already in effect in New York; that it invited perjury, he abhorred as an attack on the honesty of Americans; that its predecessor was unpopular, he refuted by quoting Senator Sherman and others; that some might flee to avoid it, he refuted by pointing to the rates elsewhere.

Not only had Bryan prepared his rebuttal as thoroughly as a rebuttal in court, without emotion giving the lie to those who opposed the bill, but he turned then, in conclusion, to an effective device, the simple, nonpartisan appeal to patriotism:

But whither will these people fly? If their tastes are English, "quite English, you know," and they stop in London, they will find a tax of more than 2 per cent. . . . I repeat, Whither will they fly?

Mr. Weadock: The gentleman will allow me to suggest that at Monte Carlo such a man would not have to pay any tax at all. [Laughter.]

[Mr. Bryan]: Then , Mr. Chairman, I presume to Monte Carlo he would go, and there he would give up to the wheel of fortune all the wealth of which he would not give a part to support the Government which enabled him to accumulate it.

Are there really such people in this country? Of all the mean men I have ever known, I have never known one so mean that I would be willing to say of him that his patriotism was less than 2 per cent deep. (S, 1:178)

Bryan's last words were a peroration and a declamation: "If we are to lose some of our 'best people' by the imposition of an income tax, let them depart, and as they leave without regret the land of their birth, let them go with the poet's curse ringing in their ears." He concluded with a ringing recitation of Sir Walter Scott's "Breathes there the man with soul so dead? . . . (S, 1:179).

Bryan's ploy and his speech were successful; the Wilson tariff bill, with its income tax provision riding upon it, was passed, substantially as he had demanded it. Cleveland could not veto it and open the possibility of a lower tariff and higher income tax in future bills.

In the debates over the income tax issue Bryan had not only enhanced his reputation as a champion of the people against those who would exploit them, thus preparing the way for his candidacy in 1896, but he had also tested some of the phraseology that would prove so effective in the Chicago convention that would nominate him. In debate with Cochran he improvised what would become the opening of the "Cross of Gold" speech: "If this were a mere contest in oratory no one would be presumptuous to dispute the prize with the distinguished gentleman from New York . . . but clad in the armor of righteous cause I dare expose myself to the shafts of his genius, believing that pebbles of truth will be more effective than javelins of error even when hurled by the giants of the Philistines. . . ."[4]

On 22 December 1894, in the waning weeks of his congressional career, Bryan rose again to attack Cleveland's money programs, concluding in the words that were to be forever linked to his name: the demand for a gold standard was insolent, and "I for one will not yield to that demand. I will not help to crucify mankind upon a cross of gold. I will not aid them to press down upon the bleeding brow of labor this crown of thorns."[5]

III   *Speech on Memorial Day, 1894*

During 1894 Bryan spoke at every opportunity. On 22 February, at a celebration chaired by William McKinley, he spoke on "Patriotism," a topic that would become a favorite of his future audiences, but he was particularly pleased to be invited to speak at the Memorial Day observance in Arlington National Cemetery, with President Cleveland and his cabinet in attendance. It was a brief but superb performance:

> With flowers in our hands and sadness in our hearts we stand amid the tombs where the nation's dead are sleeping. . . .
> We, who are of the aftermath, cannot look upon the flag with the same emotions that thrill you who have followed it as your pillar of cloud by day and your pillar of fire by night, nor can we appreciate it as you can who have seen it waving in front of reinforcements when succor meant escape from death; neither can we, standing by these covered mounds, feel as you have often felt when far away from home and on hostile soil you have laid your companions to rest. . . .
> To us who were born too late to prove upon the battlefield our courage and our loyalty it is gratifying to know that opportunity will not be wanting to show our love of country. In a nation like ours, where the government is founded upon the principle of equality and derives its just powers from the consent of the governed; in a land like ours, I say, where every citizen is a sovereign and where no one cares to wear a crown, every year presents a battlefield and every day brings forth occasion for the display of patriotism.
> And on this memorial day we shall fall short of our duty if we content ourselves with praising the dead or complimenting the living and fail to make preparations for those responsibilities which present times and present conditions impose on us. We can find instruction in that incomparable address delivered by Abraham Lincoln on the field of Gettysburg.
> "The Unfinished Work." Yes, every generation leaves to its successor an unfinished work. The work of society, the work of human progress, the work of civilization is never completed. We build upon the foundation which we find already laid and those who follow us take up the work where we leave off. . . .
> Aye, let us here dedicate ourselves anew to this unfinished work which requires of each generation constant sacrifice and care. . . .
> The strength of a nation does not lie in forts, nor in navies, nor yet in standing armies, but in happy and contented citizens, who are ever ready to protect for themselves and to preserve for posterity the blessings which they enjoy. It is for us of this generation so to perform the duties of citizenship that a "government of the people, by the people, and for the people shall not perish from the earth." (S, 2:384–88)

If Bryan had declared war on Cleveland on 16 August of the previous year, in this speech he gave that war its underlying philosophy, as Lincoln had done for his war on that November day in 1863 and Jefferson had done on 4 July 1776. The continuum is unmistakable, as it must have been to Cleveland in the audience. As he and his cabinet returned to Washington, Secretary of State Walter Q. Gresham is reported to have commented that "We can be sure of one thing; while he lives he must be reckoned with as a force in American politics."[6] There is no record of Cleveland's reply.

With his congressional career at its end on 4 March 1896, Bryan had already the previous fall made a strenuous, popularly successful but politically unsuccessful bid for election to the Senate. In that case, although senators were elected by the state legislature, Bryan had been successful in insisting that a neglected state law be enforced that placed senatorial candidates on the statewide ballot to enable voters to express their choice. In the election Bryan won what was to remain his greatest popular triumph with seventy-five percent of the popular vote. But Nebraska, like the nation, went Republican, and the legislature elected his opponent, John M. Thurston, who had won only two percent of the popular vote.

Politically unemployed, Bryan returned to Lincoln to practice law, to edit—actually to write editorials for—the *Omaha World-Herald's* weekly issue, and to begin a new career as a lecturer, a venture that was to prove as enjoyable as it was successful. In all three dimensions of his new life he was careful to keep his political fences in good repair and to meet, greet, and talk with as many people as he could. At the same time he worked tirelessly to bring about the fusion between Populists and Democrats that he was convinced would prove politically successful.

In 1895 Bryan turned thirty-five, old enough to be elected president, and many of his friends were already booming him for the nomination. On 15 November 1894, James Dahlman wrote him that "I have begun to talk you for president—and I mean it"; but Mary was skeptical, pointing out that the family finances were depleted and they had children to raise. Bluntly she asked him to give up politics and concentrate on his family and its needs. But Bryan could not; as he made clear in his Memorial Day address at Arlington, he saw a higher duty to his country and his countrymen. And the forces of silver were uniting, with meetings in Washington and Salt Lake City early in 1895. All roads, he knew, pointed to Chicago in 1896, and he was determined to travel that way with a united, fused, silver-dominated party behind him.

Of his three interim careers, the law received comparatively little attention, and his editorship was clearly a device to keep his name and ideas before the public rather than a serious career venture. His principal contributions to the paper were political editorials and detailed accounts of his speaking engagements. Political editorials, particularly when they deal with the technicalities of economic issues, are, like speeches dealing with similar issues, usually dull. But while Bryan quickly gave life, drama, and excitement to those issues on the platform, not only through his inimitable voice and dramatic talent but also with his quick wit and endless supply of anecdotes, stories, and illustrations from a wide variety of his own experiences, he did not do so in his editorials, and they rarely rise above the mundane and routine. Bryan's talents showed best on the platform rather than on the printed page.

His career on the lecture platform was not only lucrative but for him genuinely enjoyable, and he thrived on what must have been an onerous schedule. Registered with several lecture bureaus, his fees began at $50 and rapidly rose to $100 and more as he became the Midwest's favorite speaker on economic issues. He became increasingly popular in the South and West as well. Although his lectures were profitable as well as wearing, they were particularly valuable during the fifteen months before the national convention because he received a maximum amount of public exposure at the same time that his name was fixed permanently in the public mind as the nation's leader in the cause of reform. The schedule provided, too, a maximum amount of flexibility, allowing him to participate in silver conventions throughout the country. Although his enemies accused him of accepting pay from the silver mining interests at the time, particularly the Western Silver Mining Association, there is no evidence of any such arrangement; Bryan was not only too clever to have done so, but there was no need for him to supplement his income.

On the road, Bryan usually accepted four or five formal speaking engagements a week, but he often spoke without fee as well, particularly in the small towns. In the larger cities he often spoke twice, at an outdoor site in the afternoon and in a more formal indoor setting, usually in the local opera house, in the evening. Often the result was the founding of a local or state silver league or club.

Nevertheless his topic might better be described as reform rather than silver, although silver was his major subject. He spoke on the income tax; he denounced recent Sugar Trust decisions; and he attacked the jailing of Eugene V. Debs for contempt of court during the Pullman strike. In the latter case he insisted that the Supreme

Court was a tool of the wealthy, and he attacked what he called government by injunction or ukase, demanding that the Democratic party adopt an anti-injunction plank in its 1896 platform.

In June 1895, Governor John Peter Altgeld of Illinois sponsored a silver convention at Springfield that was typical of others in Texas, Mississippi, Missouri, and Tennessee. The convention adopted a strong resolution demanding the coinage of silver at the ratio of 16 to 1. Bryan spoke eloquently, declaring that "We are confronted with a conspiracy greater than that attacked by Jackson, one international in extent and destined in its consummation to produce more misery than war, pestilence, and famine," three of the legendary Horsemen of the Apocalypse. Echoes of "Bryan for President" reverberated through the hall.

During these fifteen months Bryan determined to capture the presidential nomination in 1896, but it is impossible to determine the point at which he made the decision, although it was evidently made early. During his tours he contacted local Democratic and Populist leaders and determined their preferences for the nomination. When it was evident that they preferred another, usually Richard Bland of Missouri, he implanted the idea that he would make a suitable second or third choice. At the same time he charmed the leaders as he did the rank and file at conventions and the public at his lectures.

In his meetings and his extensive correspondence, he stressed principles rather than personalities, declaring that the convention and the candidate must be pledged to free silver and reform. The cause rather than the man was, he insisted again and again, his most important interest. But at the same time he made clear his dedication to the cause, and it became increasingly evident, particularly to the uninstructed delegates whom he sought out, that he was the man. When occasionally, as in Nebraska, he was asked whether he was a Democrat or a Populist he insisted on principle rather than party.

As the date for the convention approached, fortunately for Bryan scheduled for July, he had many unresolved problems between him and the nomination: he was barely thirty-six; he was from an obscure, Western, traditionally Republican state; he was at odds with the incumbent Democratic president; he had not yet made his peace with such leaders as Altgeld; he had never controlled patronage; his following and appeal were sectional. But he had a program, a following, and an incomparable talent.

CHAPTER 5

The First Battle and the War

LATE in 1896 William Jennings Bryan published a remarkable volume unprecedented in the literature of American politics. This was *The First Battle*, the story of his first unsuccessful campaign for the presidency as he experienced it. The book is honest and thorough, it is deeply felt, and it is complete.

It is also, however, almost entirely political, omitting important personal details. It begins, after a brief biographical sketch by Mary, with Bryan's nomination for Congress in 1890 and his acceptance of the silver question as the dominant political problem of the age. Then it traces his political career from that point, largely tying together documents, particularly speeches, by narrative. It neglects such important personal details as the deaths, in quick succession, of his mother, Mariah, in Salem, Illinois, and his old mentor, Lyman Trumbull, in Chicago. Both affected him deeply, but he was unable to give expression to his grief as he became immediately caught up in the preconvention maneuvering among the silver forces who met to define their convention strategy for 1896.

As the Bimetallic Democratic National Committee, the loose alliance of Democratic silver forces, met in Chicago on 30 June, the formal, legitimate National Committee was in the hands of the Gold Democrats, and Bryan was clearly at best a dark-horse candidate, placing no higher than fifth in preconvention polls of several newspapers. Others, however, acknowledged that he could become the nominee only if the silver forces captured control of the convention. He himself, perhaps as a result of his personal grief, was deeply pessimistic. No major political leader had yet declared his support, and even such Republicans as William McKinley, soon to be the nominee of his own party, were certain that if the silver party did capture the convention, the nominee would not be Bryan but Richard P. Bland.

The drama and the political details of the convention have been recaptured many times before and since Bryan wrote *The First Battle*, but his account forsakes drama for detail as it gives the lie to the still-enduring myth that an unknown Bryan had come from nowhere with the text of a speech in his pocket that, if given, would, he was certain, turn the convention into a stampede. *The First Battle* makes clear the extent of his preparation for the office, the depth as well as the length of his commitment to the silver issue, and the degree to which his name had become associated with reform, particularly silver reform, in the West and South. If indeed Bryan was an unknown come to capture the convention through the magic of his voice, he was unknown only to the northeastern quadrant of the country, and even there his reputation had penetrated before the convention.

Bryan had attended the Republican National Convention in St. Louis beginning 15 June 1896 (not 16 July as Bryan recalled in *The First Battle*), ostensibly in his capacity as editor of the *Omaha World-Herald*, but in reality, as he recounted in his *Memoirs*, to do whatever he could to assist the Silver Republicans and to observe the silver bolt that he had anticipated. McKinley's nomination was also expected, as was a strong gold-standard platform. As he left the convention, Bryan knew that if the Democrats declared for silver, the issues would be clear, and the Democrats had an excellent chance of remaining in power. As he went to Chicago he kept in close touch with Silver Republican leadership.

A not entirely unexpected problem occurred at the beginning of the Democratic convention: the legitimacy of Bryan's Nebraska silver delegation was challenged, and those of the Gold Democrats were temporarily accepted until, after a good deal of debate, the credentials committee, chaired by Bryan's friend John H. Atwood, seated Bryan's delegation. When the committee unseated four Michigan gold men and replaced them with silver—Michigan was subject to the unit rule—the silver forces controlled two thirds of the delegates, enough, barring defections, to dominate the convention, to write the platform, and to name the nominee.

The Bryan delegation, led by the William J. Bryan Club of Nebraska, entered the hall dramatically, and the delegates and galleries roared as the silver delegates chased the gold supporters from their seats. In spite of the high drama of the moment, Bryan kept out of sight. He was determined to save his appearance—and his speech—for the most psychologically appropriate moment.

That moment came during the closing moments of the debate over the platform. The majority report of the Resolutions Committee, of which Bryan was a member and which he had scrupulously avoided chairing, was clear on the silver issue: written by Bryan, it demanded "the free and unlimited coinage of both gold and silver at the present legal ratio of 16 to 1," as well as the monetization of silver and any other "kind of legal-tender money"; it was a clear demand for an inflated currency that had been sought by reformers for two decades.

The minority report was equally clear: bimetallism "would . . . impair contracts, disturb business, diminish the purchasing power of the wages of labor, and inflict irreparable evils upon our nation's commerce and industry." The minority report expressed Cleveland's convictions as surely as the majority report expressed Bryan's. As an interesting sidelight, the majority report had obliquely criticized Cleveland by declaring against the principle of a third term, while the minority report demanded recognition of Cleveland's services as president, an acknowledgment that was not forthcoming from the majority. The split between the two forces seemed irreparable.

Of most importance, however, was the fact that bimetallism was the chief issue, to which the other elements of reform were subordinated; even the perennial tariff issue was relegated to the background: "Until the money question is settled we are opposed to any agitation for further changes in our tariff laws, except such as are necessary to meet the deficit in revenue caused by the adverse decision of the Supreme Court on the income tax."

In its other details the platform was not radical; it was liberal. There were no ringing demands for public ownership of banks and railroads, no denunciations of wealth or industry, no calls to the barricades. It was a platform that could be shared by silver Democrats, silver Republicans, and Populists. At the same time, it was a complete break with the traditional Democracy of the past, represented by Grover Cleveland, and it pointed the way toward the Democracy of the twentieth century, that marked by the New Freedom of Woodrow Wilson, the New Deal of Franklin Roosevelt and the various Frontiers, Deals, and Societies that have marked Democratic policy and platforms in the second half of this century.

Bryan's personal strategy was as careful as his concern for the platform: he was determined to remain out of the convention's eye while the preliminary battles were being fought. Then, relatively unscathed, at the proper moment he could make his voice heard, his presence felt, and his bid for the nomination evident to supporters, sympathizers, and those who were looking for a winner. That opportunity, it appeared, would be during the debate over the platform. Bryan, in charge of majority strategy for the platform debate, scheduled himself as the last speaker, to whom was given the opportunity to stir the delegates to support the platform.

Whether or not it is true that, as folklore insists, Bryan had said that he had a speech in his pocket that, if he were given the opportunity to present it, would sweep the convention in his favor, Bryan did have such a speech; its elements had been tested countless times in party conventions, silver congresses, congressional debates, and rural stumping tours across half the nation. In it he determined to include the appeals that he knew would arouse the destined responses; and he had determined to use the art and skill of the orator's craft as effectively as he had learned to do. He knew his voice would reach every seat in the auditorium. He was confident. He told friends that the "logic of the situation" demanded his nomination, but on the eve of his speech, he remained a dark horse, and the betting odds favored Bland's nomination on the third ballot.

The platform debate began promptly at 10:00 A.M. on 9 July. Organizational trivia were disposed of quickly, bands played, and banners waved. Senator "Pitchford Ben" Tillman spoke first, demagogically eloquent, strongly sectional, to an increasingly hostile audience. When he sat down, he and his supporters knew he had lost whatever chance he might have for the nomination.

Senator David Hill, a sound-money man who, in another time in another convention might himself be nominated, spoke next, attacking the platform and presenting a reasoned plea for restraint. He was followed by the lackluster sound-money supporter Senator William F. Vilas, who spoke too long, leading Bryan to suggest that the time on both sides be extended ten minutes. Governor William E. Russell of Massachusetts spoke next, his physical weakness failing to project his calm progold arguments beyond the first rows of delegates.

I   *The Cross of Gold*

The debate had been unsatisfactory at best, and often dull, but the sequence had been staged very carefully by Bryan. As he strode confidently to the platform and bounded up the stairs, cheers echoed through the hall. He paused dramatically, and delegates climbed to their feet, on their chairs, into the aisles. Finally he motioned for a reluctant silence; from his first word, without apparently raising his voice, he reached every delegate in a silent, tension filled hall:

Mr. Chairman and Gentlemen of the Convention: I would be presumptuous, indeed, to present myself against the distinguished gentlemen to whom you have listened if this were a mere measuring of abilities; but this is not a contest between persons. The humblest citizen in all the land, when clad in the armor of a righteous cause, is stronger than all the hosts of error. I come to speak to you in defense of a cause as holy as the cause of liberty— the cause of humanity. [1]

In his introductory paragraph Bryan not only set the tone for the speech, stressing neither partisanship nor personality, neither sectionalism nor nationalism, but he set the tone for the campaign to follow, a tone in keeping with his past insistence on the priority of principles over parties or persons. In this spirit, he turned then to the competing resolutions concerning the Cleveland administration:

When this debate is concluded, a motion will be made to lay upon the table the resolution offered in condemnation of the administration, and also the resolution offered in commendation of the administration. We object to bringing this question down to the level of persons. The individual is but an atom; he is born, he acts, he dies; but the principles are eternal; and this has been a contest over a principle. (F, 199)

The issue, to Bryan, was as divisive as that which destroyed parties and threatened the existence of the nation a generation before: "Never before in the history of this country has there been witnessed such a contest as that through which we have just passed. Never before in the history of American politics has a great issue been fought out as this issue has been, by the votes of a great party . . ." (F, 199).

Bryan then traced the history of the silver question as it had affected the course of party affairs; and his retelling was skillful: the issue, rather than members of the party, had begun a grass-roots movement that had grown until it had become the paramount issue of the age and the convention, an issue already resolved by common standards of morality and by the common people of the country:

With a zeal approaching the zeal which inspired the crusaders who followed Peter the Hermit, our silver Democrats went forth from victory unto victory until they are now assembled, not to discuss, not to debate, but to enter up the judgment already rendered by the plain people of this country. In this contest brother has been arrayed against brother, father against son. The warmest ties of love, acquaintance and association have been disregarded; old leaders have been cast aside when they have refused to give expression to the sentiments of those whom they would lead, and new leaders have sprung up to give direction to this cause of truth. Thus has the contest been waged, and we have assembled here under as binding and solemn instructions as ever were imposed upon representatives of the people. (*F*, 200)

Still insisting that the problem was not one of persons but of principle, Bryan dismissed those who spoke against the platform with kindness. Of Senator Hill, he said, "it is not with gladness, my friends, that we find ourselves brought into conflict with those who are now arrayed on the other side" (*F*, 200); to Governor Russell, he expressed sympathy with his concern for business, but he insisted that Russell's definition of the businessman was not satisfactory:

You have made the definition of a business man too limited in its application. The man who is employed for wages is as much a business man as his employer; the attorney in a country town is as much a business man as the corporation counsel in a great metropolis; the merchant at the cross-roads store is as much a business man as the merchant of New York; the farmer who goes forth in the morning and toils all day . . . and who by the application of brain and muscle to the natural resources of the country creates wealth, is as much a business man as the man who goes upon the board of trade and bets upon the price of grain; the miners who go down a thousand feet into the earth, or climb two thousand feet upon the cliffs, and bring forth from their hiding places the precious metals to be poured into the channels of trade are as much business men as the few financial magnates who in a back room, corner the money of the world. We come to speak for this broader class of business men. . . . (*F*, 200)

Like Tillman, Bryan's appeal was sectional, but unlike his, it was not vituperative. It was the sectionalism of a westward movement passing rapidly from reality to myth as stagnation threatened what had become a principle foundation of the democratic society under Jefferson and Jackson:

Ah, my friends, we say not one word against those who live upon the Atlantic coast, but the hardy pioneers who have braved all the dangers of the wilderness, who have made the desert to blossom as the rose . . . who rear their children near to Nature's heart, where they can mingle their voices with the voices of the birds—out there where they have erected schoolhouses for the education of their young, churches where they praise their Creator, and cemeteries where rest the ashes of their dead—these people, we say, are as deserving of the consideration of our party as any people in this country. It is for these that we speak. We do not come as aggressors. Our war is not a war of conquest; we are fighting in the defense of our homes, our families, and posterity. We have petitioned, and our petitions have been scorned; we have entreated, and our entreaties have been disregarded; we have begged, and they have mocked when our calamity came. We beg no longer; we entreat no more; we petition no more. We defy them. (F, 200)

If any doubt remained among Bryan's listeners of the extent to which he saw economic and political conflict in terms of warfare, indeed, in terms of revolution, no less for being waged on the podium, the platform, the stump, and at the ballot box, his call for a leader erased that last question: "The gentlemen from Wisconsin [Senator William Vilas] has said that he fears a Robespierre. My friends, in this land of the free you need not fear that a tyrant will spring up from among the people. What we need is an Andrew Jackson to stand, as Jackson stood, against the encroachments of organized wealth."

Bryan turned then to the objections raised by the minority speakers to the platform reported by the majority, and he disposed quickly of each objection. To the accusation that it was a political document designed to lure votes, he did not object, but insisted that it was based upon old Democratic principles reinterpreted to meet new conditions; to the statement that the proposed income tax was a new idea that should not have been introduced, he pointed out that the significance of the tax was that it was just, concluding that "When I find a man who is not willing to bear his share of the burdens of the government which protects him, I find a man who is unworthy to enjoy the blessings of a government like ours" (F, 203).

But to Bryan the objections were largely trivial and the other planks in the platform of secondary importance; the most important plank in the platform and the issue upon which the Democratic party must stand or die was for him the currency issue:

And now, my friends, we come to the paramount issue. If they ask us why it is that we say more on the money question than we say upon the tariff question I reply that, if protection has slain its thousands, the gold standard has slain its tens of thousands…. When we have restored the money of the Constitution all other necessary reforms will be possible; but until this is done there is no other reform that can be accomplished. (*F*, 204)

The complexity of the issue, the success of the prosilver forces in making it appear simple, and the ambiguity of the gold forces, both Democrat and Republican, in responding to the silver forces provided the substance of Bryan's attack:

We go forth confident that we shall win. Why? Because upon the paramount issue of this campaign there is not a spot of ground upon which the enemy will dare to challenge battle. If they tell us that the gold standard is a good thing, we shall point to their platform and tell them that their platform pledges their party to get rid of the gold standard and substitute bimetallism. If the gold standard is a good thing, why try to get rid of it? I call your attention to the fact that some of the very people who are in this convention today and who tell us that we ought to declare in favor of international bimetallism—thereby declaring that the gold standard is wrong and that the principle of bimetallism is better—these very people four months ago were open and avowed advocates of the gold standard, and were then telling us that we could not legislate two metals together, even with the aid of all the world. (*F*, 205)

Of most importance to Bryan was the need to demonstrate the relationship between the platform and Democratic tradition, between economic principle and the association with Western silver mining interests; and in the attempt he used two simplistic explanations so easily understood and propagated that they are occasionally heard even yet. The first deals with what has been called the "trickle down," or conversely the "trickle up," theory:

The sympathies of the Democratic party, as shown by the platform, are on the side of the struggling masses who have ever been the foundation of the Democratic party. There are two ideas of government. There are those who believe that, if you will only legislate to make the well-to-do prosperous, their prosperity will leak through on those below. The Democratic idea, however, has been that if you legislate to make the masses prosperous, their prosperity will find its way up through every class which rests upon them. (*F*, 205)

The second view is that of the relationship between cities and farms as indicative of the flow of wealth, raw materials, food, and fibre as well as of the foundation of the country:

You come to us and tell us that the great cities are in favor of the gold standard; we reply that the great cities rest upon broad and fertile prairies. Burn down your cities and leave our farms, and your cities will spring up again as if by magic; but destroy our farms and the grass will grow in the streets of every city in the country. (F, 205)

Like Bryan's other political speeches, this one had been well constructed to build to this point; it is a partisan speech designed not merely to support the majority view at the expense of the minority, but also to establish a common traditional Jeffersonian bond between them so that, in the final analysis, it encourages partisanship over principle in the guise of defining the contemporary application of a century-old tradition. But this speech had another purpose. In its early moments Bryan had called out for an Andrew Jackson, an activist to lead the people. Now, it its closing lines, Bryan was determined to suggest that such a man had already appeared:

If they dare to come out in the open field and defend the gold standard as a good thing, we will fight them to the uttermost. Having behind us the producing masses of this nation and the world, supported by the commercial interests, the laboring interests, and the toilers everywhere, we will answer their demand for a gold standard by saying to them: You shall not press down upon the brow of labor this crown of thorns, you shall not crucify mankind upon a cross of gold. (F, 206)

Numerous accounts of the reactions, immediate and long range, to the speech have appeared, and they continue to play an important role in the literature about Bryan and of the histories of politics and public address in America. Bryan's own comments in *The First Battle* are prosaic and perhaps overly sensitive and apologetic; close to the fact, they reflect his awareness of its imperfections and his response to some of the criticism directed at it:

The concluding sentence of my speech was criticized both favorably and unfavorably. I had used the idea in substantially the same form in a speech in Congress, but did not recall the fact when I used it in the convention. A portion of the speech was extemporaneous, and its arrangement entirely so, but parts of it had been prepared for another occasion. Next to the conclusion the part most quoted was the definition of the term, "business men." (F, 206)

More than twenty-five years later, in the *Memoirs*, he recalled the speech and its aftermath in more detail:

After an unsatisfactory opening of the debate and after our side had been pounded unmercifully by the giants of the other side, all that was necessary to success was to put into the words the sentiments of a majority of the delegates to the convention—to be the voice of a triumphant majority. . . . I had no doubt that I could meet the expectations that had been aroused by this extraordinary combination of circumstances, because I had spent three years studying the question from every angle and I had time and again answered all the arguments that the other side had advanced. . . .

The delegates had been hammered by the very able speech of Senator Hill; they had been provoked by the language of General Vilas, and still further irritated by the speech of Governor Russell, and they were in a mood to applaud. Fortunately my voice filled the hall, and as I was perfectly familiar with the subject, I was prepared to answer in an extemporaneous speech the arguments which had been presented—that is, extemporaneous in so far as its arrangement was concerned. No new arguments had been advanced and therefore no new answers were required.[2]

Regardless of his familiarity with the material and his confidence as he approached the platform, Bryan must have been gratified by a response unique even in his broad and successful platform experience:

The excitement of the moment was so intense that I hurried to the platform and began at once. My nervousness left me instantly and I felt as composed as if I had been speaking to a small audience on an unimportant occasion. From the first sentence the audience was with me. My voice reached to the uttermost parts of the hall. . . .

I shall never forget the scene upon which I looked. I believe it unrivaled in any convention ever held in our country. The audience seemed to rise and sit down as one man. At the close of a sentence it would rise and shout, and when I began upon another sentence, the room was still as a church. . . .

The audience acted like a trained choir—in fact, I thought of a choir as I noted how instantaneously and in unison they responded to each point made.

The situation was so unique and the experience so unprecedented that I have never expected to witness its counterpart.

At the conclusion of my speech the demonstration spread over nearly the entire convention.[3]

The demonstration to which Bryan refers has been described many times: his dramatic conclusion, a graphic reenactment of his last metaphors, in which he first raised his hands, fingers spread, to his temples so that his audience was almost mesmerized into seeing the bloody crowning, and then, with his arms straight out from his sides, the final image, resulted in a long moment of silence. Then, the spell broken, the hall erupted with shouts, cheers, rebel and Indian yells, brass bands playing, as twenty thousand people responded to Bryan's plea. Almost with one voice the delegates called for Bryan to lead them, and cooler heads, including John Peter Altgeld, conceded him the nomination in a foreshortened convention ritual. Nevertheless, when Murat Halstead phoned McKinley, the Republican nominee, that Bryan would be the convention's nominee, McKinley called the pronouncement "Rot!"[4] Bryan's platform was passed by a two to one majority, and as the convention recessed to meet again that evening for the nominating ritual, the silver Democrats and their young leader had driven Cleveland's Democrats from party control. A new Democratic era had begun.

Bryan's coverage of the ritual of nomination in *The First Battle* is restrained, depending upon the statistics of the five ballots necessary for his nomination to provide insight into a process that he knew was inevitable. From the beginning it was evident that two of the thirteen candidates were serious. On the first ballot, Bland, the long-time leader of the silver forces, received 235 votes and Bryan 137 out of a total of 930; on the second, Bland received 281 and Bryan 197; on the third, Bland received 291 and Bryan 219; on the critical fourth, Bland dropped to 241, while Bryan climbed to 280. The fifth gave Bryan 652, and Bland 11; the nomination was declared unanimous and, as the *New York Sun* declared with dubious logic, "an ugly little Anarchist from Illinois" had become the presidential nominee of a major American party.

Bryan's nomination was not, however, as it has often been called, a historical accident resulting from the emotional impact of a speech. Rather, it was the culmination of the forces of protest and reform which over the previous two decades had attempted to make themselves heard in the councils of the major political parties. Bryan was a product of those forces, and he became their servant and their voice, a voice that could and would be heard, long before his nomination. As the voice of the voiceless masses of the South and West, as the articulate spokesman for inarticulate delegates who had come out of their regions seeking a leader who would make clear their needs and demands as well as their dreams, Bryan had become at once the leader and the symbol of a movement that was to redirect the political and economic evolution of the nation as it made the Democratic party, for the first time since Jackson's day, the party of reform in America. He was indeed, as Edgar Lee Masters has commented, "the beginning of a changed America,"[5] a manifestation of the rebirth of the American dream.

II   *The 1896 Campaign*

Bryan's campaign for the presidency in 1896 was the most strenuous in American political history. While McKinley waged his "front-porch campaign" from his home in Canton, Ohio, Bryan traveled more than 18,000 miles by train, thus inventing the whistlestop while giving almost three thousand speeches during the course of dozens of days of eighteen hours of campaigning. Although the campaign began officially on 10 August 1896 with a speech accepting the nomination at a rally in Madison Square Garden in New York, it had actually begun on Bryan's return trip to Lincoln after a pause on Sunday, 12 June.

Bryan passed through Illinois in a tour that was almost triumphal, foreshadowing the enthusiasm with which he was to be met during his trips South and West in the campaign. After brief, informal speeches at Champaign and Mattoon as well as smaller towns, he and his party stopped overnight in Salem, where on 15 June he spoke at length in the afternoon and more briefly in the evening. Determined to avoid politics, he reminisced about the lessons learned in Salem:

It was in this city that I received my first instructions in democracy—I do not use the word in a party sense, but in the broader sense in which democracy recognizes the brotherhood of man. It was here that I learned the truth expressed by the poet, that "Honor and fame from no condition rise." It was here that I learned that clothes do not make the man; that all who contribute to the nation's greatness and have the good of the country at heart—no matter what their position in life, their ancestry or their surroundings—stand upon a common ground and share in a common citizenship. It was here, too, that I was taught to believe in freedom of conscience—that principle which must go hand in hand with a broad democracy; that every man has a right to worship God according to the dictates of his own conscience, and that no government like ours can dictate how a man shall serve his God. (*F*, 234)

That evening, he was less nostalgic but no less philosophic:

If there is one lesson taught by six thousand years of history it is that truth is omnipotent and will at last prevail. You may impede its progress, you may delay its triumph; but after awhile it will show its irresistible power, and those who stand in its way will be crushed beneath it. You ask me if these reforms which we advocate will be accomplished. I say that if they are right they will be accomplished. We who believe that they are right can only do our best and give such impetus to them as we are able to give, and then trust to the righteousness of our cause to prevail over those who oppose us. (*F*, 235)

These speeches were not only typical of Bryan's attempt to rise above partisanship before beginning the formal campaign, but they were typical too of an attempt, somewhat misguided, to rise above partisanship in the campaign itself. Stung by accounts in the Eastern press describing him as a Western anarchist or demagogue, he was determined to refrain from the exuberance for which he was noted in the West, to minimize departures from his prepared speeches, and to exhibit in every way the decorum suitable for one who aspires to the presidency.

Nevertheless, as hostile newspapers began to intensify their attacks during his journey East, Bryan moved to the attack. In Chicago, stung by newspaper assertions that he had no influential support, he said,

When I see this assemblage tonight and then remember what the newspapers of this city say, I am reminded of an expression recently made by one of our friends: "There is nobody on our side but the people." And as I look into the faces of these people and remember that our enemies call them a mob, and say they are a menace to free government, I ask: Who shall save the people from themselves? I am proud to have in this campaign the support of those who call themselves common people. If I had behind me the great trusts and combinations, I knew that I would no sooner take my seat than they would demand that I use my power to rob people in their behalf. (*F*, 303–4)

As he moved East he began to hear rumors of what was to become a real fear as the campaign progressed: the attempts of employers to coerce or frighten their employees into voting for McKinley. In Alliance, Ohio, in McKinley's Ohio back yard, Bryan referred to that threat for the first time while continuing to keep his remarks on a suitable high plane: "The employer and the employee have a right to differ in politics. Remember that we live in a nation where the salary which a man receives does not purchase his citizenship. The dollars which are paid for the labor of the hand or mind are paid for labor and not for votes" (*F*, 305–6).

III   *The Acceptance Speech*

As the train moved into what Bryan had referred to as "the enemy's country"—he had been criticized for the remark by the Republicans—he was pleased by the sizes of the crowds who came to see him and hear him speak. References to leaving the "Wild West," only to find an equally "Wild East" met with applause, and he began to regard his Eastern strategy as already successful. In order to continue to project an image of moderation, he determined to read his acceptance speech at Madison Square Garden, knowing, as he later said, that to many of his audience it would be a disappointment. After introductory remarks by Governor William J. Stone of Missouri, who referred to Bryan as "a plain man of the people," and a reading of the letter from the Democratic National Committee officially notifying Bryan of his nomination, Bryan stepped forward and, with neither drama in his gestures nor fire in his voice, began to read.

Much of the speech was defensive in tone, with the early portions devoted to the denial of charges raised against the platform, particularly the continued assertion that it was radical, dangerous, and un-American. To these charges Bryan replied firmly and with dignity:

We are not surprised that some of our opponents, in the absence of better argument, resort to abusive epithets, but they may rest assured that no language, however violent, no invectives, however vehement, will lead us to depart a single hair's breadth from the course marked out by the National Convention. The citizen, either public or private, who assails the character and questions the patriotism of the delegates assembled in the Chicago convention, assails the character and questions the patriotism of the millions who have arrayed themselves under the banner there raised. (*F*, 305)

From his general defense he turned to charges against specific details of the program:

While the money question overshadows all other questions in importance, I desire it distinctly understood that I shall offer no apology for the income tax plank of the Chicago platform. . . .
I shall also refuse to apologize for the exercise by it of the right to dissent from a decision of the Supreme Court. (*F*, 319–20)

Then Bryan turned to "the paramount question of this campaign—the money question," and attempted to present a reasoned, logical analysis and defense of the Democratic demand for currency reform:

It is scarcely necessary to defend the principle of bimetallism. No national party during the entire history of the United States has ever declared against it, and no party in this campaign has the temerity to oppose it. Three parties—the Democratic, Populist, and Silver parties—have not only declared for bimetallism, but have outlined the specific legislation necessary to restore silver to its ancient position by the side of gold. The Republican platform expressly declares that bimetallism is desirable when it pledges the Republican party to aid in securing it as soon as the assistance of certain foreign nations can be obtained. . . . The gold standard has been weighed in the balance and found wanting. Take from it the powerful support of the money-owning and the money-changing classes and it cannot stand for one day in any nation in the world. It was fastened upon the United States without discussion before the people, and its friends have never yet been willing to make a verdict before the voters on that issue. (F, 320–21)

From this restrained assertion, Bryan went on to recite the damage done the farmers and workers, the small businessmen, merchants, and manufacturers, each of whom found it difficult or impossible to borrow or earn the cash necessary to do business freely in a free economy; conversely, he insisted that those investors who might be expected to profit from a gold standard often found their well-being and security nonexistent as the nation's economy suffered the continued effect of too little money in too few hands.

Bryan's conclusion was equally restrained, recognizing that sectional differences separated the electorate but insisting that the differences were illusory, that the welfare of the rural sections would rise or fall only in relation to the urban areas:

Citizens of New York, I have traveled from the center of the continent to the seaboard that I might, in the very beginning of the campaign, bring you greeting from the people of the West and South and assure you that their desire is not to destroy but to build up. They invite you to accept the principles of a living faith, rather than listen to those who preach the gospel of despair and advise endurance of the ills you have. The advocates of free coinage believe that, in striving to secure the immediate restoration of bimetallism, they are laboring in your behalf as well as in their own behalf. . . . You cannot sell unless the people have money with which to buy, and they cannot obtain the money with which to buy unless they are able to sell their products at remunerative prices. . . . You cannot afford to join the money changers in supporting a financial policy which, by destroying the purchasing power of the products of toil, must in the end discourage the creation of wealth.

I ask, I expect, your cooperation. It is true that a few of your financiers would fashion a new figure—a figure representing Columbia, her hands bound fast with fetters of gold and her face turned toward the sea—but this figure can never express your idea of this nation. You will rather turn for inspiration to the heroic statue which guards the entrance to your city. . . . That figure—Liberty enlightening the world—is emblematic of the mission of our nations among the nations of the earth. With a government which derives its powers from the consent of the governed, secures to all the people freedom of conscience, freedom of thought and freedom of speech, guarantees equal rights to all and promises special privileges to none, the United States should be an example in all that is good, and the leading spirit in every movement which has for its objective the uplifting of the human race. (*F*, 337)

The speech was restrained; indeed, it might have been considerably more successful as a nonpartisan lecture—as some parts of it were to be on occasion in the future—than as the partisan speech more than twelve thousand Democrats had gathered in Madison Square Garden to hear. Reaction too was restrained: nearly half of Bryan's audience left the auditorium before it was over.

In its place at the beginning of what was to be perhaps the hardest-fought campaign in American political history, the speech was both a tactical and a strategic error. Not only did it fail to arouse faithful Eastern Democrats of the silver persuasion, the party faithful, or those not firmly aligned with the gold forces, but it gave many of them the impression that what they had heard of the young giant-killer from the West was erroneous or exaggerated. Nor, in terms of the strategy of the campaign, did it alleviate Eastern fears of economic anarchy or worse. Bryan had made a major gesture of political good-feeling, and, whether it was the result of his own decision or of bad advice from the East, it was not successful.

Nevertheless, the speech was praised by the Bryan loyalist press; it was "distinctly creditable and dignified" according to the *Chicago Record,* and "unanswerable" to the *New York Journal.* But to Theodore Roosevelt, Bryan "fell perfectly flat," and to others he was now "the Boy Reader of the Platte." But neither McKinley nor Mark Hanna underestimated Bryan, the latter insisting that the Republicans would need a campaign chest of three million dollars, a sum far beyond the expenses of any previous campaign, to defeat him. Hanna, James J. Hill, William Rockefeller, and Cornelius Bliss became active in fund-raising, declaring to frightened businessmen that if Bryan won, they might as well turn their assets into cash and leave the country, and they encouraged businessmen and industrialists to use whatever means necessary to induce their employees to vote for McKinley. Anyone with doubts about the relationship between the new capitalists and the Republican party had them resolved before the first ballots were cast.

IV   The Long-Distance Campaign

Evident, too, was the fact that Eastern Democratic leaders were largely frightened of Bryan. Gold Democrats selected Bourke Cochran, an eloquent Irish-born former congressman, to speak against Bryan, and on 18 August he spoke to a large audience on the topic "In Opposition to Repudiation" and announced his support for McKinley. But the rural Easterners, like the Westerners and Southerners, saw Bryan as their spokesman, and they refused to follow their leaders into the Republican camp. In the East as well as the West Bryan's reputation as a man of the people was secure. He must have sensed this when with a good deal of satisfaction he spoke to rank and file Democrats outside Madison Square Garden:

> Some of your financiers have boasted that they favor gold, but you shall teach them that they must carry their ideas far enough to believe, not in gold, but in the golden rule. Our opponents have been threatening to organize a gold standard Democratic party, but be not afraid; you will search the pages of history in vain to find a battle ever won by an army of generals. They have not a private in their ranks. Now, my friends, I want you to set an example for your opponents which they have not set for you. They claim that they represent the respectable element of society. Teach them that a man's respectability cannot be proven by slandering every one who differs from him in opinion. (*F*, 338)

Nevertheless, the combination of the hostility and indifference of Eastern Democratic leaders, together with a severe shortage of funds, a problem that was to persist throughout Bryan's campaign, led him to abandon plans for a two-week campaign tour in the East and spend the greater part of his time, money, and energy in the West and South, where he hoped to put together his winning combination of electoral votes. At Modalin, New York, on his journey West to give a Labor Day speech in Chicago, he gave what he considered his first campaign speech. It was the first in the sense that, like the bulk of the speeches to follow, it stressed the money problem as the most important in the campaign, and it attempted to convey the complexities of economic principles and practice in

terms sufficiently simply so that the electorate understood what it
was that he insisted he and his party stood for:

> I want you to remember that in the discussion of this money question
> there are certain fundamental principles; and when you understand those
> principles you understand the money question.
>
> What is the principle that underlies it all? It is that the law of supply and
> demand applies to money as it does to everything else.
>
> You know that if the world's crop next year of a certain article is very
> much greater than the crop this year, that article will fall in price; if the
> crop is much smaller than this year, the article will rise in price. You know
> that the law of supply and demand reaches and controls money, as well as
> other forms of property. It reaches and controls all sorts of property.
>
> Increase the amount of money more rapidly than the demand for money
> increases, and you lower the value of a dollar; decrease the quantity of
> money while the demand for it increases, and you increase the value of a
> dollar. When you understand that, you understand the essence of the
> money question. When you understand that, you understand what its effect
> is on you; and then you can tell where your interest lies. When you
> understand that principle, then you understand why the great crusade in
> favor of the gold standard finds its home among the holders of fixed
> investments, who, by such legislation, raise the value of the property which
> they hold.
>
> I am not giving you my authority for it; I can quote you authority which
> our opponents dare not question. (*F*, 347–48)

While Bryan began to take his campaign to the people, thus
beginning a tradition that still endures, McKinley insisted that the
people come to him, to his front porch in Canton; aided by
excursion rates on the railroads, they did so in droves. According to
Charles G. Dawes, McKinley had said that "I will not try to compete
with Bryan. I am going to stay here and do what campaigning is to
be done. If I took a whole train, Bryan would take a sleeper; if I
took a sleeper, Bryan would take a chair car; if I took a chair car, he
would ride a freight train. I can't outdo him, and I am not going to
try."[6] Apocryphal or not, as the story suggests, Bryan's reputation
for dramatics as well as eloquence had already become part of the
folklore of American politics. He found it amusing that McKinley
had freed him to travel through much of the campaign undisturbed
in a private car called "The Idler," an irony that apparently escaped
his opponent's attention.

Although Bryan determined that he would not engage in ex-
changes of invective, he determined also that he would not use the

restrained tactic which had proved so unsuccessful in New York, where he lost an audience for the first time in his life. Most of his campaign energies were to be devoted to the Ohio and Mississippi Valleys; there he made the bulk of his major addresses, and there, often throwing away his text, he never lost an audience. Conversely, visits by Bryan were festive occasions, often enjoyed as much by local Republicans as by Democrats and Populists. He spoke to crowds of 50,000 in Columbus, 10,000 in Springfield, and 40,000 in Toledo, all in McKinley's own Ohio; so large were his crowds elsewhere that predictions of his victory were commonplace, the *New York Herald* anticipating in October that he would win 237 electoral votes, thirteen more than sufficient for election. Others predicted that he would carry thirty-six of the forty-five states. Terrified, Republican supporters among the businessmen and industrialists conveyed their fears to their employees, the great McCormick Machine Company, for example, announcing that it would be forced to shut down if Bryan won. Other firms threatened cancellation of orders in case of a Bryan victory.

Stung by particularly vituperative criticism from what he termed "gold standard ministers," at Wilmington, Delaware, Bryan commented extemporaneously, according to the *Wilmington Evening Journal,* that

You will find in our cities preachers of the gospel, enjoying every luxury themselves, who are indifferent to the cries of distress which come up from the masses of the people. It was told of a princess in a foreign land that, when someone said to her, "the people are crying for bread," she replied, "Why don't they eat cake?" Tell some of these ministers of the gospel that men out of work are driven into crime, and they cannot understand why everyone is not as well off as themselves. When I have seen preachers of the gospel using even more bitter speech than politicians against the clamorings of the people, I have wondered where they got the religion that they preach. My friends, the common people were never aided in their struggles by those who were so far beyond them that they could not feel their needs and sympathize with their interests. (*F,* 469)

Bryan was unwilling to accept the accuracy of the garbled prose in the paper's account, but he did admit that it was "substantially correct." Indeed, he recalled in *The First Battle* that

The Republican National Committee sent a circular letter to various church societies, pointing out the harm which, according to the gold standard doctrine, free coinage would bring to those engaged in church work. I referred on a few occasions to this appeal to the churches.

At Albany I suggested that there was one argument which might be made by the gold standard advocates, if they could find a minister who looked at the question purely from the standpoint of dollars and cents. The argument was this, that the gold standard produces want and destitution; that want and destitution result in an increase in crime; that an increase in crime might increase the demand for ministers to counteract it. . . . (*F*, 470)

As the election neared, the Republican won victories in Vermont on 1 September and Maine two weeks later, both by substantial margins that suggested the defection of gold Democrats. Nevertheless, predictions of Bryan's election increased. On 8 September he accepted the National Silver Party nomination and on 13 October he accepted that of the Populists, leading John Hay to comment "What a dull and serious campaign we are having! The Boy Orator makes only one speech—but he makes it twice a day. . . . He has succeeded in scaring the Goldbugs out of their wits. . . ."

The tempo of Republican attacks increased each time Bryan ventured East. At Yale University he was heckled viciously, leading him to remark that "I have been so used to talking to young men who earn their own living that I hardly know what language to use to address myself to those who desire to be known, not as the creators of wealth, but as the distributors of wealth which somebody else created." Edward Atkinson described him as "leading the army of the half-witted." When President E. Benjamin Andrews of Brown University invited Bryan to speak, he was fired by his board of trustees. According to the *New York Times*, increasing numbers of manufacturing plants in New England were marked by signs proclaiming that "This factory will be closed on the morning after the November election if Bryan is elected. If McKinley is elected, employment will go on as usual." Henry Cabot Lodge called Bryan "The Boy Orator of the Platte" and then reminded his audience that "The Platte is a stream 1,250 miles long, with an average depth of six inches and a wide mouth."

As the campaign entered its last month, Republican attacks continued, and Bryan campaigned constantly, giving the lie to the name of his campaign private car; "The Idler" traveled 12,837 miles through the Midwest and Upper Mississippi Valley. As he began to fear increased Democratic defections as the result of Republican threats, Bryan said,

I am not going to say one word to prevent any Democrat doing what his conscience tells him to be right, but if any Democrat is going to leave the Democratic party, I want him to find his reason in his head or in his heart, and not in his pocketbook. If he finds his reason in his pocketbook, I want him to be man enough to say that that is where the reason is, and not say that he leaves because all the rest of the Democrats have become anarchists. If a Democrat is connected with a trust and loves the trust more than he does his country, let him say so, and we will bid him Godspeed. If there is any Democrat who is connected with a corporation and prefers to retain his connection with that corporation rather than to stand with the Democratic party in its effort to bring the Government back to the position of Jefferson and Jackson, let him say so. (F, 536–37)

In Minneapolis Bryan spoke on bimetallism to a group of ladies, discussing "an economic question before those who do not vote upon it, and yet I offer no apology" (F, 547); although he was not to align himself with the women's suffrage movement for another two decades, he must have sowed some of the seeds for that act when, in a highly innovative approach to politics, perhaps the first such action in a political campaign, he assured these women that "The money question is not too deep to be understood by the American people" (F, 548) and then went on to explain it in simple, clear terminology and vivid metaphor. As he neared home again, perhaps sensing defeat, he spoke once more in the Chicago of his triumphal nomination:

I may be wrong—I have never claimed infallibility—but when I examine a question and reach a conclusion, I am willing to stand by what I believe, I care not what may happen. In this struggle for the restoration of bimetallism there was a time when I had less company than I have now. Some of the Chicago papers have called me a demagogue. If there is one thing which I am not, it is a demagogue. A demagogue is a man who advocates a thing which he does not believe in order to conciliate those who differ from him. A demagogue is a man who is willing to advocate anything, whether he believes it or not, which will be advantageous to him and gain him popularity. Now, my friends, I have never advocated, during my public life, a single thing which I did not myself believe. I have proven my willingness to go down in defeat when I was in a minority rather than surrender my convictions, and I have always been willing to accept defeat when it came. I say this here because in this city most of the papers are against us, and I must defend myself. (F, 581)

Bryan's last trip took him from Chicago through rural Iowa and

Nebraska to his home in Lincoln; during the campaign he had traveled more miles than any American presidential contender had ever done before, and he had spoken to more people, records that would in both cases endure until the advent of faster transportation, the public address system, and electronic media of communication. He had taken his case to the people, a case that was indeed based upon one issue, as his critics maintained; but it was, he was convinced, the most important issue that the American people faced, an issue that he believed transcended all others, and he waited for the people to speak to him. On 5 November 1896 they did so, and he sent William McKinley the following telegram: "Senator Jones has just informed me that the returns indicate your election, and I hasten to extend my congratulations. We have submitted the issue to the American people and their will is law."

Convinced that he had fought the good fight, Bryan did not indulge in hindsight, analysis, explanation, or apologies in the last chapters of *The First Battle;* he knew that it was just the good fight and no more. After careful computation of McKinley's pluralities in some states, his own in others, and the relation between each and the electoral voting, he concluded "This calculation is made to show how narrow was the defeat of bimetallism and what is possible for the future" (*F*, 607). The future that concerned him was only four years away.

V Aftermath—and Prelude

The last chapter in *The First Battle* is called "The Future"; it is devoted to the few months between the election and the book's publication, but it is concerned, too, with the strategy for maintaining the party control necessary to support a bimetal platform and candidate in the last election of the nineteenth century.

The most important part of a successful strategy for 1900 was, Bryan knew, maintaining and strengthening the loose coalition of bimetal Democrats, Republicans, Populists, and Independents that had emerged under his candidacy in 1896. Consequently, convinced that the major issue of 1896 would again be the major issue in 1900, he issued a statement, not to Democrats, but to bimetallists, in which he made clear what he saw to be the path of the future. From the beginning he was convinced and in turn sought to convince his fellow bimetallists that the setback was temporary:

Conscious that millions of loyal hearts are saddened by temporary defeat,

I beg to offer a word of hope and encouragement. No cause ever had supporters more brave, earnest and devoted than those who have espoused the cause of bimetallism. They have fought from conviction, and have fought with all the zeal which conviction inspires. Events will prove whether they are right or wrong. Having done their duty as they saw it, they have nothing to regret. . . . The friends of bimetallism have not been vanquished; they have simply been overcome. They believe that the gold standard is a conspiracy of the moneychangers against the welfare of the human race, and they will continue their warfare against it. (F, 625)

After providing moral and psychological encouragement, Bryan turned then to political encouragement:

But in spite of the efforts of the Administration and its supporters; in spite of the threats of money loaners at home and abroad; in spite of the coercion practiced by corporate employers; in spite of trusts and syndicates; in spite of an enormous Republican campaign fund, and in spite of the influence of a hostile daily press, bimetallism has almost triumphed in its first great fight. The loss of a few States, and that, too, by very small pluralities, has defeated bimetallism for the present, but bimetallism emerges from the contest stronger than it was four months ago.

In the face of an enemy rejoicing in its victory, let the roll be called for the next engagement. I urge all friends of bimetallism to renew their allegiance to the cause. If we are right, as I believe we are, we shall yet triumph. Until convinced of his error, let each advocate of bimetallism continue the work. Let all silver clubs retain their organization, hold regular meetings and circulate literature. Our opponents have succeeded in this campaign and must now put their theories to the test. Instead of talking mysteriously about "sound money" and an "honest dollar" they must now elaborate and defend a financial system. Every step taken by them should be publicly considered by the silver clubs. Our cause has prospered most where the money question has been longest discussed among the people. During the next four years it will be studied all over this Nation even more than it has been studied in the past. The year 1900 is not far away. Before that year arrives international bimetallism will cease to deceive; before that year arrives those who have called themselves gold standard Democrats will become bimetallists and be with us, or they will become Republicans and be open enemies; before that year arrives trusts will have convinced still more people that a trust is a menace to private welfare and to public safety; before that year arrives the evil effects of a gold standard will be even more evident than they are now, and the people, then ready to demand an American financial policy for the American people, will join with us in the immediate restoration of the free and unlimited coinage of gold and silver at the present legal ratio of 16 to 1, without waiting for the aid or consent of any other nation. (F, 625–26)

Bryan ended *The First Battle* optimistically; he believed that "1900 will mark the overthrow of the single gold standard" (*F*, 628–29). *The First Battle* was actually the first document of that campaign rather than the last of 1896. It is in no sense either a history or a memoir of the campaign, although it contains the raw material of both; it is a record and a political document valuable for what it contains not only about Bryan personally but also about his cause. Loose in structure, nearly but not entirely chronological in order, combining personal and public elements in what is a permanent public record, it expresses confidence as it attempts to retain Bryan's political organization intact and to give it spirit and energy to provide the momentum for 1900 that had been lacking before 1896. That momentum alone, Bryan was convinced, would make the difference between the results of 1896 and 1900. Much would happen during those four years, not all of it unpredictable, but Bryan was confident that the issue of 1896 would be that of 1900. He was prepared to fight, and he was reasonably confident of victory.

CHAPTER 6

The Second Battle

THE First Battle was not only a record of the campaign of 1896 and an anticipation of that of 1900, but it was effective in alleviating one of Bryan's perennial problems—a personal money shortage. It was financially successful far beyond anything Bryan had anticipated, selling more than a thousand copies a day during the first two months of 1897, the total sales reaching more than two hundred thousand copies. By 31 August 1897 it had paid Bryan $35,643 in royalties, much of which he distributed directly to silver organizations in proportion to votes they had secured for him in the election.

Early in 1897 Bryan made public his conviction that the currency issue would be the major issue again in 1900. He committed himself at the Jackson Day dinner in Chicago on 7 January 1897, asserting that "The contest for the restoration of the money of the Constitution will go on with renewed vigor. The people who advocated free silver before the election advocate it now. The election . . . has not overthrown the convictions of those who believe that the gold standard is a conspiracy against the welfare of the producing masses."[1] During the rest of the year he addressed the bimetallism issue on almost every occasion, although he did speak, particularly to state legislatures, on other aspects of reform, including railroad regulation, direct election of United States senators, trust control, and progressive constitutional reform.

But the key issue to Bryan remained the silver issue, and second to that was his practical political concern for fusion among the prosilver parties. Free Silver Clubs—no longer "Bryan" Free Silver Clubs but "1900" Free Silver Clubs in deference to Bryan's wishes—remained active, and plans were made to field 5,000 or more free-silver speakers across the country. Bryan determined to make Nebraska the bastion of the cause, with a model fusion party.

That September the three Nebraska prosilver parties—Silver

96

Democrat, Silver Republican, and Populist—held their conventions in Lincoln simultaneously, and, although the three parties met and deliberated separately, there was a remarkable degree of accord in their pronouncements. Bryan spoke at all three conventions and, although he feared that an eloquent young rising star in the Democratic party named A. C. Shallenberger had overshadowed him, he was pleased with his reception. At the gathering of the three groups at the Lincoln capitol grounds, he asserted again that the silver issue was the basic problem in the drive toward economic and social reform: "The money question must be settled before other questions can be seriously considered. To fight each other in the face of a united and unscrupulous enemy would not only postpone the restoration of bimetallism but endanger the success of every other necessary reform."[2]

As 1898 neared, Bryan made clear the program under which he sought fusion of the silver parties and which he predicted would lead them to victory in 1900. Silver coinage at the ratio of 16 to 1 led the list, but also included were retention of greenbacks, the outlawing of paper money issued by national banks and of interest-bearing bonds in time of peace, and the forbidding of government by injunction. Also listed were trust and railroad regulation, the establishment of an income tax, and the use of arbitration in labor disputes. On 15 February 1898 the three parties, as nearly one as they were ever to be, issued a call for victory in 1900.

However, the next day, 16 February 1898, the American political landscape was changed almost beyond recognition. Early that morning, the second-line battleship U.S.S. *Maine*, in the harbor of Havana, Cuba, on what was either a good-will mission or a show of force, was rended by a submarine mine or an internal explosion and sent to the bottom at the cost of 250 American lives. The explosion brought to the forefront of public attention the Cuban crisis, a three-year struggle between Cuban rebels and Spanish troops, the pressures of which had increased dramatically while Bryan and McKinley were pursuing a solution to the money question and related domestic problems. The explosion revived American expansionism, the reflection of a faith in American manifest destiny that had taken the American republic from the east bank of the Mississippi River to the Pacific Coast in less than a century and promised to make the Pacific an American lake. Expansionism had never been the prerogative of either political party, and Bryan's idols Jefferson and Jackson had both shared the vision, while others,

including Lincoln, had denied it. Much of the expansionist sentiment early in the century had been Western; as the twentieth
century approached, however, it had largely become Eastern and
Republican, the group including Senator Henry Cabot Lodge,
Assistant Secretary of the Navy Theodore Roosevelt, and others. To
their voice was added that of the so-called "yellow" press, particularly William Randolph Hearst's *New York Journal* and Joseph
Pulitzer's *New York World.*

I   *Intervention in Cuba*

While McKinley, supported by Bryan, counseled moderation and
discretion, the yellow press, the expansionists, and a congressional
faction demanded war. While Bryan refused to discuss the Cuba
question until a full report on the *Maine* sinking was available, and
he continued to insist that the money problem would remain
paramount in 1900, the nation moved toward war. On 9 March,
however, he supported a defense appropriation, saying that it would
make clear the fact that "Congress and the American people,
without regard to political differences, are ready to support the
Administration in any action necessary for the protection of the
honor and welfare of the nation." Thereafter convinced that the
United States must defend Cuba, he appeared on lecture platforms
waving a small American flag in one hand and a Cuban flag in the
other. His patriotism had superseded his pacifism, as it was to do
again in 1917 when, under a Democratic administration, the United
States entered the European war.

Nevertheless, Bryan did not take political advantage of the
situation; although he had virtually ignored foreign policy questions
in Congress, even while Cleveland was involved in the Hawaii and
Venezuela problems, thus suggesting his concern with domestic
rather than foreign affairs, he might have captured the jingoist
leadership, thus undermining McKinley's leadership, but he did
not. Conversely, he did not attack McKinley's drift toward war. On
21 April McKinley issued a congressional ultimatum to Spain; on
the twenty-third he issued a call for 125,000 volunteers; on 25 April
Congress declared war, and Bryan, in Boston, led the cheers of a
crowd of more than 20,000 people.

Bryan had not become a jingoist, however, nor had he become an
expansionist; his remarks on intervention made his position clear.
Not only did they provide his rationale for acceptance of the war,

but they provided the foundation for his attitude toward its aftermath:

Yes, the time for intervention has arrived. Humanity demands that we shall act. Cuba lies within sight of our shores and the sufferings of her people cannot be ignored unless we, as a nation, have become so engrossed in money making as to be indifferent to distress.

Intervention may be accompanied by danger and expense, but existence cannot be separated from responsibility and responsibility sometimes leads a nation, as well as an individual, into danger. A neighbor, must sometimes incur danger for a neighbor, and a friend for a friend.[3]

For Bryan, the world of international affairs was not unlike the neighborhood of small-town Illinois in which his values had been formed. Like his political mentors—indeed, like the image of Christ that dominated his religious convictions—he did not subscribe to peace at any price, nor did he seek quarrels or propose violence, except upon the strongest provocation.

With the declaration of war on 25 April, for Bryan the die was cast, and on the same day he offered himself to President McKinley: "I hereby place my services at your command during the war with Spain and assure you of my willingness to perform to the best of my ability any duty to which you, as the commander-in-chief of the Army and Navy may see fit to assign me." To McKinley, faced not only with prosecuting a war but maintaining his position for the election in 1900, the letter was a dilemma. Twelve days later he asked Bryan which branch of service he felt best qualified to serve in. Bryan, of course, had no special qualification for any branch.

This exchange was simply an exercise in political one-upmanship, but there is no real reason to doubt either man's integrity. Bryan did want to serve, but his flair for the dramatic and his political instinct led him to volunteer directly to the president rather than anonymously to a recruiting sergeant. Conversely, apparently McKinley could not make an acceptable decision, and his best course was to delay, hoping that no decision would be necessary.

As McKinley anticipated, no decision was necessary as Bryan sought his place through a more receptive and friendlier political structure. His first preference was to serve on the staff of General Joseph Wheeler, former Confederate general, a member of Congress, and an old friend. But he had to be a commissioned officer first. With the First and Second Nebraska regiments activated, he hoped for a commission in a third. That regiment, when it was authorized, was understood to be Bryan's regiment, and he enlisted immediately, to be elected its colonel by its members and confirmed by Governor Holcomb of Nebraska. On 13 July 1898 he became colonel of the Third Nebraska Regiment, United States Volunteers—the "Silver Regiment," as it quickly became known.

II   *Imperialism*

Bryan's military experience was not unlike that of the majority of his contemporaries, except for the added complication of its political dimension. Like almost all his military colleagues, Bryan was an enthusiastic amateur, but he was fortunate in having as lieutenant colonel the experienced Victor Vifquain, a graduate of the military school in his native Belgium and winner of the Congressional Medal of Honor in the Civil War. On 18 July 1898 the regiment left Omaha for Camp Cuba Libre, near Jacksonville, Florida, where it spent the war fighting malaria and typhoid rather than Spaniards. On 12 August the war was over, and on 17 August McKinley announced the release of 75,000 to 100,000 volunteers. But the Third Regiment and Bryan were not among them. Instead, the Third was slated for occupation duty in Cuba.

On 8 September the regiment moved to what was hoped to be a healthier camp, but it was no better, and Bryan, falling ill himself, declared that they had "volunteered to attempt to break the yoke of Spain in Cuba, and for nothing else. They did not volunteer to attempt to subjugate other peoples, or establish United States sovereignty elsewhere."[4] He went to Washington to carry the case for the Third's release to the War Department, but he promptly fell ill. In the war's aftermath he had found another cause for 1900; whether or not it would supplant silver remained to be seen.

On 12 December in Savannah, while awaiting shipment to Cuba, Bryan was honorably discharged by order of the adjutant general. The next day he held a press conference, at which he addressed the new issue:

I may be in error, but in my judgement our nation is in greater danger just now than Cuba. Our people defended Cuba against foreign arms; now they must defend themselves and their country against a foreign idea—the colonial idea of European nations. Heretofore greed has perverted the government and used its instrumentalities for private gains, but now the very foundation principles of our government are assaulted. Our nation must give up any intention of entering upon a colonial policy, such as is now pursued by European countries, or it must abandon the doctrine that governments derive their just powers from the consent of the governed.[5]

After paraphrasing Lincoln's insistence that the country must be undivided philosophically as well as physically and attempting to justify past expansion while rejecting this phase of it, Bryan turned to the political issue which had already split the anti-imperialist forces: the debate over ratification of the peace treaty. Bryan, favoring ratification, took this opportunity to explore why he did so:

Some think that the fight should be made against ratification of the treaty, but I would prefer another plan. If the treaty is rejected, negotiations must be renewed and instead of settling the question according to our ideas we must settle it by diplomacy, with the possibility of international complications. It will be easier, I think, to end the war at once by ratifying the treaty and then deal with the subject in our own way. The issue can be presented directly by a resolution of Congress declaring the policy of the nation upon this subject. The President in his message says that our only purpose in taking possession of Cuba is to establish a stable government and then turn that government over to the people of Cuba. Congress could reaffirm this purpose in regard to Cuba and assert the same purpose in regard to the Philippines and Porto Rico. Such a resolution would make a clear-cut issue between the doctrine of self-government and the doctrine of imperialism.[6]

Bryan did indicate that he had read Admiral Alfred Thayer Mahan, who had become the philosopher of imperialism, or at least listened to his arguments in recommending that coaling stations be reserved in Puerto Rico, the Philippines, and Cuba. Some critics have seen in his rejection of annexation of the Philippines not only because of their remoteness but because "their people [are] too different from ours" traces of the racism they attribute to Populism, but Bryan's position leaves no room for debate: he was opposed to imperialism on moral as well as philosophical and political grounds, and he could not reconcile himself with what his conscience told him was evil.

Bryan returned home in time to celebrate Christmas with his family; on 23 December he was welcomed at a reception by the silver forces of Lincoln, the Women's Bimetallic League, the Lancaster County Bimetallic League, and the University Bimetallic Club, and he leaped to the attack on gold with all his old fire: "The

American people have not accepted the gold standard as final," he declared; "It has wrought more injustice in our country during the last twenty-five years than Spain has wrought in all her colonies." He attacked the trusts, the proposed expansion of the Regular Army, and other trappings of empire, and then he turned to the immediate issue:

The flag is a national emblem and is obedient to the national will. It was made for the people, not the people for the flag. When the American people want the flag raised, they raise it; when they want it hauled down, they haul it down. The flag was raised upon Canadian soil during the war of 1812 and it was hauled down when peace was restored. The flag was planted upon Chapultepec during the war with Mexico and it was hauled down when the war was over. The morning papers announce that General Lee ordered the flag hauled down in Cuba yesterday because it was raised too soon. The flag will be raised in Cuba again on the 1st of January, but the President declares in his message that it will be hauled down as soon as a stable government is established. Who will deny our people the right to haul the flag down in the Philippines, if they so desire, when a stable government is established there?

Our flag stands for an indissoluble union of indestructible states. Every state is represented by a star and every territory sees in the constitution a star of hope that will some day take its place in the constellation. What is there in the flag to awaken the zeal or reflect the aspirations of vassal colonies which are too good to be cast away, but not good enough to be admitted to the sisterhood of states?

Shall we keep the Philippines and amend our flag? Shall we add a new star—the blood-star, Mars—to indicate that we have entered upon a career of conquest? Or shall we borrow the yellow, which in 1896 was the badge of gold and greed, and paint Saturn and his rings, to suggest a carpet-bag government, with its schemes of spoilation? . . .

No, a thousand times better that we haul down the stars and stripes and substitute the flag of an independent republic rather than surrender the doctrines that give glory to "Old Glory."[7]

Bryan had made up his mind that the war had been fought for justice and freedom rather than acquisition, and because most leading annexationists were Republicans and many of them were industrialists—Andrew Carnegie was a major exception—he found it easy to construct a program of opposition to a closely linked triumvirate: imperialism, gold, and trusts. As the year 1899 began Bryan determined to stump the country opposing all three individually and collectively. In the first few months of 1899 he spoke in

Cincinnati, Chicago, Denver, St. Paul, and elsewhere, in almost every case hitting the triumvirate hard, but giving increasing attention to the expansionists and the trusts. In Denver, at a joint meeting of the Colorado state committees of the Democratic, Populist, and Silver Republican parties, he used a biblical parable in his denunciation of the motivation behind those who, under one pretext or another, coveted or stole what belonged to another:

> The Bible tells us that Ahab, the king, wanted the vineyard of Naboth and was sorely grieved because the owner thereof refused to part with the inheritance of his fathers. Then followed a plot, and false charges were preferred against Naboth to furnish an excuse for getting rid of him.
> "Thou shalt not covet!" "Thou shalt not bear false witness!" "Thou shalt not kill"—three commandments broken, and still a fourth, "Thou shalt not steal," to be broken in order to get a little piece of ground! And what was the result? When the king went forth to take possession, Elijah, that brave old prophet of the early days, met him and pronounced against him the sentence of the Almighty. "In the place where the dogs licked the blood of Naboth shall the dogs lick thy blood, even thine." (S, 2:6)

To Bryan the moral implications of imperialism were as clear as those of gold worship and monopoly: covetousness, lying, killing, and stealing were morally reprehensible. Bryan, the prophet of the common people, was determined to bring that message to as many Americans as he could. The three issues, he was convinced, were those over which the political battles of 1900 would be fought.

Nevertheless, Bryan knew that he, too, must pursue money. He had left the army owing debts, primarily for land purchases for what was to be his farm, Fair View, four miles outside of Lincoln, and he had no job or source of income; his immediate prospects were much less bright than they had been a year earlier. Consequently, many of his lectures during the first months of 1899 were delivered for fees. Furthermore, he enjoyed lecturing, both because of the sheer pleasure he found in speaking and because he was determined to keep in touch with Americans, particularly those of the rural areas and the small towns. Perhaps he needed contact with them as much for psychological stimulation and self-identity as for political purposes.

III   *Girding for Battle*

Consequently, in the spring of 1899 Bryan became associated with an institution that seemed to be made for him, just as he and his talents seemed to be made for it. This institution was called

"Chautauqua," whose working motto, "Religious-Democratic Faith in the Popularization of Knowledge," could well serve as Bryan's own. From its origins as a summer assembly for religious revivals, Bible-study seminars, and Sunday School teacher-training at Lake Chautauqua, New York, in the 1870s, the institution had evolved to traveling programs, held in tents or opera houses throughout the Midwest during late spring and summer. Its curriculum had expanded to include music, history, literature, and the practical arts, and, although secularized, it never forgot its Christian evangelical origins until its demise in the second decade of this century.

Chautauqua's high motives were matched by low admission fees—never more than twenty-five cents for a single admission or a dollar for an entire family—but it became as profitable as it was popular. When Bryan signed with the Redpath Agency, one of four which recruited talent for the shows, he was promised at least a thousand dollars for a ten-engagement week.

Charles Horner, Redpath's manager, described the activities to Bryan in classic terms: "Like the great Julius Caeser . . . we campaign only in the most suitable weather, carrying our own accouterments," and when Bryan began his first tour in June 1899, he found that he liked it. It was strenuous, including much travel, usually at night by day coach, but often by buggy, wagon, horseback, or afoot. Bryan found that it had, with the inclusion of frequent political chicken dinners, a great deal in common with campaigning: it had the same hazards—bad weather, bad food, and accidents—and the same reward—warm, receptive audiences. In the years between 1899 and 1912 he was to return to Chautauqua again and again, each time leaving the circuit renewed and refreshed.

Nevertheless, during the remainder of 1899 and the early months of 1900, Bryan kept his eye on the main chance, the nomination for the presidency. He was convinced that, with issues as momentous as gold, trusts, and imperialism, the grand prize would be his.

In 1900, his fortieth year and either the last year of the old century or the first of the new—he preferred the latter definition—William Jennings Bryan was at the peak of his powers. Thinner after his military service and sickness, his appearance had never been more confident or commanding. To his friends and supporters, he was the incarnation of virtue in both his personal life and his political ideology and career. His handsome appearance, his eloquence, the remarkable rapport which he enjoyed with his audiences were to his supporters simply manifestations of that virtue. "Bryanism," as Senator Henry M. Teller of Colorado described the phenomenon, was not only another name for Americanism, but it was close to becoming a cult; indeed, to some it already had become one.

To Bryan's enemies, personified by Senator Marcus Alonzo Hanna of Ohio, McKinley's mentor, Bryan was a demagogue, an anarchist, and worse; to William Allen White, then Bill White of Emporia, he was none of those:

> Now the truth of the matter is that Mr. Bryan is *not* a demagogue. He is absolutely honest, which a demagogue is not. He is absolutely brave, which a demagogue is not. He is passionately sincere, which a demagogue is not. When Bryan came to Nebraska a dozen years ago, his town, his Congressional District and his state were overwhelmingly Republican. A demagogue would have joined the majority party.[8]

However, even more telling were those criticisms raised against Bryan by intellectuals, who delighted in denigrating Bryan's intellectual capabilities, an attitude one encounters even yet; Ellery Sedgwick, editor of the *Atlantic Monthly*, sounds curiously like Ray Ginger in his assessment of Bryan's mind:

> Mr. Bryan is an interesting man with an uninteresting mind. He has none of those powers of generalization which lead to the larger reaches of thought; nor has he that mental flexibility which enables a man to understand a position alien to his own. His ideas are cement hardening to stone before they can take rightful shape. To genius the great gift is given of seeing problems in their simple forms . . . but, like many uneducated men, Mr. Bryan thinks a problem simple because he sees not its complexities.[9]

Nevertheless, to his constituency, the economically deprived farmers and the disenfranchised, inarticulate poor, Bryan was wisdom itself; he was God's statesman, indeed, God's spokesman, and his ability to make the complex simple and understandable was not the least of the qualities about him that they loved.

As the preconvention conversations and meetings began to explore the issues of the new campaign, some of Bryan's followers attempted to persuade him that the major issue should be imperialism, thus broadening his appeal to embrace the Easterners, city-dwellers, and Gold Democrats and Republicans who abhorred expansionism, while downgrading or ignoring the gold and trust issues, but Bryan would have none of it. To do so, he insisted, would not merely repudiate the platform of 1896, but it would repudiate his traditional following as well, and that he would not do. He was told he could carry the East and win handily if he did not mention 16 to 1, but again he refused that counsel. In his *Memoirs* he recalled the experience in painful detail:

> About the only plank that aroused discussion was the plank restating the Chicago platform for the restoration of bimetallism and the opening of the mints to the free coinage of silver at the ratio of sixteen to one. The Eastern delegates were opposed to the restatement of this proposition, although they were willing to reaffirm the platform as a whole without any special reference to this plank. As it was intended, however, to restate nearly all the other planks of the Chicago platform, it was evident that the failure to restate this plank was equivalent to a repudiation of it, notwithstanding the general endorsement of the Chicago platform as a whole. I insisted upon the restatement of the plank because I thought that a refusal to restate it would, under the circumstances, be recognized as a repudiation of that plank.[10]

The fact was, although Bryan had not recognized it, or perhaps refused to recognize it, the money issue, unlike the traditional tariff issue and the new international issue, was no longer important.

Nevertheless, as Bryan knew, the Democrats had made substantial gains in the election of 1899, largely in the South and Midwest, including his own Nebraska, on platforms largely like that which he insisted would win nationally in 1900. Others, however, including Charles Gates Dawes and Allan Thurman, insisted that the gains were personal victories won by Bryan himself rather than gains based upon the 1896 platform reinforced by the addition of the issue of imperialism. Bryan, however, refused to acknowledge that possibility:

> I told the friends there that I could afford to lose the nomination, that it was not necessary to my happiness, but that I could not afford to lose the confidence that the voters had in my honesty and that I would decline to be a candidate if the convention in its wisdom saw fit to write the platform as was then proposed. So unwilling was I to put my judgement against the judgement of the committee that I was on the point of sending a communication to the convention declining to be a candidate under any circumstance, for I felt that the support of the convention would not be a hearty support if it approved of a platform against its own judgement, and

yet I was not willing to be a candidate under conditions that required me to apologize for the platform.[11]

Concurrently Bryan refused the overtures of an Eastern anti-imperialist group which, meeting in New York, attempted to form a third party with its major plank independence for the Philippines. Although promised the group's nomination and support if he would compromise the silver issue, he refused to do so. McKinley, he asserted, was advancing the causes of "gold and empire," and he would fight him on both fronts simultaneously. Nevertheless, he was forced or persuaded to compromise on one point: "I did agree to the plank making imperialism the paramount issue, because I believed that with changed conditions the question of imperialism was at that time more important than the money question."[12]

IV   *The Issue of 1900*

Although Bryan's personal popularity and political power were never higher (by June 1900, twenty-two of twenty-four state delegations that had met voted to support him, and he controlled nearly half of the total of 930 votes in the convention), pressures, particularly from the East and from Hearst and Pulitzer, moved him further toward compromise and acceptance of a new political reality. Hearst told him that "we cannot . . . and will not . . . take up 16 to 1 in the East," and Pulitzer insisted that he could support Bryan only if he did not mention silver east of the Blue Ridge Mountains. Perhaps as a result, in the *North American Review* for June 1900, Bryan began a redefinition of his position. In "The Issue of the Presidential Campaign" he saw a new point of controversy between the parties, a fundamental overriding struggle that went beyond the battle over currency and incorporated the traditional conflict over the tariff, the trust controversy, and the new debate over imperialism as well. It was, he insisted, "the issue between plutocracy and democracy."[13]

It was a single conflict as Bryan defined it, a conflict that originated in "the conflict between the dollar and the man—a conflict as old as the human race, and one which will continue as long as the human race endures."[14] In America, the article insists, the struggle was that which brought about the Revolution, and the political battles of each of the political heroes of Bryan's liberalism—

Benjamin Franklin, Jefferson, Jackson, Lincoln—were manifestations of that continuing war.

The article is skillfully put together, not only as a literary construction, in which it closely resembles the structure of Bryan's speeches, but also in the political context in which it was written. Bryan first traces the battles waged between economic conservatives and liberals from the nation's beginning to his own time, in each case making evident the potential for human exploitation in the causes propagated by the conservatives, until he demonstrates in the election of 1896 the most recent manifestation of that conflict: the political debate over bimetallism, with bimetallism clearly aligned with democracy and the supporters of gold advocates of plutocracy. Bryan writes, in concluding that section,

Mr. Carlisle, in his speech in 1878, divided the people into two classes. In one class he placed those described by him as "the idle holders of idle capital," and in the other "struggling masses."

When the money question is fully understood, the struggling masses and those who sympathize with them will support the double standard, and the money-owning and bond-holding classes and those who sympathize with them will favor the gold standard. [15]

From the discussion of money, the transition to the trusts is easy, and again Bryan sees the issue in terms of conflict between competing ideologies:

The trust question is more easily understood than the money question. . . .

The trust question was in the campaign of 1896, and the menace of the trust was then pointed out, but the warning was unheeded. Now the heavy hand of monopoly is laid upon so many that there is a growing protest against a system which permits a few men to control each branch of industry, fix the rate of wages, the price of raw materials and the price of the finished product.

On the trust question, as on the money question, the line is drawn between those who believe that money is the only thing to be considered and those who believe that the people have rights which should be respected. [16]

Again, Bryan moves with an easy transition:

The Philippine question is even plainer than the trust question, and those who will be benefited by an imperial policy are even less in number than those who may be led to believe that they would share in the benefits of a gold standard or of a private monopoly. . . .

If the Filipino is to be under our domination, he must be either citizen or subject. If he is to be a citizen, it must be with a view to participating ultimately in our government and in the making of our laws. . . . If the Filipino is to be a subject our form of government must be changed. A republic can have no subjects. . . . An imperial policy nullifies every principle set forth in the Declaration of Independence.[17]

With this discussion Bryan had come full circle in linking the three issues of 1900 into one, describing a relationship that is so intricate that to eliminate or ignore one issue would be to diminish the force of the others. In each case he shows the conflict in human and political terms, the masses linked together with the Democrats in support of democracy, while the Republicans, the few, together with those of the masses they have misled, are identified as the agents of plutocracy.

Bryan's conclusion, like those of his speeches, is rhetorically powerful, emotional, and pointed:

Surely, the rapid development of plutocracy during the last few years will arouse the people to the dangers which threaten our Republic. The warning voice of history cannot longer be disregarded. No nation has travelled so far, in the same space of time, from democracy to plutocracy, as has this nation during the last ten years. Foreign influence, described by Washington as "one of the most baneful foes of republican government," has been felt as never before. Fortunes have been made more suddenly than ever before. . . . Money is more freely used than ever before to corrupt elections.

What is to be the end? Can any thoughtful person believe that these conditions promise well for a republic? Are we not following in the footsteps of Rome?

Instead of regarding the recent assault upon constitutional government— the attempted overthrow of American principles—as a matter of destiny, we may rather consider it as the last plague, the slaying of the first-born, which will end the bondage of the American people, and bring deliverance from the Pharohs who are enthroning Mammon and debasing mankind.[18]

Bryan's fusion of patriotism, politics, and religious lore into a representation of American history as continued class warfare, with a major battle to be fought in the election that fall, was less effective in the party conflicts than he had hoped. Although he had determined that he would not sacrifice principle for political favor, in his *Memoirs* he remembered a shift in emphasis among the three elements that characterized the continuing battle between democracy and plutocracy:

> I did agree to the plank making imperialism the paramount issue, because I believed that with changed conditions the question of imperialism was at that time more important than the money question. The trust plank was given the second place in importance, and the money question was not discussed to any extent during the campaign. The fact that the platform reiterated the demand for independent bimetallism made it less necessary for me to discuss the question than it would have been had the platform attempted to avoid the subject.[19]

In spite of the bitter fight in the Resolutions Committee over the currency plank, which was finally won by Bryan's supporters, the convention in Kansas City that July belonged to Bryan, from the first item on the agenda to the adjournment. The convention opened with an indication of the depth of the personal loyalty to Bryan in the party and an indication of his personal triumph in the convention to follow: the unveiling of a huge bust of Bryan, which set off a massive demonstration among the delegates, 2,000 strong, and the more than 20,000 spectators.

From the beginning it was evident that if Bryan were the convention's choice, as indeed he was, imperialism was the convention's issue. When Benjamin Tillman read to the delegates the statement that "We recognize imperialism as the paramount issue of the campaign," stressing the word "paramount," he set off a sustained if contrived twenty-one minute demonstration, but the silver plank led to only four and a half minutes of cheering. To many of Bryan's supporters, those who still insisted that the currency issue was more significant, it was evident that compromise was the price of victory, and a floor fight was averted.

When nominations were in order, Alabama yielded to Nebraska, William Oldham nominated Bryan in impressive terms; a thirty-one minute demonstration followed his sonorous pronouncement of the magic name, and after the formality of assorted seconding speeches, led by that of David Bennett Hill of New York, the nomination was made unanimous. Bryan's victory was in no way diminished by the nomination of Adlai Stevenson for the vice-presidency in an attempt to soothe Democratic factionalism at the expense of fusion with the Populists.

Although friends had urged him to attend the convention, Bryan remained at home, insisting that it was questionable taste for him to attend. But he had made it clear that without the 16 to 1 plank he would refuse the nomination; if the threat did not prevail, he would go to the convention and carry the fight to the floor. But the silver plank, although downgraded, was as he wanted it, and the convention adjourned with a measure of good feeling that promised a successful campaign.

V   *The Second Acceptance Speech*

Bryan's position at the time might well be envied by a good many presidential candidates since then. He was the unanimous choice of his party's convention, so honored for the second time; he was the nominee of a number of other antiadministration parties, large and small; he was running on a platform of his choice; and he had a host of devoted personal followers. His reputation for integrity was never higher, and his refusal to compromise the currency plank reinforced it. His name had become synonymous with reform. Consequently, in his acceptance speech, scheduled for Military Park, Indianapolis, on 8 August rather than the Madison Square Garden of four years earlier, he knew that he could be magnaminous in accepting the collected wisdom of the convention. In the speech, then, he would focus on imperialism, carefully defined.

As he had in the past, Bryan had tested his opening lines and the controlling idea, in this case in his essay in the *North American Review* of two months before. The contest, he said, would be, again, between democracy and plutocracy, and "on the important issues of the day the Republican party is· dominated by those influences which consistently tend to substitute the worship of mammon for the protection of the rights of man" (*S*, 2:17).

Not unexpectedly the introduction suggested that Bryan would, as of old, focus on economic issues, and he opened with an attack on the Republicans by turning Lincoln's statement about the relationship between the man and the dollar against them before examining their handling of the issues of 1896:

Republicans who used to advocate bimetallism now try to convince themselves that the gold standard is good; Republicans who were formerly attached to the greenback are now seeking an excuse for giving national banks control of the Nation's paper money; Republicans who used to boast that the Republican party was paying off the national debt are now looking for reasons to support a perpetual and increasing debt; Republicans who formerly abhored a trust now beguile themselves with the delusion that there are good trusts and bad trusts, while in their minds, the line between the two is becoming more and more obscure; Republicans who, in times past, congratulated the country upon the small expense of our standing army, are now making light of the objections which are urged against a large increase in the permanent military establishment; Republicans who gloried in our independence when the Nation was less powerful now look with favor upon a foreign alliance. (S, 2:19)

But all Bryan's remarks to this point were prefatory to his major thrust: his insistence that as the Republicans had betrayed their own principles in these economic areas, they had begun to do it in another, and they would do it if the McKinley administration were continued:

Republicans who three years ago condemned "forcible annexation" as immoral and even criminal are now sure that it is both immoral and criminal to oppose forcible annexation. That partizanship has already blinded many to present dangers is certain; how large a portion of the Republican party can be drawn over to the new polities remains to be seen. (S, 2:19-20)

The rest of the speech, which Bryan read to the assembled 50,000 partisans, was not the rousing attack that some of them expected, but a reasoned, intelligent attack on imperialism. In it, after examining specific issues of the peace treaty and the reasons for his own support of it, Bryan rejected the retention of the Philippines from the perspective of American tradition. Particularly contrary to tradition as he saw it was the problem of what some had begun to call "pacification" in the Philippines:

When hostilities broke out at Manila Republican speakers and Republican editors at once sought to lay the blame upon those who had delayed the ratification of the treaty, and during the progress of the war, the same Republicans have accused the opponents of imperialism of giving encouragement to the Filipinos. This is a cowardly evasion of responsibility.

If it is right for the United States to hold the Philippine Islands permanently and imitate European empires in the government of colonies, the Republican party ought to state its position and defend it, but it must expect the subject races to protest against such a policy and to resist to the extent of their ability.

The Filipinos do not need any encouragement from Americans now living. Our whole history has been an encouragement, not only to the

Filipinos, but to all who are denied a voice in their own government. If the Republicans are prepared to censure all who have used language calculated to make the Filipinos hate foreign domination, let them condemn the speech of Patrick Henry. When he uttered that passionate appeal, "Give me liberty or give me death," he exprest a sentiment which still echoes in the hearts of men.

Let them censure Jefferson. . . . Let them censure Washington . . . let them censure Lincoln, whose Gettysburg speech will be quoted in defense of popular government when the present advocates of force and conquest are forgotten. (*S*, 2:23–24)

Particularly upsetting to Bryan was the insistence of a number of supporters of acquisition that the policy toward the Philippines was merely an extension of that begun by Jefferson with the annexation of Louisiana, which had since become the course of America's manifest destiny. This position, to Bryan, was nonsense:

Our opponents, conscious of the weakness of their cause, seek to confuse imperialism with expansion, and have even dared to claim Jefferson as a supporter of their policy. Jefferson spoke so freely and used language with such precision that no one can be ignorant of his views. On one occasion he declared: "If there be one principle more deeply rooted than any other in the mind of every American, it is that we should have nothing to do with conquest." And again he said: "Conquest is not in our principles; it is inconsistent with our government." (*S*, 2:26)

To make this distinction clear, Bryan turned then to define differences between traditional nineteenth-century American—and Democratic—attitudes toward national expansion and that of fin de siècle American imperialism:

The forcible annexation of territory to be governed by arbitrary power differs as much from the acquisition of territory to be built up into States as a monarchy differs from a democracy. The Democratic party does not oppose expansion when expansion enlarges the area of the Republic and incorporates land which can be settled by American citizens, or adds to our population people who are willing to become citizens and are capable of discharging their duties as such.

The acquisition of the Louisiana territory, Florida, Texas, and other tracts which have been secured from time to time enlarged the Republic and the Constitution followed the flag into the new territory. It is now proposed to seize upon distant territory already more densely populated than our own country, and to force upon the people a government for which there is no warrant in our Constitution or our laws. (*S*, 2:27)

More devastating to Bryan were the inherent and to him dangerous precedents provided by imperialism elsewhere:

> After a century and a half of English domination in India, less than one-
> twentieth of one per cent of the people of India are of English birth, and it
> requires an army of seventy thousand British soldiers to take care of the tax
> collectors. . . .
> A colonial policy means that we shall send to the Philippine Islands a few
> traders, a few taskmasters and a few office-holders and an army large
> enough to support the authority of a small fraction of the people while they
> rule the natives.
> If we have an imperial policy we must have a great standing army as its
> natural and necessary complement. (S, 2:27)

The clear and present danger presented by imperialism to the
United States, its values, and its people, was to Bryan too great to
question; he saw, however, another solution to the Philippines
problem more in keeping with American tradition:

> There is an easy, honest, honorable solution of the Philippine question. It
> is set forth in the Democratic platform and it is submitted with confidence
> to the American people. This plan I unreservedly endorse. If elected, I will
> convene Congress in extraordinary session as soon as inaugurated and
> recommend an immediate declaration of the nation's purpose, first, to
> establish a stable form of government in the Philippine Islands, just as we
> are now establishing a stable form of government in Cuba; second, to give
> independence to the Filipinos as we have promised to give independence to
> the Cubans; third, to protect the Filipinos from outside interference while
> they work out their destiny, just as we have protected the republics of
> Central and South America and are, by the Monroe Doctrine, pledged to
> protect Cuba. (S, 2:46)

In his conclusion Bryan became a visionary, a role he had rarely if
ever permitted himself before:

> I can never fully discharge the debt of gratitude which I owe to my
> countrymen for the honors which they have so generously bestowed upon
> me; but, sirs, whether it be my lot to occupy the high office for which the
> convention has named me, or to spend the remainder of my days in private
> life, it shall be my constant ambition and my controlling purpose to aid in
> realizing the high ideals of those whose wisdom and courage and sacrifices
> brought this republic into existence.
> I can conceive of a national destiny surpassing the glories of the present
> and the past—a destiny which meets the responsibilities of to-day and

measures up to the possibility of the future. Behold a republic, resting securely upon the foundation stones quarried by revolutionary patriots from the fountain of eternal truth—a republic applying in practice and proclaiming to the world the self-evident propositions that all men are created equal; that they are endowed by their Creator with inalienable rights; that governments are instituted among men to secure these rights, and that governments derive their just powers from the consent of the governed. Behold a republic in which civil and religious liberty stimulate all to earnest endeavor and in which the law restrains every hand uplifted for a neighbor's injury—a republic in which every citizen is a sovereign, but in which no one cares or dares to wear a crown. Behold a republic standing erect while empires all around are bowed beneath the weight of their own ornaments— a republic whose flag is loved while other flags are only feared. Behold a republic increasing in population, in wealth, in strength and in influence, solving the problems of civilization and hastening the coming of an universal brotherhood—a republic which shakes thrones and dissolves aristocracies by its silent example and gives light and inspiration to those who sit in darkness. Behold a republic gradually but surely becoming the supreme moral factor in the world's progress and the accepted arbiter of the world's disputes—a republic whose history, like the path of the just, "is as the shining light that shineth more and more unto the perfect day." (*S*, 2:48–49)

The speech contained no less fire and eloquence for having been read, and to its audience it was another of Bryan's personal triumphs, maintaining its place on the political high road, lofty in spirit, eloquent in purpose and lacking the fanaticism that many contemporary reformers found necessary on public occasions. Essentially a one-topic speech that focused on what was to be the one topic of the Bryan campaign, it was widely circulated in pamphlet form, becoming a major campaign document and winning Bryan prominent support in the East, including that of Thomas W. Higginson, John P. Hopkins, E. L. Godkin, Perry Belmont, and others.

The speech was not only statesmanlike in tone, but in its optimism it provided a glimpse of America's future that was not only visionary but utopian, reflecting the utopian vision of Edward Bellamy's *Looking Backward*, Ignatius Donnelly's *The Golden Bottle*, and others. But Bryan's vision was not rooted in the social or economic structure, nor was it to be found in the remote future or in a magic potion; it was to be found in American tradition and the American political reality.

As imperialism was to remain the Democratic issue for the

campaign, Bryan's economics was to be the Republican issue. Although Bryan's advisors had recommended that he curtail travel, depending on a campaign more nearly like that of McKinley's front porch campaign instead of carrying on the extensive whistle-stop touring he had done in 1896—and party finances dictated that such a course would be wise—Bryan was eager to get in touch with the people again. When the campaigns of both candidates seemed to engender little enthusiasm, neither the imperialism nor the economic issue stirring much interest in the electorate, Bryan determined on two changes in campaign tactics: the first was a personal swing through ten states in the Midwest and East leaning to the Republicans; and the second was to make strong appeals to specific interest groups. He hoped to combine both in his speaking tours.

Bryan's targets were labor, German and Irish Americans, and blacks, three groups who, when combined, particularly in narrow or doubtful states, held a balance of power. On Labor Day in Chicago and again in Wisconsin and New York he attacked the Republican promise of "the full dinner pail," pointing out the natural affinity and shared interests of labor and agriculture: "Our desire should be not to separate the people into warring factions, but to bring them into better acquaintance and greater sympathy with each other," he declared in Chicago; "Why should the man who eats at a well-supplied table forget the man whose toil furnished the food? Why should the man who warms himself by the fire forget the man whose labor in the forest or in the mine brings forth the fuel?" But radical labor, led by Eugene Debs, was scornful; the more restrained labor leaders were delighted with Bryan and with the Democratic platform, which included a denunciation of the injunction, the blacklist, Asian immigration, and militarism; promised a labor bureau; and contained Bryan's own plan of arbitration between capital and labor.

Bryan depended upon the issue of imperialism and the threat of a large standing army to win support among German-Americans and, to a lesser extent, among Irish-Americans. For the latter he occasionally twisted the tail of the British lion, charging that McKinley's policy in the Philippines was not unlike that of the British in South Africa and by implication, in Ireland.

Bryan's attempt to bring black voters into the Democratic party and to gain their support personally faced two obstacles: the traditional allegiance of the blacks to the Republican party and the racism of Southern Populists and Democrats, but he did make some inroads. "The Republican party," he pointed out, "has taken the Negro for thirty years to an office door and then tied him on the outside. The Negro has bestowed Presidents on the Republican party—and the Republican party has given to the Negro janitorships in return." Two organizations which gave Bryan a good deal of support and which he in turn worked to bring into the mainstream of the party were the United Colored Democracy of Greater New York and the Negro National Democratic League. Other black groups traveled to Lincoln to meet with him on the problems of Negro rights and a place for them in the party. But it was not until the New Deal and Franklin Delano Roosevelt that blacks in substantial numbers began to ally themselves with the Democratic party.

The success of his publication of *The First Battle,* a postelection compilation of his campaign record of 1896, led Bryan to adapt the technique into a campaign tool for 1900. The result was *The Second Battle,* published that year. Like its predecessor, it is a valuable collection of documents that provide the raw material of history, but its usefulness is limited by inadequate identification of sources. Furthermore, its documentary record is that of Bryan's political career to the drive for the nomination in 1900, covering much of the material that he had included in *The First Battle* and focusing on the questions that he saw as crucial in 1900. However, the description of the convention in Kansas City, with which the volume opens, is factual and well-done, and the platform included is complete.

After chapter 3, the "Biography of Hon. William J. Bryan," by Mary Bryan, reprinted from *The First Battle,* the book focuses on imperialism as the major issue, devoting one chapter to excerpts from Bryan's speeches and interviews on the topic, largely from 1898 and 1899, and a second to his articles on the topic from the same years. His Baltimore speech of 20 January 1900 is reprinted in full, as is his antitrust speech of 16 September 1899. Much of the remainder of the text is devoted to the Chicago convention, drawn largely from *The First Battle,* and to speeches by an even dozen other anti-imperialists ranging from Ben Tillman to Adlai Stevenson, all of whom opposed McKinley's policies in the Philippines.

The First Battle is weak because it was put together hurriedly, but it is complete, including Bryan's immediate postelection reactions, but *The Second Battle,* in the tradition of campaign materials, is weak not only because it was hurriedly put together, but because it lacks the drama of the immediate as it pretends to be complete;

its title page as well as advertising implying a relationship to *The First Battle* that does not exist. The ruse apparently had only limited success. Thousands of copies of the first volume are still extant, while the later had only limited sales and is relatively rare.

Unfortunately, too, Bryan had little to do with the volume's publication other than turning manuscripts over to his publishers, and he did not see it through the press. Campaigning at his usual pace, in the last six weeks covering more than 16,000 miles and speaking more than 600 times, most of the time traveling in railway coaches rather than private cars, he focused on imperialism, trusts, and the exploitation of labor. Not only were the trips largely repetitions of 1896, active montages of movement, masses, and receptions, each one hailed as greater than the last, but the campaigning was repetitious too in the Republican counterattack, which drew upon a campaign fund of $5,000,000, ten times that available to Bryan; it included the warnings to workmen that a Bryan victory would result in loss of jobs and attacks on Bryan's integrity, many of which were directed at his alliance with Tammany Hall.

Added to the Republican campaign were two potent weapons: postwar prosperity and the magic name and presence of Theodore Roosevelt, whose Rough Riders and skirmish at San Juan Hill had already begun to take on mythic proportions. As the campaign moved into the final week Bryan was exuberant, but the betting odds were four and a half to one for McKinley.

Election night was also repetitious of 1896. Early optimism faded quickly, but Bryan could console himself with the fact that it was not a Republican landslide, although McKinley made only modest gains. In electoral votes McKinley polled 292 to Bryan's 155, a gain of twenty-one for McKinley. In popular vote, McKinley increased his total over 1896 by about 100,000; Bryan lost about 150,000. It was a respectable showing, but it was defeat, and Bryan pondered its meaning and his future.

VI   *"The Election of 1900"*

In December Bryan published his assessment of the campaign in the *North American Review*. He knew, as the statistics of the election demonstrated, that it was not a landslide for McKinley in spite of the assertions of the Republican press, and his essay, "The Election of 1900," is a restrained, intelligent assessment of the elements that contributed to the Republican victory.

In the essay Bryan attributes the Republican success to three major advantages: almost unlimited financial resources, the heady atmosphere engendered by an easily won war, and the nation's prosperity, the combination of which was unbeatable. The first he attributed to the growth of the trusts, their strength during the previous four years, and their support of the Republicans:

All of these trusts [seventeen of which he describes] and many others, had a pecuniary reason for supporting the Republican ticket, for they have not only enjoyed immunity during the present Administration, but they had every reason to expect further immunity in case of Republican success; while the Democratic platform and the Democratic organization were outspoken in their condemnation of private monopolies, and the candidates were pledged to aggressive measures for the extermination of all combinations formed in restraint of trade.[20]

The results of this political-economic alliance were, Bryan points out, already evident:

Since the election the meat combine at Chicago has raised the price of meat. One paper estimates that the increase will amount to thirty-nine millions in one year. . . . On the day before the election of 1900, the stock of the Standard Oil Company was worth six hundred and twenty-five dollars per share, the par value being one hundred dollars. According to report of Henry Clews & Co., the Standard Oil Co. paid twelve per cent dividends from 1891 to 1895. In 1899 it incorporated under the laws of New Jersey, and controls two-thirds of the output of oil in the United States. This year its dividends will aggregate about fifty per cent on the capital stock.[21]

To Bryan, the situation had no place in a democratic society:

The political objections to a private monopoly are scarcely less serious than the moral and economic objections. Daniel Webster said: "The freest government cannot long endure where the tendency of the law is to create a rapid accumulation of property in the hands of a few, and to render the masses of the people poor and dependent." When hundreds of thousands of workingmen must go down on their knees each morning, and, addressing their petition to trust magnates, say, "Give us this day our daily bread," a government of the people, for the people and by the people will be a thing of the past.[22]

For Bryan this battle, the second battle, was, like the first, another battle in the long, hard-fought war between privilege and human rights, between economic and political power and human dignity, and it was a war that would go on:

> Back of all the questions which have been referred to, lies the deep and lasting struggle between human rights and inhuman greed. If greed triumphs, its victory will transform our government into a plutocracy and our civilization into barbarism.
>
> Those who believe in equal rights before the law, and desire a government which rests upon the consent of the governed and deals justly with all who are under its jurisdiction, must continue the contest in triumph or defeat. Success may be the measure of enjoyment, but it cannot be the measure of duty.[23]

With those words, Bryan, who at forty had twice come close to the heights, pledged to continue that war.

CHAPTER 7

The Voice and Hope of the People

WITH his second defeat for the presidency behind him, Bryan entered the twentieth century wth his identity secure, his conviction in the rightness of his cause unshaken, and his temperament serene. Defeat, he believed, was not a sign of weakness, of a lost or mistaken cause, or of God's disfavor; it was a stimulus to further action and a call to greater service. And he enjoyed a faithful following and an international reputation that few men before or since have known.

To his followers in 1900 and to much of the reform-minded population of the world he was indeed the Great Commoner; he was the symbol as well as the leader of an outraged people; and he was seen as the embodiment of the spirit of reform at the dawning century. To his followers as well as to himself, he was twice defeated; in all probability he had carried the banner of his party for the last time; but he was unvanquished, and millions of Americans would follow wherever he led them.

Though there is no evidence to suggest that he knew he had reached his political peak as a presidential candidate in 1896, he did know that his chances for a third nomination were few. Therefore, his prime political task was to retain control of the party, not as an instrument of his own political fortunes but as an agent for reform in the nation. But, with his fortunes as a presidential aspirant behind him, he planned to spend a sustantially greater portion of his time in activities other than political or only peripherally so.

Although his immediate personal need was to earn a living, he turned down several offers of lucrative newspaper jobs, preferring instead to follow his own interests, and he began immediately to put his plans into effect. Although Republicans had raised the issue of his personal wealth, insisting that he was a plutocrat as well as a demagogue, his personal worth was little more than $20,000, much of it balanced by campaign and other debts, so his immediate plans

121

included lecturing and writing for money, activities that comple-
mented each other and enacted his determination to keep the
Democratic party on its reform course.

I   The Commoner

Shortly after his defeat he decided to carry out an idea that he
had had since 1895: founding his own weekly newspaper, a national
journal that would serve as a forum for reform, keep in touch with
his national following, and, while sold inexpensively enough to be
within the reach of everyone, provide him with a modest but steady
income.

The paper appeared for the first time on 23 January 1901; its
name, suitably, was *The Commoner*, dedicated to aiding "the
common people in the protection of their rights, the advancement
of their interests, and the realization of their aspirations"; "as an
exponent of Democratic sentiment and as a defender of Jeffersonian
principles it hopes to make itself useful." It was to pursue both
ideals for twenty-two years.

The first issue of *The Commoner* was eight pages, 10½ by 13½
inches in size—it became twelve pages, with two pages of unpaid
advertisements for worthy causes, in April, and sixteen pages a year
later—and initially it focused almost exclusively on Bryan's causes,
often to a ponderous degree. But its expansion permitted additional
departments and paid advertising, both of which contributed to its
success. More than 17,000 subscriptions at a dollar each were
received before the initial edition was printed, and its total sales of
the first issue exceeded 50,000 copies.

Bryan himself was editor and publisher, and the first issue bears
much of his personal imprint, but he recruited an effective staff,
including his brother Charles as business manager, Richard Metcalf
as associate editor, and J.R. Farris as superintendent of publications,
and he delegated much of the day-to-day operation of the paper to
them. Rejecting William Randolph Hearst's suggestion that he
move the paper to New York or Washington, he determined to keep
it in Lincoln for symbolic as well as practical reasons.

Bryan's introductory editorial in the first issue of *The Commoner*
defines his chosen title and the badge he had worn with pride
through two presidential campaigns. The name was not chosen, he
insisted, because it would serve to inflame class feelings or contribute to prejudice and hate, as editorials in the Republican press

maintained, and it was not un-American; it was chosen because it was descriptive of the majority of Americans; it indicated the nature of their character, and it was deeply rooted in American and Christian tradition:

It has . . . an eminently respectable origin. In the same chapter in which Christ condensed man's duty to his fellows into the commandment: Thou shalt love thy neighbor as thyself; in the same chapter in which he denounced those who devour widow's houses and for a pretense make long prayers—in this same chapter it is said of Him: The common people heard him gladly! [1]

No higher compliment was ever paid to any economic class. Bryan's definition of the commoner, like his definition of the true business man in his "Cross of Gold" speech, excluded only those who exclude themselves in one way or another:

The term, the common people, is properly used to describe the large majority of the people—those who earn their living and give to society a fair return for the benefits bestowed by society—those who in their daily lives recognize the ties which bind together the mass of the people who have a common lot and a common hope. Sometimes they are called "the middle classes" because paupers and criminals are excluded on the one hand, while on the other hand some exclude themselves because of wealth or pride of birth. The common people form the industrious, intelligent and patriotic element of our population. . . . They ask of government nothing but justice and will not be satisfied with less. . . .

Anyone can become a member if he is willing to contribute by brain or muscle to the nation's strength and goodness. Only those are barred—and they are barred by their own choice—who imagine themselves made of a superior kind of clay and who deny the equality of all before the law

A rich man, who has honestly acquired his wealth and is not afraid to intrust its care to laws made by his fellows, can count himself among the common people, while a poor man is not really one of them if he fawns before a plutocrat, and has no higher ambition than to be a courtier or a sycophant.

The Commoner will be satisfied, if by fidelity to the common people, it proves its right to the name which has been chosen. [2]

Bryan's oratorical rhetoric is evident in this introductory editorial. It is unsigned, as most editorials and similar items were to be unsigned in the future; that fact has led scholars to complain that, because editorial material was written by Bryan, Mary, Charles, and

Metcalfe, all of whom agreed on issues, it is difficult to tell who wrote what. But often, as here, Bryan's style is evident; his prose flows on the page as it did from the platform or stump, and the work is without question his. As in his attitudes, his causes, and his values, the stamp of his use of the language is unmistakable.

The first issue is firmly rooted in the campaign of 1900. Bryan's sensitivity to accusations that he was too wealthy to be a commoner and hence was a demagogue is evident in his introductory editorial, but evident too is his concern with continuing issues. Items define the relationship between the tariff and the trusts, they emphasize the dangers of militarism, they criticize McKinley's appointments, support unionism, and denounce imperialism. But the first issue shows too Bryan's determination to direct the faithful and the party in the path of the future. It examines the American role in the Philippines and in Cuba, often drawing on news or editorial items from other journals to make its point; it challenges governmental subsidies; and it attacks trusts—all of which Bryan saw as significant issues in Congress as well as important questions for 1904 and beyond.

Evident, too, in a more subtle way, is the clear indication of the turn of Bryan's thinking and the development of his issues in the future. Bryan's fusion of Christian morality and political virtue is more evident than in his political speeches; equally evident is a strong concern with personal morality; in a brief sermonette on the value of truth and in those items dealing with imperialism and war, there are clear indications of a pacifism no longer latent. If *The Commoner* was to be Bryan's voice, it was also to serve as a means by which his own thinking would be clarified and directed as it evolved.

In the first issue Bryan, perhaps in a search for filler, but more likely because he delighted in sharing, included a quotation from Tolstoy, whom he greatly admired and was to meet in Russia several years later; he reprinted William Cullen Bryant's "To a Waterfowl," perhaps the most complete poetic expression of his own personal philosophy; he included a great many of his own favorite humorous stories and jokes; even attempted a bit of culture. *The Commoner*, in effect, was Bryan's concept of what a newspaper should be: a Chautauqua in print, issued weekly.

Two other aspects of the paper bear Bryan's unmistakable imprint. Each item is written simply and clearly, so that, as in his speeches, the complex is understandable to a simple but serious audience. Typically, too, the paper was not copyrighted; its contents belonged to the people, and Bryan wanted it disseminated to them, whether or not he received either credit or payment.

From the first, *The Commoner* was controversial. Not only did its faithful largely remain so, but its enemies also remained relatively constant throughout its existence. Mary Bryan remembered that "A hostile press often took up his writings and pursued his editorial utterances with merciless criticisms," [3] and, although the pressures of his appointment as secretary of state in the Wilson administration later forced Bryan to reduce its publication to a monthly, he remained close to it to the end. As his personal crusades changed over the years, so did the editorial focus of *The Commoner*. In its last years it became increasingly dominated by religious matters, and it ceased publication after Bryan moved to Florida. Its last issue was that of April 1923.

II   *Chautauqua*

If *The Commoner* was Bryan's first interest and love during those years, lecturing, particularly on the Chautauqua circuits, was a very close second. Mrs. Bryan, often at home in Lincoln while her husband toured the towns and countryside, nevertheless felt with him the closeness to the Midwestern grassroots that the movement engendered in him and in two generations of Midwesterners:

Upon the Chautauqua platform Mr. Bryan was always perfectly at home. He met the perpetual heat, the restlessness of the great throngs which usually overspread the adjoining grove, with genial ease and command. His leisurely approach, his humanity and humor soon won the audiences and continued to hold them to the end. . . .

But Chautauqua is something deeper than concerts or inspirational lectures. It is more than the gathering together of great crowds in the interest of civic progress.

When Mr. Bryan stood in the Chautauqua tent at night under the electric lights and the starlight, with practically every adult and most of the children from miles around within sound of his voice, he could forget the hardships and weariness of travel. His voice would grow deep and solemn, for he knew he was speaking to the heart of America.

It is not too much to say that Mr. Bryan has remained the most popular Chautauqua lecturer in this country for thirty years. Each year when he returned from his tours he had not only spoken to, but had listened to the mind of America. He had had an opportunity to know what America was thinking and he had helped America to make up her mind. [4]

Together with its founders, Bryan saw Chautauqua as morally uplifting as well as inspirational, and his lectures, refined through much repetition, were rarely politically partisan, although, particularly in his last years, he was often called upon to give his "Cross of Gold" speech. Among his lectures, two of the most popular were "The Value of an Ideal," first presented in 1901, and "The Prince of Peace," which was first given in 1904.

Both lectures are intensely personal; they are, in keeping with the tone of Chautauqua, morally uplifting and inspiring; and they are indicative of Bryan's own active faith in the people as well as in God. Often criticized by intellectuals and enemies because of their commonplace morality, they are important as articulations not only of Bryan's ideals but also of those of his people, his time, and his place.

"The Value of an Ideal" was as popular on Midwestern college campuses as on the Chautauqua circuit, and Bryan gave it at dozens of commencement exercises over a period of twenty years, perhaps because it had its origins in Bryan's own college days in Jacksonville. As with others of Bryan's lectures the text was not fixed, and he included new illustrations or anecdotes, usually in the nature of his experiences, from time to time. The "standard" text, if one can be said to exist, is that in *The Speeches of William Jennings Bryan*, which he saw through the presses in 1912, but some of its content dates back to his college days, and in this as in other lectures his trip around the world in 1905–1906 contributed details.

Typical, too, in the lecture are the elements which pleased his Chautauqua audience and his personal followers but have engendered a good deal of criticism from a more sophisticated age: its commonplace, highly moral but ambiguous subject matter and its intensely personal development. The former, to Bryan's critics, is intellectually unacceptable, and the latter is sometimes cited as the evidence of a colossal ego that was eventually to lead him to his conflict with Clarence Darrow in Dayton, Tennessee. Both criticisms are unfair to his sincerity and ignorant of the closeness between Bryan and his audience and of the fact that he voiced the aspirations, ideas, and convictions of an age equally sincere but inarticulate. In "The Value of an Ideal" Bryan's rhetorical opening lays the foundation for his remarkable rapport with his audience:

What is the value of an ideal? Have you ever attempted to estimate its worth? Have you ever tried to measure its value in dollars and cents? If you would know the pecuniary value of an ideal, go into the home of some man of great wealth who has an only son; go into that home when the son has gone downward in a path of dissipation until the father no longer hopes for his reform, and then ask the father what an ideal would have been worth that would have made a man out of his son instead of a wreck. He will tell you that all the money that he has or could have he would gladly give for an ideal of life that would turn his boy's steps upward instead of downward.

An ideal is above price. It means the difference between success and failure—the difference between a noble life and a disgraceful career, and it sometimes means the difference between life and death. Have you noticed the increasing number of suicides? I speak not of those sad cases in which the reason dethroned leaves the hand no guide, but rather of those cases, increasing in number, where the person who takes his life has nothing to live for. When I read of one of these cases I ask myself whether it is not caused by a false ideal of life. (*S*, 2:235–36)

Bryan turns then to the nature of the ideal, defining it in ambiguous terms as the measuring of life by what one does for others; it "must be far enough above us to keep us looking up toward it all the time, and it must be far enough in advance of us to keep us struggling toward it to the end of life" (*S*, 2:236). Bryan illustrates this striving with the first of his personal anecdotes:

I was once made an honorary member of a class and asked to suggest a class motto. I suggested "Ever-Green" and some of the class did not like it. They did not like to admit that they ever had been green, not to speak of always being green. But it is a good class motto because the period of greenness is the period of life. When we cease to be green and are entirely ripe we are ready for decay. I like to think of life as a continual progress toward higher and better things—as a continual unfolding. There is no better description of a really noble life than that given in Holy Writ where Solomon speaks of the path of the just as "like the shining light that shineth more and more unto the perfect day." (*S*, 2:236–37)

Bryan returns to the ideal: it "is permanent; it does not change . . . [it] must be a worthy one" (*S*, 2:237), and then he turns again to a long series of personal anecdotes: his earliest ambition to be a Baptist preacher until he saw his first total immersion; his second ambition to be a farmer ("there are doubtless a great many people who are glad that I now have a chance to realize my second ambition without having my agricultural pursuits interrupted by official cares," *S*, 2:238); his third ambition to be a lawyer; his "accidental" entry into politics and his remaining there "by design," in effect, pursuing his ideal:

My term in Congress brought me into contact with the great political and economic problems now demanding solution and I have never since that time been willing to withdraw myself from their study and discussion, and I offer no apology at this time for being interested in the science of government. It is a noble science, and one to which the citizen must give his attention. . . . But while my plans and ambitions have been changed by circumstances, I trust that my ideals of citizenship have not changed . . . an ideal that will place above the holding of any office, however great, the purpose to do what we can to make this country so good that to be a private citizen in the United States will be greater than to be a king in any other nation. (S, 2:239–40)

He then cited his observations of people he had known who have shared that ideal: a young foreigner who had come to America to learn about democracy so that he might teach the ideal in his own country; Jane Addams of Hull House; Leo Tolstoy, who shared his ideal with the world; an anonymous former classmate who, after a life of dissipation, had found God and devoted his life to serving Him.

Then, foreshadowing the last great crisis of his life in Dayton, Tennessee, he digressed:

I have been reading a book recently on materialism and I have been interested in the attempt of the author to drive God out of the universe. He searches for Him with a microscope and because he cannot find him with a microscope, he declares that he is too small to see; then he searches for Him with a telescope, and because he cannot see Him among the stars or beyond, he declares that there is no God—that matter and force alone are eternal, and that force acting on matter has produced the clod, the beast that feeds upon the grass, and man, the climax of created things. I have tried to follow his reasoning and have made up my mind that it requires more faith to accept the scientific demonstrations of materialism than to accept any religion I have ever known. . . . In the journey from the cradle to the grave we encounter nothing so marvelous as the change in the ideals that works a revolution in the life itself, and there is nothing in materialism to explain this change. (S, 2:244–245)

Bryan then defines other ideals: of domestic life, of the professions, and finally, of politics, where he found what was perhaps his highest ideal: the ideal of the party and of the nation, in the process preaching a brief homily on politics as he practiced it, as it was, and as he believed it should be:

And so if you ask me how we can win an election this year, I do not know. If you ask me how we can insure a victory four years from now, I cannot tell, but I do know that the party which has the highest ideals and that strives most earnestly to realize its ideals will ultimately dominate this country and make its impress upon the history of this nation. . . .

The country is suffering today from a demoralization of its ideals. Instead of measuring people by the manhood or womanhood they manifest, we are too prone to measure them by the amount of money they possess, and this demoralization has naturally and necessarily extended to politics. Instead of asking "Is it right?" we are tempted to ask "Will it pay?" and "Will it win?" As a result the public conscience is becoming seared and the public service debauched. (*S,* 2:251–52)

Nevertheless, Bryan's optimism remains. He asserts that "a conscience is stronger than money" (*S,* 2:253) and will win against corruption; that in a popular government, the people will prevail, and, however many mistakes they make, they will eventually see the right; that he had witnessed the right prevail only recently:

It was my good fortune to be in Cuba on the day when the formal transfer took place, and I never was more proud of my nation in my life than I was on the 20th of May, 1902, when this great republic rose superior to a great temptation, recognized the inalienable rights of the people of Cuba and secured to them the fruits of a victory for which they had struggled and sacrificed for more than a generation. We hauled down the flag, it is true, and in its place they raised the flag of the Cuban republic, but when we lowered the flag we raised it higher than it ever had been raised before, and when we brought it away we left it enshrined in the hearts of a grateful people. (*S,* 2:259)

For Bryan the rest is anticlimax:

We shall not fulfill our great mission, we shall not live up to our high duty, unless we present to the world the highest ideals in individual life, in domestic life, in business life, in professional life, in political life—and the highest national ideal that the world has ever known. (*S,* 2:260)

"The Value of an Ideal" shows Bryan at his best and at his worst. As a speech it makes evident the affinity which he sought with his audience, and it demonstrates too that he was of them, not apart from them, as he gave voice to their aspirations for themselves and their children and to their faith in a fundamental Christianity and a virtuous nation. He could give voice to those aspirations and that faith because he shared them, and he was determined to make them more than aspirations and faith; he wanted them as a way of life for himself, his people, and his nation. But Bryan also depended heavily on strong emotional appeal and upon commonplace ideas, themselves often ambiguous and emotional rather than rational. Those elements show Bryan at his worst, unoriginal and simplistic in ideas and in presentation. But, as in his political speeches, it is unfair to question his sincerity or his motives; he asked no more of his audience than he was convinced he asked of himself, and, like Whitman's concept of himself in "Song of Myself," his identity and his experience, he believed, were the identity and the experience of other Midwestern Americans of his time and place; he, he was convinced, had been privileged to give them voice.

Whereas "The Value of an Ideal" is perhaps as secular as Bryan found it possible to be, "The Prince of Peace" is unembarrassedly religious, yet with major secular—and in terms of Bryan's future, prophetic—overtones. In it, Bryan not only defines an ideal in religious terms for individual emulation, but he implies too that the ideal is suitable for emulation by peoples and nations as well. As in "The Value of an Ideal," the lecture is strongly personal:

> I offer no apology for speaking upon a religious theme, for it is the most universal of all themes. I am interested in the science of government, but I am more interested in religion than in government. I enjoy making a political speech—I have made a good many and shall make more—but I would rather speak on religion than on politics. I commenced speaking on the stump when I was only twenty, but I commenced speaking in the church six years earlier—and I shall be in the church even after I am out of politics. (S, 2:261)

Bryan turns then to the nature of religion and the "First Cause," both of which he interprets in conventional terms, and then addresses, again in personal terms, skepticism, modernism, and scientific theory:

> There are difficulties to be encountered in religion, but there are difficulties to be encountered everywhere. If Christians sometimes have doubts and fears, unbelievers have more doubts and greater fears. I passed through a period of scepticism when I was in college and I have been glad ever since that I became a member of the church before I left home for college, for it helped me during those trying days. And the college days

cover the dangerous period in the young man's life. . . . He thinks he knows more than he ever does know. (*S*, 2:265–66)

Concerning Darwinism and creation he is clearer and more precise before friendly audiences than he was to be under the probing questions of Clarence Darrow in July of 1925:

It was at this period that I became confused by the different theories of creation. But I examined these theories and found that they all assumed something to begin with. . . . The nebular hypothesis, for instance, assumes that matter and force existed—matter in particles infinitely fine and each particle separated from every other particle by space infinitely great. Beginning with this assumption, force working on matter—according to this hypothesis—created a universe. Well, I have a right to assume, and I prefer to assume, a Designer back of the design—a Creator back of the creation; and no matter how long you draw out the process of creation, so long as God stands back of it you cannot shake my faith in creation. . . . We must begin with something—we must start somewhere—and the Christian begins with God.

I do not carry the doctrine of evolution as far as some do; I am not yet convinced that man is a lineal descendant of the lower animals. I do not mean to find fault with you if you want to accept the theory; all I mean to say is that while you may trace your ancestry back to the monkey if you find pleasure or pride in doing so, you shall not connect me with your family tree without more evidence than has yet been produced. (*S*, 2:266–67)

With most of his contemporary—and some current—religious critics of Darwinism, Bryan continues to insist that Darwin's "common ancestor" is instead the monkey or the ape as they exist today. But his objections to the theory in "The Prince of Peace" are rational as well as theological, though his reasoning is largely that of other critics rather than his own:

One does not escape from mystery, however, by accepting this theory, for it does not explain the origin of life. When the follower of Darwin has traced the germ of life back to the lowest form in which it appears—and to follow him one must exercise more faith than religion calls for—he finds that scientists differ. Those who reject the idea of creation are divided into two schools, some believing that the first germ of life came from another planet and others holding that it was the result of spontaneous generation. Each school answers the arguments advanced by the other, and as they cannot agree with each other, I am not compelled to agree with either. (*S*, 2:267–68)

But for Bryan the principal reason, personal, theological, and rational, for rejection of Darwinian theory is one of the great strengths that he found in Christianity: the subject of his lecture and the foundation of his political philosophy:

> The Darwinian theory represents man as reaching his present perfection by the operation of the law of hate—the merciless law by which the strong crowd out and kill off the weak. If this is the law of our development then, if there is any logic that can bind the human mind, we shall turn backward toward the beast in proportion as we substitute the law of love. I prefer to believe that love rather than hatred is the law of development. How can hatred be the law of development when nations have advanced in proportion as they have departed from that law and adopted the law of love? (*S*, 2:268–69)

Bryan then turns to the point which he intends to emphasize: the nature of God and particularly of Christ as the source of all virtues in human life; the greatest virtues for Bryan are forgiveness and love, the latter the means of his striving toward perfection and the former the measure of his achievement. Interestingly, however, Bryan does not see what others have seen: the relationship between man's instinct for violence and his Darwinian origins:

> The most difficult of all the virtues to cultivate is the forgiving spirit. Revenge seems to be natural with man; it is human to want to get even with an enemy. It has even been popular to boast of vindictiveness; it was once inscribed on a man's monument that he had repaid both friends and enemies more than he received. This was not the spirit of Christ. He taught forgiveness and in that incomparable prayer which he left as a model for our petitions, He made our willingness to forgive the measure by which we may claim forgiveness. . . .
> But love is the foundation of Christ's creed. . . . Jesus gave a new definition of love. . . . Christ's plan was to purify the heart and then leave love to direct the footsteps. . . . Here is the great fact of history; here is One who has with increasing power, for nineteen hundred years, moulded the lives of men, and He exerts more influence today than ever before. (*S*, 2:277–78)

From this point Bryan explicates the role of Christ as "Prince of Peace." He brings "peace to each individual heart," "assurance that a line of communication can be established between the Father above and the child below," "and immortality. . . . Who will estimate the peace which a belief in a future life has brought to the sorrowing hearts of the sons of men?" Bryan reiterates his faith in the future as he concludes:

> I am glad that He, who is called the Prince of Peace—who can bring peace to every troubled heart and whose teachings, exemplified in life, will bring peace between man and man, between community and community, between State and State, between nation and nation throughout the world—I am glad that He brings courage as well as peace so that those who follow Him may take up and each day bravely do the duties that to that day fall. (*S*, 2:290)

"The Prince of Peace" and "The Value of an Ideal" have much in common structurally and rhetorically with each other and with Bryan's political speeches. They represent, too, the substance and techniques of Bryan's other lectures, including "Man," first given at the Nebraska State University Commencement on 15 June 1905 and at Illinois College and elsewhere; "Missions," a favorite at church societies, beginning in the fall of 1906; "Faith," given at colleges beginning in 1907; and "The Price of a Soul," given at Northwestern Law School in Chicago, the Pierce School in Philadelphia, and then incorporated into his Chautauqua lectures in 1909.

Of most importance, in all of his speeches, political, religious, or ethical, Bryan ranges widely, incorporating his fundamental faith in God and his democratic faith in man, but focusing in more detail on the particular topic. Fundamental to his personal philosophy and underlying the intensely personal nature of each of them is his conviction that faith, morality, and service are one, and that he who would accept one must accept all. In them Bryan displays a philosophy that, developed in his youth, remained consistent to the end, and it is this consistency, this faith, that brought thousands to hear him on the stump, the platform, or the pulpit. A man who loved to speak, who spoke well, and who spoke for and with as well as to his audience, he was, during those years in the Midwest heartland when transportation had become easier and mass communications media had not yet begun their exploitative domination, the most authentic voice of the time and place.

Bryan spoke to all who would come to hear him, and his topics on the platform were always the old verities: faith, brotherhood, forgiveness, and ultimate social change. All of these truths were summed up in "Faith," the lecture which first attracted Woodrow Wilson to him and provided the basis of their ultimate friendship:

Have faith in mankind. The great fault of our scholarship is that it is not sufficiently sympathetic. It holds itself aloof from the struggling masses. It is too often cold and cynical. It is better to trust your fellowmen and be occasionally deceived than to be distrustful and live alone. Mankind deserves to be trusted. There is something good in every one, and that good responds to sympathy. If you speak to the multitude and they do not respond, do not despise them, but rather examine what you have said. If you speak from your heart, you will speak to their hearts, and they can tell very quickly whether you are interested in them or simply in yourself. The heart of mankind is sound; the sense of justice is universal. Trust it, appeal to it, do not violate it. . . . I fear the plutocracy of wealth; I respect the plutocracy of learning; I thank God for the democracy of the heart. (S, 2:332)

That Bryan, throughout his long career, spoke to the heart is evident in the masses who thronged to hear him, and he knew it. He spoke at every opportunity, for pay—often earning a thousand dollars a week on the summer Chautauqua circuit—but often free, usually at his own expense; but he never spoke for pay and always on religious themes on Sunday.

On the platform and off, Bryan practiced what he preached, and inevitably his lecturing came under attack from his political enemies. These attacks, accusing Bryan of using the Chautauqua medium as a means of getting rich, especially while serving as secretary of state, apparently stung Bryan and his wife, and Mrs. Bryan replied to them at length in the *Memoirs*:

Mr. Bryan recognized Chautauqua as an opportunity for listening to and speaking to the mind of his country, but he also saw in his lecturing an honorable way to make a living. Mr. Bryan's public life did not mean perpetual office-holding, and the exactions of his political work prevented him from devoting himself to the legal profession. The lecture platform furnished him with a means of livelihood as well as a medium for presenting his thoughts and ideals to the public.[5]

Nevertheless, in spite of criticism he continued to lecture, because he loved it and believed in its utility. During the first decade of this century, when it was of particular importance to him financially, he lectured extensively, at the same time editing *The Commoner*, contributing to other periodicals, maintaining political ties, and twice organizing national political campaigns. If that were all he did, it would have been a virtuoso performance.

CHAPTER 8

Keeper of the Political Faith

IN spite of his preoccupation with *The Commoner*, the eagerness with which he pursued opportunities to speak, a trip to Havana in 1902 to celebrate Cuba's independence, and a trip to England, Germany, and Russia in the winter of 1903–1904, Bryan's mind was seldom far from Democratic politics, particularly those that pointed toward the presidential campaign of 1904. Although he insisted in *The Commoner* that the Democratic party had a wealth of candidates—Senator Francis Marion Cockrell of Missouri, John W. Bookwalter of Ohio, and others whom his enemies described as "The Little Unknowns from Nowhere"—it was evident that Bryan was determined to keep open his options in 1904. With his strength he could virtually choose the party nominee or capture the nomination himself, and he determined to fight the gold Democrats to a standstill.

Nevertheless, much had happened in the four years between Bryan's candidacy in 1900 and the convening of the Democratic convention in St. Louis in July 1904: McKinley's assassination had brought Theodore Roosevelt to the White House, and he had belatedly but fervently espoused reform causes; the midterm elections saw Bryan Democrats lose control of their state parties and many of their seats in Congress; Populists and independents virtually vanished as viable political forces. While Bryan carried his message to rural America and abroad, more and more Democrats began to listen to those who, with Congressman Jacob Bromwell of Ohio, insisted that "The Democratic party can never make any headway until it gets rid of Bryan. He is a millstone around its neck."[1]

While Democratic reform seemed in a shambles, the new, popular president turning toward a reform program of his own and Judge Alton B. Parker, newly elected to the New York Court of Appeals, looming as a conservative champion who would stop Bryan as well

135

as the rising star of William Randolph Hearst, Bryan expressed unconcern. Of the nomination, he said if the party chose "to bid for the plutocratic element, it will nominate a gold Democrat; it it wants to bid for support of the masses, it will nominate a silver Democrat. If it does not want any support at all and does not care to take part in the contest between man and Mammon, it will find a man who lacks neither the brains [n]or the heart to take a position."

Whether Bryan thought that the convention would inevitably turn to him as its nominee is debatable; certainly he felt the weight of his two losses, but he had told the Cubans at the inauguration of their first president on 16 May 1902 that "the work of self-government is a continuous work and one that taxes both the patience and the energy of the citizen" (S, 2:192), and in London on 26 November 1903 he declared his admiration for those "who have dared to stand out against overwhelming odds and assert their opinions before the world" (S, 2:200). As the convention neared, he was asked what he thought of Judge Parker. "I am not thinking about Judge Parker at all," he snorted. He was ready once again for a fight.

I   The Campaign of 1904

Bryan arrived in St. Louis on 3 July, determined to maintain the reform momentum in the party. But he continued to refuse to name a candidate in spite of what seemed to be an unsurmountable lead for Parker. He insisted only that Parker's nomination was "highly improbable if not impossible." As chairman of the Nebraska delegation he opened the battle by challenging the seating of the Illinois delegation, supporting instead a group pledged to Hearst, but the Parker men in control ruled against him. His minority report, however, brought the cry of "Bryan, Bryan, Bryan," from the galleries and an impromptu demonstration that seemed for a moment to resurrect the spirit of 1896. But order was restored until he proclaimed in conclusion that "No band of train robbers ever planned a robbery upon a train more deliberately or with less conscience" than did the Parker forces, and the gallery erupted again. He was defeated by more than two to one, but he had made his presence known.

In the Committee on Resolutions Bryan fought for a liberal money platform, including reaffirmations of the platform of 1896 and 1900, and he fought desperately for an income-tax plank and an antitrust plank against the full power of the Parker forces. Forced to compromise on the first, he traded the income-tax plank for a strong antitrust plank, weakened his tariff plank, and secured passsage of a plank to pledge Philippine independence. It was a platform on which he could stand, but there was little room for Parker, who was to object to it strongly a day later.

Although Bryan had not yet named a candidate when nominations began, he determined to speak for Senator Francis M. Cockrell, a Southerner, an ex-Confederate, and a Bryan supporter, and at 4:30 a.m., last to the dais and with an extension of time, he began his statement. After a ten-minute demonstration, he launched into what he later called his best speech:

> Eight years ago a Democratic national convention placed in my hand the standard of the party and commissioned me as its candidate. Four years later that commission was renewed. I come tonight to this Democratic national convention to return the commission. You may dispute whether I have fought a good fight, you may dispute whether I have finished my course, but you cannot deny that I have kept the faith. (S, 2:50)

He turned then to Roosevelt, as he was to do in the pages of *The Commoner* and on the stump during the campaign:

> This Republican president, a candidate for reelection, is presented as the embodiment of the warlike spirit as "the granite and iron" that represent modern militarism.
> Do you, men of the East, desire to defeat the military idea? Friends of the South, are you anxious to defeat the military idea? Let me assure you that not one of you, North, East, or South, fears more than I do the triumph of that idea. If this is the doctrine that our nation is to stand for, it is retrogression, not progress. It is a lowering of the ideals of the nation. It is a turning backward to the age of violence. More than that, it is nothing less than a challenge to the Christian civilizations of the world. (S, 2:51–52)

Addressing the means by which Roosevelt could be defeated, he looked back at his own experience, addressing but not easing the fears of those who thought he might bolt the party and carry his supporters with him:

> As your candidate I tried to defeat the Republican party. I failed, you say? Yes, I failed. I received a million more votes than any Democrat had ever received before, and yet I failed. Why did I fail? Because some who

had affiliated with the democratic party thought my election would be injurious to the country, and they left the party and helped to elect my opponent. That is why I failed. I have no words of criticism for them. I have always believed, I believe tonight, I shall ever believe, I hope, that a man's duty to his country is higher than his duty to his party. I hope that men of all parties will have the moral courage to leave their parties when they believe that to stay with their parties would injure their country. The success of our government depends upon the independence and the moral courage of its citizens. (S, 2:53)

After retracing his role in the convention—"I have said that I thought certain things ought to be done"—he turned to the issue of the campaign as he saw it:

The great issue in this country today is "Democracy versus Plutocracy." I have been accused of having but one idea—silver. A while back it was said that I had only one, but then it was tariff reform. But there is an issue greater than the silver issue, the tariff issue or the trust issue. It is the issue between the democracy and plutocracy—whether this is to be a government of the people, and administered by officers chosen by the people, and administered in behalf of the people, or a government by the moneyed element of the country in the interest of predatory wealth. This issue is growing.

I ask you to help us meet this issue. You tell me that the Republican candidate stands for militarism. Yes, but he also stands for plutocracy. . . . The laws are being violated today, and those laws must be enforced. The government must be administered according to the maxim. "Equal rights to all and special privileges to none."

Bryan concluded then with a personal plea:

I am here . . . because I owe a duty to more than six million brave and loyal men who sacrificed for the ticket in recent campaigns. I came to get them as good a platform as I could; I have helped to get them a good platform. I came to help to get as good a candidate as possible, and I hope that he will be one who can draw the factions together; one who will give to us who believe in positive, aggressive, democratic reform, something to hope for, something to fight for—one who will also give to those who have differed from us on the money question something to hope for, something to fight for. And I close with an appeal from my heart to the hearts of those who hear me: Give us a pilot who will guide the Democratic ship away from the Scylla of militarism without wrecking her upon the Charybdis of commercialism. (S, 2:61–62)

Bryan had, almost incidentally, seconded Cockrell's nomination, but that went unnoticed in the tumult that followed; in the speech he had, according to Josephus Daniels, "converted a convention hostile to him into one that gave him a larger measure of applause than he ever received, before or afterwards," and his enemy August Belmont declared, "My God! Now I can understand the power of the man."[2] But Bryan was exhausted; he did not remain in the convention to see Parker's nomination. He returned to his hotel room to sleep and to plan for 1908.

Although Bryan announced from Fair View that he would support the Parker ticket against the militarism of Roosevelt, he warned that a Parker victory would mean little progress on economic questions. After a month in Arizona in September, he returned to the Chautauqua circuit, lecturing on "A Conquering Nation" as a means of attacking Roosevelt. In October he spoke throughout Indiana, Missouri, Illinois, West Virginia, Ohio, and Kentucky, advocating a Democratic victory but saying little of Parker, confessing later that he "found it difficult to arouse enthusiasm" for a gold Democrat. But as he looked toward 1908 he knew that silver was a dead issue.

Parker ran badly, Roosevelt winning the strongest Republican victory since 1872 and Parker receiving 1,400,000 fewer votes than Bryan in 1896 and 1,300,000 fewer than Bryan in 1900. He carried only the South. The Populists were in shambles, and Bryan knew that they and the reform Democrats would look West again in 1908.

Almost immediately after the election Bryan began a heavy speaking schedule. Visiting Congress and the White House, where he was pleased to find Roosevelt putting together his Square Deal program, he announced his pleasure publicly, saying that "I believe in speaking well of any policy that is good, regardless of which party is supporting it." As he increased the tempo of his speaking, meanwhile exhorting Democrats through the editorials in *The Commoner* to act, he found himself under attack again from Parker Democrats and from Secretary of War William Howard Taft, already being groomed as Roosevelt's successor.

Neither the world nor the place of the United States in it were, in the middle of the first decade of the new century, what they had been in 1896, and in September 1905 Bryan and his family embarked from San Francisco on a year-long journey around the world. During the trip he spoke on numerous occasions in many places, but always, even in the Philippines, with decorum and restraint, almost as though the world had become an extended

Chautauqua circuit. When he reached London in July 1906, he was met by an evolving American political scene as wealthy Democrats, disenchanted with Roosevelt, sought him out to extract promises of conservative programs in exchange for their support in 1908.

When his ship approached New York, the harbor took on the spectacle of a political campaign. Whistles blew, two tugs loaded with supporters escorted the ship to the dock, and he was met by a party of dignitaries. Again he was promised support in exchange for restraint, but he made no commitments.

II   *The Campaign of 1908*

The next day, 30 August 1906, in a massive welcome home rally in Madison Square Garden, he gave his reply in what was his first speech of the 1908 campaign. He had been silent for nearly a year, but he had lost none of his eloquence or his principles. First he spoke as the world statesman he had become:

The first messsage that I bring from the old world is a message of peace. The cause of arbitration is making real progress in spite of the fact that the nations most prominent in the establishment of the Hague tribunal have themselves been engaged in wars since that court was organized. There is a perceptible growth in sentiment in favor of the settlement of international disputes by peaceful means. It was my good fortune to be present at the last session of the Inter-parliamentary Union, which convened in London on the 23rd of July. Twenty-six nations were represented, and these included all the leading nations of the world. This peace congress, as it is generally known, not only adopted resolutions in favor of the limitation of armaments and the arbitration of all questions relating to debts, but unanimously endorsed the proposition that all disputes of every nature should be submitted to an impartial tribunal for investigation, or to the mediation of friendly nations before hostilities were commenced.

It is not necessary to point out the importance of the position taken. . . .
(S, 2:65)

Having presented his diplomatic credentials, he answered those who sought his views and laid out the path that would take him to 1908 and the nomination:

Our nation has lost prestige rather than gained it by our experiment in colonialism. . . .

Congress does not meet in regular session until thirteen months after the election. . . .

I return more strongly convinced than before of the importance of a change in the methods of electing United States Senators. . . .

The income tax, which some in our country have denounced as a socialistic attack upon wealth has, I am pleased to report, the endorsement of the most conservative countries in the old world. . . .

[Arbitration] can be used in disputes between capital and labor. . . .

. . . No reference to the labor question is complete that does not include some mention of what is known as government by injunction. . . .

The struggle to secure an eight-hour day is an international struggle, and it is sure to be settled in favor of the workingman's contention. . . . (*S*, 2:67–73)

Then he turned to "those policies for which the Democratic party stands:"

The unlooked-for and unprecedented increase in the production of gold has brought a victory to both the advocates of gold and the advocates of bimetallism—the former keeping the gold standard which they wanted and the latter securing the larger volume of money for which they contended. . . .

I congratulate President Roosevelt upon the steps which he has taken to enforce the anti-trust law, and my gratification is not lessened by the fact that he has followed the Democratic rather than the Republican platform in every advance he has made. . . .

Legislation which prevents monopoly not only does not injure legitimate business, but actually protects legitimate business from injury. . . .

The tariff question is very closely allied to the trust question and the reduction of the tariff furnishes an easy means of limiting the extortion which the trusts can practice. . . .

I have already reached the conclusion that railroads partake so much of the nature of a monopoly that they must ultimately become public property. . . . I do not know that the country is ready for this change. . . .(*S*, 2:74–84)

Bryan's speech was clear, concise, and carefully organized; there could be no mistake as to his intent. In his closing lines he turned to the kind of eloquent plea that had won so many loyalties over the years:

Plutocracy is abhorrent to a republic; it is more despotic than monarchy, more heartless than aristocracy, more selfish than bureaucracy. It preys upon the nation in time of peace and conspires against it in the hour of its calamity. Conscienceless, compassionless and devoid of wisdom, it enervates its votaries while it impoverishes its victims. It is already sapping the strength of the nation, vulgarizing social life and making a mockery of morals. The time is ripe for the overthrow of this giant wrong. In the name of the counting rooms which it has defiled; in the name of business honor which it has polluted; in the name of the home which it has despoiled; in the name of religion which it has disgraced; in the name of the people whom it has opprest, let us make our appeal to the conscience of the nation. (S, 2:91)

As the opening cannonade in the campaign for the nomination in 1908, the speech was carefully prepared, Bryan reading from a text as he had on other occasions when he wanted no misunderstanding; but he scored only one direct hit with the carefully controlled shot, aimed for the future, concerning government ownership of the railroads. To his immediate audience and to his constituency beyond the Appalachian mountains the whole address was a great success, evidence of greater things to come, but to the Eastern press he had returned from Europe more reckless and dangerous than ever before.

Back in Lincoln, Bryan jumped into state and national politics as though he had never been away, but with the perspective that his world trip had given him. While stumping the Midwest for Democratic candidates in the midterm elections he began publication of his observations and experiences. In *The Old World and Its Ways*, released early in 1907, he observed imperialism in action; it was as he expected:

The government of India is as arbitrary and despotic as the government of Russia ever was, and in two respects it is worse. First, it is administered by an alien people, whereas the officials of Russia are Russians. Second, it drains a large part of the taxes out of the country, whereas the Russian government spends at home the money which it collects from the people. A third disadvantage might be named since the czar has recently created a legislative body, whereas England continues to deny to the Indians any form of representative or constitutional government. Under British rule there is no official corruption and the government is probably as impartial as an alien government can be expected to be, but British rule has the defects which are inherent in a colonial policy.[3]

Nevertheless, his observations appealed to his sense of irony:

But why is there a lack of intelligence among the Indians? Have they not had the blessings of British rule for several generations? Why have they not been fitted for self-government? Gladstone, whose greatness of head and heart shed a lustre upon all Europe, said, "It is liberty alone which fits men for liberty. This proposition, like every other in politics, had its bounds, but it is far safer than the counter doctrine, 'wait till they are fit.' "[4]

The implications for American policy in the Philippines were obvious to Bryan, but he saw some signs of progress, however limited, which were equally significant:

The Netherlands have large colonial possessions in the Malay archipel-ago, but they have been compelled to abandon the culture system—a form of slavery—and there are signs of a political development which will some day make it necessary for Holland to consult the wishes of the people more than she has in the past.[5]

Europe and the labor problem also had lessons for America:

In Europe it is a question between capital and labor and the laborer is organizing for the advancement of his welfare. The guild and the labor organization have long sought to enlarge the laborer's share of the joint profit of labor and capital and to improve the conditions which form his environment. The efforts of these societies have mainly been directed, first, toward the improvement of sanitary conditions; second, toward the short-ening of hours; and third toward an increase in wages. It looks like a reflection on mankind in general to say that laboring men should have to ask for legislation to protect their lives while at work.[6]

Bryan's critics insisted that he had learned no more through his extensive trip than he had on the Chautauqua circuit; others insisted that he chose to ignore the plight of the Negro in the South while castigating the British in India. But these critics ignored Bryan's denunciation of Roosevelt for his treatment of black troops in the Brownsville, Texas, incident, leading W. E. B. Dubois to declare that "It is high noon, brethren—and you are free, sane, and twenty-one. If between two parties who stand on identically the same platform you can prefer the party who perpetrated Brownsville, well and good! But I shall vote for Bryan."[7] Bryan had planted what Franklin Roosevelt was to reap.

Progressive gains in both parties during the midterm elections marked out the path that led Bryan inexorably to the nomination. Eastern Democrats met to stop him; Woodrow Wilson, refusing to become an active candidate, nevertheless wrote, "Would that we could do something, at once dignified and effective to knock Mr.

Bryan once and for all into a cocked hat."[8] But it was Wilson who, in the next four years, would learn his progressivism from Bryan, and it was to be Bryan's vote that gave the nomination and the presidency to Wilson.

As Bryan continued his intense schedule of political, Chautauqua, and Lyceum speeches—leading George L. Miller of Nebraska to declare that "He is a thrifty fellow. All this talking over the country brings him in money, and keeps up his political machine at the same time"—state after state in the West and South instructed their convention delegates for Bryan. His eloquence and political skill were reinforced by the Panic of 1907, which led him to demand governmental programs to supply aid and employment a quarter century before Franklin Roosevelt. Government, he insisted, existed for as well as by and of the people, and it must act.

Although no serious Democratic rival to Bryan had emerged in 1907, he published his usual list of possible candidates in *The Commoner*, including Senator George Gray, Woodrow Wilson, Governor Joseph Falk, and Governor John A. Johnson, a better slate of prospects than he had customarily offered. In an article published in the *Century Magazine* in October 1906 he refuted the charges leveled against him after his misinterpreted railroad statement by attempting to carve out a third path for himself between plutocracy and socialism, asserting that

> There should be no unfriendliness between the honest individualist and the honest socialist; both seek that which they believe to be best for society. The socialist, by pointing out the abuses of individualism, will assist in their correction. At present private monopoly is putting upon individualism an undeserved odium, and it behooves the individualist to address himself energetically to this problem in order that the advantages of competition may be restored to industry.[9]

As he approached the nomination and it became increasingly evident that it would be his, he looked beyond the election to insure that he would be recognized as that individualist, midway between competing ideologies, reiterating the principles of democratic government.

Roosevelt, perhaps seeking to blunt Bryan's offensive, invited him to the White House conference on the conservation of resources on 13–14 May 1908, but Bryan as an individualist took the opportunity not only to compliment Roosevelt for his purpose but to express alarm at the centralizing tendency of Roosevelt's program. In supporting the conservation of the nation's resources, he warned against the threat of growing federalism as well as the everpresent threat of private exploitation:

> I am a strict constructionist if that means to believe that the Federal Government is one of delegated powers and that constitutional limitation should be carefully observed. I am jealous of any encroachment upon the rights of the States, believing that the States are as indestructible as the Union is indissoluble. It is, however, entirely consistent with this theory to believe, as I do believe, that it is just as imperative that the general Government shall discharge the duties delegated to it, as it is that the States shall exercise the power reserved to them. *There is no twilight zone between the Nation and the States, in which exploiting interests can take refuge from both.*[10]

As he spoke, the *New York Times* had already conceded his nomination, and again he was speaking for a postconvention audience. By mid-June he had more than enough delegates pledged to win the nomination, he had written a platform that he knew would be accepted, and he retired to his front porch at Fair View to greet delegates passing through and to give them newly printed copies of "The Prince of Peace." The theme he had chosen for his campaign was "Shall the People Rule?"

For the third time in his life and for the second time at a convention at which he was not present, Bryan won the Democratic nomination. It was a one-ballot victory. When he was notified at 4:30 A.M. on 11 July, he pledged that if defeated he would not run again, and he was already at work on the two documents that would portray him in his new role as defender of the middle ground.

The first of these was an article published in *Collier's Weekly* of 18 July. In it Bryan examined an issue that he had addressed in much of his thinking for more than a decade: his concept of the presidency. His view is both traditional and innovative, Jeffersonian and Jacksonian in inspiration, and it is dominated by his own strong sense of personal morality and responsibility. First, he examines the traditional limitations on the office:

> The President's power for good or for harm is often overestimated. Our government is a government of checks and balances; power is distributed among different departments, and each official works in cooperation with others. In the making of laws, for instance, the President joins with the Senate and the House; he may recommend, but he is powerless to legislate,

except as a majority of the Senate and the House concur with him. The Senate and the House are also independent of each other, each having a veto over the other; and the President has a veto over both; except that the Senate and the House can, by a two-thirds vote, override the President's veto.[11]

After this elementary lesson in constitutional law, he offers his personal concept of the presidency, and not only defines the nonconstitutional dimensions of the office but also makes evident his own qualifications for the office:

The most important requisite in a President, as in other officials, is that his sympathy shall be with the whole people, rather than with any fraction of the population. . . . They act only at elections; and must trust to their representatives to protect them from all their foes.

Second, the President must have a knowledge of public questions and the ability to discern between the true and the false . . . and to detect the sophistries that are always employed by those who seek unfair advantage.

He must possess the moral courage to stand against the influences that are brought to bear in favor of special interests. In fact, the quality of moral courage is as essential in a public official as either right sympathies or a trained mind.[12]

Particularly innovative—and a change that would not be effected for a half-century—was his concept of the proper role of the vice-president, a logical extension of his concept of the role of the president's advisors and of the party platform in determining presidential policy:

A President must have counselors, and to make wise use of counselors, he must be open to convictions. *The President is committed by his platform to certain policies, and the platform is binding.* . . . *The law provides these [counselors], to a certain extent, in giving him a Cabinet, and the Vice-President ought to be made a member of the Cabinet ex-officio, in order, first, that the President may have the benefit of his wisdom and knowledge of affairs, and, second that the Vice-President may be better prepared to take up the work of the President in case of a vacancy in the Presidential office.*[13]

Bryan's conclusion was compounded of his zeal for service and his reverence for an office once more apparently within his grasp:

But the Presidency is the highest position in the world, and its occupant is an important factor in all national matters. If he is a devout believer in our theory of government, recognizes the constitutional distribution of powers, trusts thoroughly in the people and fully sympathizes with them in their aspirations and hopes, he has an opportunity to do a splendid work; he occupies a vantage ground from which he can exert a wholesome influence in favor of each forward movement.

The responsibilities of the office are so great that the occupant ought to be relieved of every personal ambition, save the ambition to prove worthy of the confidence of his countrymen; for this reason he ought to enter the position without thought or prospect of a second term.

While the burdens of such an office are heavy, and while the labors of the office are exacting and exhausting, the field of service is large, and, measuring greatness by service, a President, by consecrating himself to the public weal, can make himself secure in the affections of his fellow citizens while he lives, and create for himself a permanent place in his nation's history.[14]

The essay has obvious political overtones, largely a result of recent experiences, including the impact of Theodore Roosevelt's accession to office upon the continuity of policy on the one hand and Alton B. Parker's refusal to accept a platform with which he disagreed upon the other, and it is certainly a campaign document. But, in retrospect, it is much more. Bryan's concern for the danger inherent in the President's search for reelection was deeply felt, and he was largely responsible for writing a commitment to one term into the party platform in 1912, a commitment that Woodrow Wilson was to ignore in 1916.

III   *The Third Acceptance Speech*

The second document was his speech of acceptance, given in Lincoln on 12 August. Titled "Shall the People Rule?" after the slogan of his campaign, it made clear who now ruled the nation as power had passed into a few private hands:

Four years ago the Republican platform boastfully declared that since 1860—with the exception of two years—the Republican party had been in control of part or all of the branches of the federal Government; that for two years only was the Democratic party in a position to either enact or repeal a law. Having drawn the salaries; having enjoyed the honors; having secured the prestige, let the Republican party accept the responsibility!

Why were these "known abuses" permitted to develop? Why have they not been corrected? If existing laws are sufficient, why have they not been enforced? All of the executive machinery of the federal Government is in the hands of the Republican party. Are new laws necessary? Why have they

not been enacted? With a Republican President to recommend, with a
Republican Senate and House to carry out his recommendations, why does
the Republican candidate plead for further time in which to do what should
have been done long ago? Can Mr. Taft promise to be more strenuous in
the prosecution of wrongdoers than the present executive? Can he ask for a
larger majority in the Senate than his party has? Does he need more
Republicans in the House of Representatives or a speaker with more
unlimited authority? (S, 2:104–5)

Bryan saw the cure as both obvious and morally necessary:

> So long as the Republican party remains in power, it is powerless to
> regenerate itself. It cannot attack wrongdoing in high places without
> disgracing many of its prominent members, and it, therefore, uses opiates
> instead of the surgeon's knife. Its malefactors construe each Republican
> victory as an endorsement of their conduct and threaten the party with
> defeat if they are interferred with. Not until that party passes through a
> period of fasting in the wilderness will the Republican leaders learn to study
> public questions from the standpoint of the masses. Just as with individuals,
> "the cares of this world and the deceitfulness of riches choke the truth," so
> in politics, when party leaders serve far away from home and are not in
> constant contact with the voters, continued party success blinds their eyes
> to the needs of the people and makes them deaf to the cry of distress. (S,
> 2:107–8)

Bryan turned then to the abuses that had prevented the people
from ruling, and in each instance pointed out the remedy promised
in the Democratic platform:

> An election is a public affair. The people, exercising the right to select
> their officials and to decide upon the policies to be pursued, proceed to their
> several polling places on election day and register their will. What excuse
> can be given for secrecy as to the influences at work? If a man, pecuniarily
> interested in "concentrating the control of the railroads in one manage-
> ment" subscribes a large sum to aid in carrying the election, why should his
> part in the campaign be concealed until he has put the officials under
> obligation to him? If a trust magnate contributes $100,000 to elect political
> friends to office with a view to presenting [preventing?] hostile legislation,
> why should that fact be concealed until his friends are securely seated in
> their official positions? How can the people hope to rule? (S, 2:109)

For Bryan, the remedy was the prevention of corporate gifts, a
limitation on individual gifts, and disclosure of all but minor gifts

before the election. The Democrats, he pointed out, had already promised to abide by that plank in the present campaign. He did not, of course, point out that corporate gifts to the Democrats were already minimal, as were individual gifts, but he did present a plan which, he insisted, was "complete and effective."

Two other matters, both also addressed in the Democratic platform, were defined as preventing the people from ruling: "Next to the corrupt use of money the present method of electing United States Senators is most responsible for the obstruction of reforms" (*S*, 2:110). The Democratic platform in 1908, as it had in 1904 and 1900, called for a constitutional amendment providing for the direct election of senators. The other issue was the great concentration of power in the hands of the speaker of the house, Joe Cannon:

> Our party demands that "the House of Representatives shall again become a deliberative body, controlled by a majority of the people's representatives, and not by the speaker," and is pledged to adopt "such rules and regulations to govern the House of Representatives as will enable a majority of its members to direct its deliberations and control legislation." (*S*, 2:114)

The platform, as Bryan stressed its importance, was clearly a conservative document, as was his speech, and Bryan emphasized that conservatism as he moved toward his conclusion:

> "Shall the people rule?" I repeat, is declared by our platform to be the overshadowing question. . . .
> The Democratic party seeks not revolution but reformation. (*S*, 2:115–17)

He ended, appropriately, with a biblical injunction and a vision of the achievable future:

> There is a Divine law of rewards. When the Creator gave us the earth, with its fruitful soil, the sunshine with its warmth, and the rains with their moisture, He proclaimed, as clearly as if His voice had thundered from the clouds: "Go work, and according to your industry and your intelligence, so shall be your reward." Only where might has overthrown, cunning undermined or government suspended this law, has a different law prevailed. (*S*, 2:118)

Finally, unlike his earlier acceptance speeches, this one concludes with a simple promise:

I promise, if entrusted with the responsibilities of this high office, to concentrate whatever ability I have to the one purpose of making this, in fact, a government which will do justice to all, and offer to every one the highest possible stimulus to great and persistent effort, by assuring to each the enjoyment of his just share of the proceeds of his toil, no matter in what part of the vineyard he labors, or to what occupation, profession, or calling he devotes himself. (*S*, 2:118–19)

Bryan's speech, intentionally low-keyed and conservative, reflected both the theme of the campaign and the platform which, by long distance, he had supported, and he determined that the campaign would exude that atmosphere. It would be financed by individual one-dollar donations, antedating the "Dollars for Democrats" campaign of the mid-fifties by nearly forty years. A note of optimism appeared early as, for the first time, a labor union, the American Federation of Labor under Samuel Gompers, pledged its support. One unfavorable note appeared, however, as many Catholic Democrats appeared to support Taft because of his close, friendly relationship with the powerful church in the Philippines while he was governor-general. That problem, together with Roosevelt's support of Taft, was eventually to be considered a major factor in Bryan's defeat.

Considering the Midwest and the West reasonably safe, Bryan planned a series of major speeches attacking Taft on the issues and a good deal of stumping in the East. He planned to ignore the prohibition issue, rapidly becoming a major emotional cause, especially in the South and West, including Nebraska, in spite of misgivings of his advisors.

IV   *Campaign Issues*

A.   *On The Trusts*

The first of his major speeches was given in Indianapolis on 25 August. Treating "The Trust Question," its major thrust was directed at the gulf between the promises in the Republican platform and the performance of the Roosevelt administration, and it emphasized the greater promise and certainty of performance of the Democratic position:

The Sherman anti-trust law was passed eighteen years ago; it has a criminal clause which provides a penitentary punishment for those who conspire together in restraint of trade. Ever since the enactment of the law, with the exception of four years, the Republican party has controlled the executive department of the government, and, during two years of the four, it controlled the House of Representatives. Instead of Democratic dereliction, the Democratic party has been urging the strict enforcement of that law, and the Republican party has been explaining year after year why it was impossible to enforce it. Instead of being a "wholesome instrument for good," it has been almost useless, so far as the protection of the public is concerned, for the trusts have grown in number, in strength, and in arrogance, at the very time the Republican party was boasting of its enforcement of the law. The Steel Trust was formed immediately after the election of 1900, and a prominent Republican said, in a speech soon after, that it might have prevented a Republican victory if it had been formed before the election.

Most of the trusts have never been disturbed and those that have been prosecuted have not had their business seriously interrupted. The President has done something toward the enforcement of the law, but not nearly enough and the Republican leaders have thwarted him at every point. (S, 2:120–21)

In contrast to Republican duplicity, Roosevelt's inaction, and Taft's inept compliance, Bryan stressed Democratic action:

I have, in discussing the tariff question, presented one of our remedies, namely, the removal of the tariff from imports which compete with trust-made goods. . . .

Because the private monopoly is indefensible and intolerable, the Democratic party favors its extermination. . . .

Our platform does not stop with the enforcement of the law; it demands the enactment of . . . additional legislation. . . .

The Democratic party does not content itself with a definition of the wrong or with a denunciation of it. It proceeds to outline remedies. (S, 2:124–25)

His attempted conservatism is clear: "In proposing the exercise of this power, the Democratic platform is not asserting a new doctrine" (S, 2:126).

In attacking Taft, Bryan portrayed his opponent as a minion of the Republican alliance with business, but only incidentally as Roosevelt's heir:

According to Mr. Taft's logic, a plan is not socialistic which is not effective, but the same would be socialistic if made effective. . . .

The trouble with Secretary Taft is that he spends so much time trying to discover excuses for inaction in trust matters that he has none left for the consideration of effective remedies. . . .

Here is a confession by Mr. Taft that he regards the trusts as necessary to the nation's prosperity. (S, 2:130–35)

His conclusion is appropriately low-keyed:

To a national conscience already aroused we appeal, with the pledge that a Democratic victory will mean the ringing out of industrial despotism and the ringing in of a new era in which business will be built upon its merits, and in which men will succeed, not in proportion to the coercion they may be able to practice, but in proportion to their industry, their ability and their fidelity. (S, 2:142)

B.   *On The Banks*

On 27 August, in Topeka, Kansas, Bryan addressed what may have been the most popular issue of the campaign in the aftermath of the Panic of 1907, that of government-guaranteed bank deposits for individual depositors. He began with a question not rhetorical but blunt:

Why not make the depositor secure? The United States Government requires the deposit of specific security when it entrusts money to a national bank, altho it can examine the bank at any time; the State requires security when it deposits money in a bank; the county requires security and the city requires security; even the banks require security from the officials who handle money. Why should the depositor be left to take his chances?

A bank asks deposits on the theory that the depositor is sure of the return of his money, and the law ought to make the facts conform to the theory. (S, 2:143))

Bryan proceeded then, logically and calmly, to establish the need for government-sponsored deposit insurance, citing factual evidence; he pointed out the silence of the Republican platform on the subject, and he noted Taft's opposition to the plank in the Democratic program. He described an incident, not entirely uncommon, from the newspaper, to make his point: "twelve hundred infuriated Italians [in Cleveland, Ohio] stormed the closed doors of the busted banking house of Costan Liopea, on Orange street today. The police drove the crowd back" (S, 2:153). The lesson was clear: Republican government was indifferent, the people were helpless, and the power of government supported those who abuse the public trust. In a democracy, the people, the majority, have a greater claim than the bankers to protection under law:

> There are only 20,000 banks, while there are 15,000,000 depositors, and I do not hesitate to declare that in a conflict between the two, the depositors have a prior claim to consideration. . . . The guaranty law, therefore, brings the greatest good to the greatest number, as well as to those who have the greater equity upon their side. (S, 2:159)

Bryan's conclusion was both a graphic summation and an unabashed plea for acceptance of the economic theory that he believed in as firmly as in his God and his party:

> I submit that in this effort to make all banks secure, the Democratic party is the champion of the farmer, the laboring man, the business man, the professional man, and the champion of the banker as well. No class is outside of the benefits of this law, for it bestows its blessings upon all. . . .
>
> When Solomon was invited to choose what he would, he asked for an understanding heart, that he might discern between the good and the bad, and he was told that, because he had chosen wisdom rather than wealth or long life, he should have, not only wisdom, but riches and length of days as well. And so when a party determines to seek first that which benefits the common people, it finds that in acting in the interest of the common people, it also promotes the welfare of the smaller classes which rest upon the masses, for when the producers of wealth prosper, their prosperity is shared by every element of society. (S, 2:153–63)

In focusing upon a single issue—as he attempted to do in each of his major speeches during the campaign—Bryan not only defined and supported an act of legislation that would not become real until another generation, another major depression, and a forceful president demanded that it be made so, but he revealed the foundation of a political and economic philosophy that he had argued on hundreds of occasions for more than a generation. In so doing, he revealed, too, the foundation of the tremendous faith in him displayed by thousands of people for more than twenty years. That secret was a compassion that transcended issues and parties, that had been part of him from the beginning and was to remain with him to the end.

C.   *On Labor*

On Labor Day, 7 September, Bryan gave his major address on labor issues at the invitation of the American Federation of Labor, thus initiating a practice that since 1932 has been traditional for Democratic candidates and organized labor. Closely related to his speech in Topeka—indeed, a logical transition as well as a common philosophy ties the two together—he began where he had ended in the earlier:

> If it were proper to speak from a text, I would select a passage from Proverbs, for I know of no better one than that furnished by the words of Solomon when he declared that as a man "thinketh in his heart, so is he." This is Bible doctrine; it is common sense, and it is human experience. We think in our hearts as well as our heads—out of the heart "are the issues of life." It is a poor head that cannot find a plausible reason for doing what the heart wants to do. I begin my speech with this proposition because I want to impress it upon the minds of those who listen to me, and upon those who read what I say to you. The labor question is more a moral than an intellectual one. (S, 2:164)

But the dimensions of that question were far broader than the labor issue:

> The world is growing toward brotherhood, and our nation is leading the way. There is more altruism in this country than anywhere else in the world, and more today than there ever has been before. There is more recognition of the kinship that exists between us, more thought about the questions which concern a common humanity, than at any preceeding time. The labor organization is a part of this great movement of the masses toward closer fellowship. It has worked wonders in the past and its work is only commenced. (S, 2:165)

Bryan's immediate concern, however, was the issue of labor, specifically of anti-injunction legislation, which the Democratic platform supported, the Republicans opposed, and labor demanded. First, he defined a fundamental difference between party and individual policies and proposals:

> There are two questions, however, intimately connected with the labor problem upon which the Democratic and Republican parties do not agree, and I not only feel at liberty to discuss these, but under the circumstances I have no right to ignore them. One relates to the issue of injunctions, and

the other to contempt cases arising under injunctions. The Republican convention did not deal candidly with the laboring man on the subject of the writ of injunction. Secretary Taft has endeavored to amend his platform in this respect and to make some promises, which are not supported by his platform, but his promises offer nothing substantial in the way of reform, and are not binding on Republican senators and members. The Republican Congress has already made a record on labor questions, and the Republican party cannot escape from that record. (*S,* 2:170)

Bryan cited the clarity with which the Democratic platform made its position known: that "all parties to all judicial proceedings shall be treated with rigid impartiality"; that "injunctions shall not be issued in any cases in which injunctions would not issue if no industrial dispute were involved"; that in cases of contempt the evidence shall be weighed by a jury. He declared,

The Democratic platform proposes no interference with the right of the judges to decide the cases of direct contempt . . . ; neither is it proposed to interfere with the right of the judge to determine the punishment for indirect contempt. All that is sought is the substitution of trial by jury when the violation of the court's decree must be established by evidence. (*S,* 2:174–75)

Labor issues were infinitely broader than the debate over the injunction, Bryan acknowledged, but he was confined to the issue at hand; nevertheless, he concluded by moving beyond it to the economic issue upon which it rested:

One of the great problems of today is to secure an equitable distribution of the proceeds of toil. The material wealth of this country is largely a joint product; in factories few people work alone, and on the farm a certain amount of cooperation is necessary. . . . The difficulty has been to divide the results fairly between the captains of industry and the privates in the ranks. As the dividing is done largely by the captains, it is not unnatural that they should magnify their part and keep too large a share for themselves. . . .
The labor question, therefore, as it presents itself at this time, is chiefly a question of distribution, and the legislation asked for is legislation which will secure to each that to which his services entitle him. . . . The Democratic platform presents the ideal toward which the Democratic party is striving, namely justice in the distribution of rewards. (*S,* 2:178–79)

Bryan concluded by tying the opening vision into an achievable political reality:

Riches may take the wings of the morning and fly away, but government is permanent, and we cannot serve posterity better than by contributing to the perfection of the Government, that each child born into the world may feel that it has here an opportunity for the most complete development, and a channel to secure, through service, the largest possible happiness and honor. (S, 2:179–80)

If Bryan's concept of the labor question was oversimplified, this was not evident to his audience or to the editor of Samuel Gompers's *Federationist*. For the first time it appeared that labor had a candidate; no more would threats, fears, or coercion drive the workingman into the camp of the Republicans. Bryan was elated by the depth of his labor support, and he began to think of it as one of the foundation stones of his victory coalition.

D.   *On the Balance of Political Power*

On 9 September he spoke in Peoria, Illinois, in friendly home country, and he presented something that was new for him on the campaign trail: a philosophical statement on the nature of the intricately balanced American system of government, a fusion of balances of federal power, state and federal power, and philosophical and pragmatic forces in the political parties. In keeping with Democratic tradition and with the East-West, country-city tension that he had known all his life, he expressed a strong bias toward state power in spite of advocating programs that would inevitably gather more power into federal hands—hands that were also Eastern and urban.

The success of our system of government rests upon the careful observance of the constitutional division of power between the State and the Nation. A number of expressions have been coined to describe the relations existing between the Federal Government and the several subdivisions, but no one has been more felicitous in definitions than Jefferson or more accurate in drawing lines of demarcation. He presented the historic position of the Democratic party when he declared himself in favor of "the support of the State governments in all their rights, as the most competent administrations for our domestic concerns and the surest bulwarks against anti-republican tendencies," and "the preservation of the general Government in its whole constitutional vigor, as the sheet anchor of our safety at home and peace abroad." The Democratic platform, adopted at Denver, quotes the language of Jefferson and declares that it expressed the party's position at this time. (S, 2:181)

Nevertheless, he pointed out, the power of the states had been eroded not only because, "in all disputes as to the relative spheres of the Nation and the States the final decision rests with the federal courts," but because another great force entered political and constitutional life, in the process extending the power of the federal government:

I refer to the great corporations. They prefer the federal courts to the State courts, and employ every possible device to drag litigants before United States judges. They also prefer Congressional regulation to State regulation, and those interested in large corporations have for years been seeking federal corporation. . . .

The predatory corporations have taken advantage of the dual character of our Government and have tried to hide behind State rights when prosecuted in the federal courts, and behind the interstate commerce clause of the constitution when prosecuted in the State courts. (S, 2:183–84)

The remedy, Bryan insisted, lay in careful, specific legislation balanced to preserve a proper relationship. Drawing an image from his speech on conservation, he defined the reality of the relationship between state and local power:

There is no twilight zone between the Nation and the State in which the exploiting interests can take refuge from both. There is no neutral ground where, beyond the jurisdiction of either sovereignty, the plunderers of the public can find a safe retreat. As long as a corporation confines its activities to the State in which it was created, it is subject to State regulation only; but as soon as it invades interstate commerce it becomes amenable to federal laws as well as to the laws of the State which created it and the laws of the States in which it does business. (S, 2:184)

The means of maintaining that balance, Bryan pointed out, was inherent in the philosophy and practice of the Democratic party:

No one can contrast the plain, straightforward declarations of our party with the vague and ambiguous utterings of the Republican leaders and the Republican candidate without recognizing that our appeal is to the judgment and good sense of the voters who desire justice for themselves and insist upon justice being done by others. Our party, if entrusted with the power, will remedy the abuses which have grown up under Republican rule, and yet remedy those abuses with due regard to constitutional limitations and without injury to any legitimate business interest. (S, 2:187)

V   *Defeat*

Bryan stumped the East and Midwest; he ventured into the South, and he received some of the greatest ovations of his life; he courted the black vote without alienating the white; he weathered the conflict-of-interest scandal of the Democratic treasurer, Charles N. Haskell of Oklahoma; he gave hundreds of brief speeches as well as revisions of his major ones; he received a standing ovation in Madison Square Garden on 18 September before and after his disclosure of "Republican Tendencies"; he drew large crowds where Taft had drawn small ones. After sixty days on the stump he returned to Lincoln on 2 November to await the results.

Before all the returns were in, he knew he had been defeated again and that it was the worst of his career. Taft amassed 321 electoral votes to Bryan's 162, and enjoyed a margin of more than a million popular votes. Postmortems suggested causes, primarily the defection of Catholics and nonunion workers. But Bryan knew that it did not matter, and that there would be no *Third Battle* written. He would never again actively pursue the presidency. His only regret, he told his daughter Grace, was that her mother would never be First Lady of the Land.

CHAPTER 9

Decline and Fall

I *Regrouping*

ALTHOUGH Bryan had sought and lost the presidency three times and determined that he would not actively seek it again, he was only forty-eight years old in November 1908, younger than many who had sought the office or would in the future and younger too than most of those who had been elected to it. Retiring from politics was unthinkable, not merely because of his relative youth, but because much remained to be done. In December 1908, in a speech called "A Battle Over, A War Begun," he made clear his determination to continue the fight for reform in the nation and to sustain the reform impetus in his own party. He could not, he said, accommodate those of both parties who clamored for his retirement, nor would he take the advice of those who regretfully advised it: the campaign of 1912 was on the horizon.

Bryan remained more than titular head of his party. No other Democratic leader of national stature had emerged, although Champ Clark, Democratic leader of the House, and Governor Woodrow Wilson of New Jersey, as well as the perennial potential candidate William Randolph Hearst, occupied places of varying degrees of prominence. The immediate task he saw was to maintain the reform thrust of the party and to insure that it was not recaptured by those of the Democratic right who had supported him reluctantly if at all in the election.

Nevertheless, during much of 1909 he remained quiet—but not silent—on political issues as he attempted to define the nature of his new but not lesser role. He spent much time on the Chautauqua circuit; he saw his two older children, William, Jr., and Ruth, married; and he determined to take an active role in what he saw as the two most important progressive issues of the time: peace and the conservation of natural resources. The former, he was convinced,

159

was a cause whose time had come, and it could be made a living reality through the efforts of men of good will; the latter was another battle in the war against those exploiting interests that he had fought so long. Increasingly, too, he began to take an active role in the leadership of his Presbyterian Church, and he moved closer to the battle line in the drive toward prohibition.

In all these activities he was determined to be neither a passive participant nor a theorizer—two years before he had declared that there was room for only one "dreamer" in the Democratic party and that place was occupied by Thomas Jefferson—but he was apparently undergoing a rigid self-examination during 1909. He had come from nowhere to the threshold of the presidency, not once but three times, and he was not only concerned with where he was going from that point but also fascinated with the means by which he had risen. Invited to speak in Springfield, Illinois, on 12 February 1909 at the centennial observance of Lincoln's birth, he chose to speak on "Lincoln as an Orator." He might have been speaking of himself:

> His power as a public speaker was the foundation of his success, and while it is obscured by the super-structure that was reared upon it, it cannot be entirely overlooked. . . . With no military career to dazzle the eye or excite the imagination; with no public service to make his name familiar to the reading public, his elevation to the presidency would have been impossible without his oratory. (S, 2:424-25)

Bryan's own oratorical skills were employed frequently for his causes in 1909 and in the midterm election year 1910. At the New York Peace Society on 29 February 1909 he declared that "war was the sum of all evils," and later denounced war as "unchristian"; on 20 June he spoke on "Arbitration" at the Lake Mohonk Peace Conference. He wrote President Taft, recommending that the United States move toward a positive peace policy by writing an arbitration treaty with Great Britain—an idea Taft found so attractive that he had his secretary of state, Philander C. Knox, draw up sample treaties with France and Great Britain. Both treaties were signed by the appropriate nations, but both were so weakened in the Senate by exclusions, especially of immigration and the provisions of the Monroe Doctrine, that Taft abandoned them. But in a brief, unsigned article in the *Outlook* for 12 August 1911, Bryan was optimistic about their passage, and he lavished praise upon Taft and Knox for initiating them:

It is universally recognized that for taking the initiative in this matter credit belongs to President Taft and his Secretary of State, Mr. Knox. Americans, while justified in taking pride in the special honor that belongs to their country in this matter should not fail to remember, however, that the achievement would have been impossible without the ready and enlightened response of the Governments of Great Britain and France.[1]

For Bryan, the peace movement and the settling of international disputes through arbitration were far more than political goals; they were deeply imbedded in his sense of Christian morality. In his summation of "The World Missionary Movement" which appeared in *Outlook* for 13 August 1910, actually a summation of a world missionary conference held at Edinburgh, Scotland, he commented,

A study of the report of the Commission and a review of the discussions ought to stimulate good citizenship by impressing Christians with their responsibility for the continued existence of governmental evils which might be corrected. Reference was made during the Conference to the Peace Movement, and a largely attended Peace Meeting, addressed by representatives of Great Britain, Germany, Japan, and the United States, declared unanimously in favor of treaties stipulating that the contracting parties will not in any case declare war or commence hostilities until the question in dispute, no matter what its nature, has been submitted to an impartial international tribunal for investigation and support.[2]

(The search for peace, not through the abstract means of prayer or exhortation, but through a practical means of agreement among nations, was to remain at the center of Bryan's thinking and action for the rest of his life. As secretary of state, peace was the cornerstone of his foreign policy; a threat to it was to prompt his resignation from that office; and it remained his most important consideration even after the American declaration of war, when he offered his services to President Wilson for the duration.)

During 1910 and 1911 Bryan was determined to direct Democratic party energies and programs toward reform, and he felt a sense of triumph in the midterm Congressional elections of 1910. In that election, spurred by conservative Democratic support of the high-tariff Payne-Aldrich Bill, he attempted to purge conservatives from among the Democratic nominees for Congress, and he was almost successful, largely by recruiting members for *The Commoner*'s "Million Army" who were pledged to support progressive candidates. When Democrats swept the election in 1910, gaining ten Senate and forty House seats, controlling the latter, Bryan saw 1912 as a Democratic year, and he increased his efforts.

In Washington early in 1911, he lobbied extensively for Champ Clark's election as speaker of the house and Clark's election was considered a Bryan victory. In the Senate he campaigned for Benjamin Shively of Indiana for minority leader, but Senator Thomas Martin of Virginia, whom Bryan considered a "tariff renegade," was elected. In an attempt at peace-making that was not entirely unsuccessful, the Democratic conservatives in Congress invited Bryan to a Jackson Day banquet, but Bryan was skeptical; he saw the overture as an attempt to forge a coalition that would nominate a conservative presidential condidate in 1912. He was determined to prevent that at all costs. At the same time, however, his control over the Nebraska party was slipping, and he cast about for an issue that would bring the Nebraska and national party back under his control.

II   *Prohibition*

The issue was prohibition. By 1910 it had become the only dominant domestic political issue that engendered strong emotions in the electorate nationwide, and the Anti-Saloon League, founded in 1893 in Oberlin, Ohio, had become the country's most powerful pressure group. By 1910 the League had succeeded in drying up thousands of townships and counties nationwide, and, beginning with Georgia and Oklahoma in 1907, it had succeeded in drying up thirteen states as well as Alaska, Puerto Rico, and the District of Columbia. In 1910 the League began to demand a local-option law in Nebraska.

The lesson of this remarkable political achievement was not lost on Bryan, although whether he threw his lot in with the prohibition-ists in 1910 for political purposes or as a matter of conviction is open to debate. Although he had abstained from drinking alcohol all his life, he had in the past studiously avoided making prohibition a political issue, and, in fact, had opposed it in his first congressional campaign in 1890. As recently as 1909 he had declined to support the drys' county-option campaign. But in 1910 he suddenly de-manded that the popular Democratic governor of Nebraska, A. C. Shallenberger, call a special session of the legislature, either to pass the county-option bill or to permit the people to vote on it through the initiative and referendum. His ostensible reason was that this action would remove the issue from the congressional campaign that year, which, he insisted, should be reserved for national issues, whereas prohibition was a local matter.

Shallenberger refused, whereupon Bryan went on a statewide speaking tour, demanding the special session and a county-option plank in the state Democratic platform. He demanded that each candidate for the governorship declare himself on the issue, and he began to attack drinking and the liquor interests. Almost overnight he became the darling of the Anti-Saloon League and the Women's Christian Temperance Union. Shallenberger, however, refused to be drawn out, and in the primary he was opposed by Bryan and defeated by James C. Dahlman, a wet. In the campaign Bryan damned Dahlman with faint praise, and Dahlman lost the election to the Republican candidate, Chester Aldrich. Bryan made peace with his third rival for Democratic leadership in Nebraska, Gilbert Hitchcock, and as 1912 loomed Bryan was again firmly in control of the party in his home state. His county-option plank had been refused by the convention that nominated Dahlman, but his move had apparently served its purpose for the moment.

During the campaign Bryan crossed oratorical swords in a debate with Clarence Darrow in Lincoln. While Bryan, perhaps foreshadowing the Scopes trial, denounced liquor and the liquor interests on moral grounds, Darrow, tongue in cheek, suggested that dancing, cardplaying, and drinking tea and coffee were equal evils, and hence all deserved to be outlawed.

Whether or not his allegiance to the prohibition cause was initially induced by political considerations, once Bryan had declared his loyalty he never again wavered. Prohibition, one of the oldest reform movements in the nation, had fought the hard-drinking American frontier tradition for more than a century. It had made alliances with other reform movements from time to time over the years, and its reform credentials were impeccable; certainly it was no more radical in its actions than the women's suffrage agitators with whom, through the W.C.T.U., the prohibitionists were allied. Prohibition's moral credentials were equally impeccable; it was endorsed by evangelical Protestantism en masse.

For Bryan the issue was essentially moral; as secretary of state he was to refuse to serve wine or other intoxicants at official functions— upon appointment he asked Wilson whether or not that would embarrass his administration and refused appointment until assured that it would not—and after his resignation from the office he lobbied for the cause. He and Josephus Daniels, Wilson's secretary of the navy, persuaded Wilson not to oppose the Eighteenth Amendment. If it worked, they pointed out, his administration would reap the political benefit. If it did not, he could not be blamed. At the Prohibition Watch Night Service in Washington's First Congregational Church on the night of 20 January 1920, Bryan declared in biblical terms, as midnight struck and prohibition became the law of the land, that "they are dead which sought the young child's life."

But his conversion to the prohibitionist cause did not affect his determination to nominate and elect a progressive Democratic president in 1912. In *The Commoner* he began to review potential candidates, breaking with Governor Judson Harmon of Ohio—the Harmon who had declared in 1908 that he would gladly suffer defeat "if that course would insure the election of Mr. Bryan"—and he turned to Governor Woodrow Wilson of New Jersey and Champ Clark, speaker of the house, as worthy of consideration. He rejected Oscar Underwood, the favorite of the conservatives, out of hand.

However, Bryan quickly lost faith in Clark as Clark supported Underwood in tariff maneuvers in Congress; when Clark later held up debate on a bill regulating the interstate shipment of liquor, Bryan was disgusted. As Clark began putting together his campaign for the nomination, Bryan noted that it was financed to a great extent by the liquor interests. He was left with one acceptable candidate, Governor Wilson of New Jersey.

III   *Woodrow Wilson*

Bryan's support of Wilson seemed unlikely to many observers, however. Not only had Wilson voted against Bryan in 1896, but he and Bryan opposed each other on issues of government control, the central bank, and the role of financial leaders in Congress. In 1907 Wilson had publicly stated that Bryan's position on many issues was absurd; on two occasions in 1908 he had refused to speak from the same platform with Bryan, and in the background there was the Joline letter, not yet made known to Bryan. To a reporter Wilson had described Bryan as "the most charming and lovable of men personally but foolish and dangerous in his theoretical beliefs."[3] It was the kind of criticism that stung Bryan more than any other, and chances of his forgiving Wilson seemed slight.

Nevertheless, Wilson began, by 1907, to draw closer to Bryan in his political beliefs. Throughout his academic career Wilson had never forgotten his youthful ambition for a political career, and his increasing difficulties in the presidency of Princeton were instrumental in his willingness to listen to conservative Democratic machine leaders who proposed to make him governor of New Jersey. He became the state's first Democratic governor in a generation.

Whether the result of political expediency, slow or sudden conversion, or his ingrained Calvinist morality, Wilson's progressivism became evident during the gubernatorial campaign of 1910; after his election by a 50,000 vote majority, he began to act upon his new convictions. A strong governor, he broke with the party bosses and forced through the legislature a corrupt practices law, railroad regulation, public utilities regulation, a direct primary, and an employers' liability law. One of the most reactionary states in the union when Wilson took office, New Jersey quickly became one of the most progressive, and he began to emerge as a national leader.

Bryan applauded Wilson's conversion in *The Commoner*, nudging him gently on occasion, while carrying on his own campaign for progressive reform, focusing particularly upon tariff reform and trust regulation. In 1911, when the Supreme Court applied its so-called "Rule of Reason" to Standard Oil and American Tobacco cases, thus limiting the effects of the Sherman Anti-Trust Act, Bryan exploded, but, in an article in the *North American Review*, he examined the issue with remarkable restraint and rationality:

The decision of the United States Supreme Court in the Standard Oil case—and the language of the opinion is repeated with emphasis in the Tobacco case—is epoch-making, although people will differ as to the character of the epoch which it ushers in. There are a number of things which impress one as he reads the majority and minority positions, and the impression made is so deep that feeling increases with contemplation. It is easier for the public to discuss the subject in diplomatic language now than it will be when the far-reaching effect of the decision is fully understood. The position one takes in regard to the majority and minority opinions depends largely upon the point of view from which he looks at the trust question. Those who regard the trust as a benevolent institution, or as a natural and necessary economic development, will be likely to approve of the position taken by the majority of the Court, and if they approve of the position taken by the Court they will quite naturally endorse the reasons given. Those, on the contrary, who look upon the trust as a real menace to economic independence and to our political institutions will applaud Justice Harlan for having so vigorously dissented, even though in dissenting he stood alone.[4]

Bryan had himself delighted in standing virtually alone on many occasions, but in this essay he examined the majority opinion on seven major points in great detail, concluding with his assessment of the effects of the bill:

The last question to be considered is, what is to be the result of this decision? We have seen one result—namely, rejoicing on the part of every man pecuniarily interested in the corporations which are exploiting the public. But what will be the effect upon the public? This question cannot be answered without entering the realm of prophecy, and prophecy is uncertain. We have seen one decision of the Supreme Court—the decision in the Dred Scott case—hasten a civil war, and we have seen another decision—the decision in the Income Tax case—compel the submission of an amendment to the Constitution. We shall see, as time goes on, whether the people will acquiesce in this decision or be aroused by it to more energetic action against combinations in restraint of trade, and the result will have its effect upon the reputations of the members of the Court. If the revolution which Chief-Justice White has led marks the beginning of a permanent policy it will be accorded a high place among our jurists. If, on the other hand, public sentiment develops along the line of the dissenting opinion, we may expect to see Justice Harlan increasingly honored. If his warning is heeded and the people assert their right to protect themselves against trusts and monopolies he will become the forerunner of a great reform, while the flame which the Court mistook for "the light of reason" will be discarded as an illusion.[5]

Bryan's position on the trusts had remained essentially unchanged through the essay, as did his determination to see them brought under government control, but his restraint is marked. His argument, however one-sided, is rational rather than emotional, and his reasoning is virtually devoid of moralizing or of biblical overtones. Increasingly he was reserving the latter technique for his promotion of prohibition, and, after his appointment as secretary of state, for the cause of peace.

As the convention of 1912 approached, Wilson, making a strong bid for the nomination, spoke in every section of the country, largely in terms that appealed to Bryan—although it became increasingly evident that Clark would inherit the support of most of Bryan's supporters who would serve as delegates to the convention. Wilson and Bryan met several times and developed a close personal friendship, especially after Wilson pointed out that he had voted "very cheerfully" for Bryan in 1900 and 1908.

Bryan, however, refused to name an acceptable candidate publicly, although he supported an unsuccessful drive for Wilson delegates in Nebraska. Clark swept the Nebraska primary handily, with Wilson a poor third, and Bryan, as a Nebraska delegate, would go to Baltimore pledged to Clark. Bryan declined to be keynote speaker lest he be accused of trying to stampede the convention to himself but insisted that the keynoter be a progressive, and that the platform and permanent chairmen be progressives also.

From 16 to 22 June he attended the Republican convention in Chicago as a newspaper syndicate correspondent, a circumstance which he enjoyed as the party split, with the Old Guard in command. Roosevelt's speech, "We Stand at Armageddon," he characterized as a rehash of Democratic speeches since 1896, and Roosevelt's bolt convinced him that a Democratic progressive nominee was essential. That he enjoyed the Republican predicament is clear; a contemporary cartoon shows him beaming as Republicans quarrel. He was determined to enjoy seeing Democratic conservatives squirm as well.

With the rumor circulating that Bryan was for Bryan, he went to Baltimore without having endorsed a candidate but convinced that he would defeat whoever the New York delegation, controlled by Parker, supported. As the convention opened, Clark had 436 pledged delegates, to Wilson's 248, with Underwood third. Bryan lost his fight to deny the temporary chairmanship to Parker, although he was supported by the Wilson forces. Thereupon, in his loud, clear voice, he introduced a resolution that was perhaps the most daring in American political convention history. He demanded that the reactionaries be purged:

Resolved, that in this crisis in our party's career and in our country's history this convention sends greetings to the people of the United States, and assures them that the party of Jefferson and of Jackson is still the champion of popular government and equality before the law. As proof of our fidelity to the people, we hereby declare ourselves opposed to the nomination of any candidate for president who is the representative of or under obligation to J. Pierpont Morgan, Thomas F. Ryan, August Belmont, or any other member of the privilege-hunting and favor-seeking class.

Be it further resolved, That we demand the withdrawal of any delegate or delegates constituting or representing the abovenamed interests.[6]

The convention gasped before erupting into cheers and catcalls; Belmont was a member of the New York delegation and Ryan of the

Virginia, leading one member to fear that Bryan was attempting to destroy the party. But Bryan was speaking for the record and for effect; a compromise was effected whereby Bryan withdrew the second part of the resolution after an exchange of vituperation and fist-shaking, and the first part carried overwhelmingly. Bryan had won what he wanted; the New York delegation would have little voice in nominating a candidate.

Bryan's role in defining the progressive limits of the convention has been misinterpreted almost constantly, immediately after the fact and since, but it was neither an attempt to destroy old enemies nor to stampede the progressive elements into nominating him. It was a courageous and skillful movement by which the reactionary power in the party was virtually neutralized; and as the balloting began, he had two more potent weapons with which to finish the fight: his vote and his voice.

In the early balloting, Clark maintained his solid lead, with Wilson an equally solid second. Nebraska voted for Clark, and New York for Harmon. On the tenth ballot, however, New York threw its ninety votes to Clark, giving him a strong majority of 556, and, with the two-thirds rule for nomination prevailing, it was presumably the signal for a landslide; not since 1844 had a candidate with a clear majority failed to win nomination. However, the Wilson and Underwood forces stood firm, and on the fourteenth ballot Bryan exploded his second bombshell.

On that ballot, Nebraska passed, signaling debate in the delegation. When it was reached again, Bryan rose, asking permission to explain his vote. The chairman refused, Bryan forces shouted demands that he be heard, and the permission was given. Clearly and incisively, Bryan defined his position in a statement he had prepared before the convention and had reserved for this moment. Nebraska, he said, had been pledged to Clark "with the distinct understanding that Mr. Clark stood for progressive democracy." Fighting his way to the platform, he continued:

Speaking for myself and for any of the delegation who may decide to join me, I shall withhold my vote from Mr. Clark as long as New York's vote is recorded for him. (Applause.) And the position that I take in regard to Mr. Clark I will take in regard to any other candidate whose name is now or may be before the convention. I shall not be a party to the nomination of any man, no matter who he may be, or from what section of the country he comes who will not, when elected, be absolutely free to carry out the anti-Morgan-Ryan-Belmont resolution, and make his administration reflect the wishes and the hopes of those who believe in a government of the people, by the people, and for the people.

Now I am prepared to announce my vote, with the understanding that I stand ready to withdraw my vote from the candidate for whom I now cast it, if Mr. Murphy casts the ninety votes of New York for him. I cast my vote for Nebraska's second choice, Governor Wilson.[7]

In the two hours of tumult that followed, it was scarcely noticed that Bryan had not endorsed Wilson, but actually had placed him under the same warning that he had placed the others, in effect merely reinforcing his initial resolution, but the effect was the same as an endorsement. Again, no landslide developed, but a steady growth of Wilson's strength began, together with discussion of a deadlock and another Bryan nomination.

But Bryan, after consulting with Mary, refused to encourage his own candidacy. Finally, on the thirtieth ballot, Wilson moved past Clark; on the forty-second, Illinois came over to Wilson; Indiana traded its votes for the nomination of Thomas Marshall as vice-president; and the Underwood forces defected to Wilson on the forty-sixth ballot. With them, Wilson won the nomination on 2 July. The rest of the convention was anticlimax. Asked if he would take the stump for Wilson, Bryan replied, "I should say I will. Just watch me," while his brother Charles went on to Sea Girt, New Jersey, to confer with the nominee.

With the Republican split, the first major three-way campaign since 1860 promised a result as foregone in 1912 as in 1860, but the campaign was no less hard fought. Wilson's "New Freedom," was little more than Bryan's traditional ideas in new clothes furnished by Louis Brandeis, but it captured the popular imagination, as Roosevelt's "New Nationalism" had done and the "New Deal" of a later generation was to do.

After his Chautauqua tour, Bryan campaigned widely, largely in his old territory, and he supported Clark for reelection to the House in Missouri as well. The last week, as was traditional, he devoted to Nebraska, making nineteen speeches on the last day, declaring in Omaha that "I am more interested in the election of a Democratic President this year than is Woodrow Wilson himself. I have travelled more miles; I have spoken more hours, and I will rejoice more next Tuesday night over the election of Woodrow Wilson than that gentlemen himself." The statement was almost literally true.

The election was not merely a victory for Wilson; it was a

progressive victory as well. Wilson's popular vote was 6,293,019, nearly 100,000 fewer than Bryan had received in 1908, to Roosevelt's 4,119,507 and Taft's 3,484,956, but in the electoral college it was a landslide: Wilson's 435 votes to Roosevelt's 88 and Taft's eight. Both the Senate and the House were Democratic, but Wilson was aware not only of his status as a minority president, but of Bryan's role in his election. There would be a major place for him in the new administration.

IV   *Secretary of State*

After some discussion, Wilson advanced a tentative offer of a major ambassadorship, which Bryan declined. He preferred appointment as secretary of the treasury, but on 21 December in Trenton, Wilson formally offered Bryan the position of secretary of state. Bryan pointed out his objection to serving intoxicants at official functions, which Wilson saw as no problem, and then he introduced the draft of a peace treaty, which he would like to negotiate with a number of foreign nations, and again Wilson saw no problem. Bryan pressed him for a declaration that making such treaties would be a major part of the administration's foreign policy; Wilson said that it would be part of his program, and Bryan formally accepted the appointment.

Both within and outside the Wilson administration objections were raised to Bryan's appointment: he had no foreign experience— although he had spent nearly two years abroad; he was sectional in orientation—although he had campaigned and drawn support in every region of the country; and he was not interested in commerce—in spite of his many tariff pronouncements.

Bryan drew his own staff together to administer the department, with one major exception that was to have serious repercussions and contribute to Bryan's resignation: as counselor to the department and chief legal advisor to Bryan, Wilson appointed John Bassett Moore, who was to be succeeded by another Wilson appointee, Robert Lansing, a strong Anglophile.

Bryan was determined that his secretaryship would be marked by an open, democratic, moral administration. To avoid conflict of interest, he turned *The Commoner* into a monthly, with his contributions limited to advice and an occasional editorial, but he continued to lecture at Chautauqua during his vacations, a factor which drew some hostile criticism. His efforts to open the department's affairs to public scrutiny were, however, frustrated by diplomatic policy, and his attacks on the ingrained bureaucracy were blunted by the career system.

However, his introduction of a moral dimension was evident not only in his teetotal entertainments, which drew more praise than condemnation, but in his determination to banish war from human affairs. He was optimistic that it could and would be accomplished, and that it could be done by moral sanctions alone. After incorporating several suggestions by Wilson, he prepared a new draft of his treaty:

> The parties hereto agree that all questions of whatever character and nature whatever, in dispute between them, shall, when diplomatic efforts fail, be submitted for investigation and report to an international commission (the composition to be agreed upon); and the contracting parties agree not to declare war or begin hostilities until such investigation is made and report submitted.
>
> The investigation shall be conducted as a matter of course, without the formality of a request from either party; the report shall be submitted within (time to be agreed upon) from the date of the submission of the dispute, and neither party shall utilize the period of investigation to change its military or naval program, but the parties hereto reserve the right to act independently on the subject matter in dispute after the report is submitted.[8]

Although questions were raised about the advisability as well as the legality of such a treaty, the procedure was put into effect as a major emphasis in American foreign policy, with results that were gratifying to Wilson as well as to Bryan, who summed up the results in his *Memoirs:*

> Upon being invited into the Cabinet of President Wilson, I secured his hearty approval of the plan. Soon after the inauguration, it was put into diplomatic form and laid before him and by him submitted to the cabinet. Before it was offered to the foreign representatives at Washington, it was submitted to the Senate Committee on Foreign Relations and approved by that committee. It was in April, 1913, submitted to the diplomatic representatives at Washington. . . .
>
> The following are the nations with whose governments these treaties were made; they are given in the order in which the treaties were executed: Salvador, Guatemala, Panama, Honduras, Nicaragua, Netherlands, Bolivia, Persia, Portugal, Costa Rica, Switzerland, Dominican Republic, Venezuela, Denmark, Italy, Norway, Peru, Uruguay, Brazil, Argentine Republic, Chile,

Paraguay, China, France, Great Britain, Spain, Russia, Ecuador, Greece, Sweden.

The United States Senate advised the ratification of all these treaties except those with Panama and the Dominican Republic. Ratification has been exchanged with twenty. . . .

The plan of these treaties, with the exception of the provision reserving the right of independent action, was embodied in the Covenant of the League of Nations.[9]

Although Bryan recognized that such a treaty was far from a renunciation of war as an instrument of national policy, nevertheless he felt that he had made substantial progress toward peace. At the same time he was faced with the inherent irony of wars threatened and in progress: the turmoil in Mexico out of which Wilson and Bryan were determined to construct a moral, consistent policy and a stable democratic government, but which instead resulted in continued confusion and the first major disagreement between the two; the search for a consistent, democratic Latin American policy, permitting the settlement of disputes through arbitration and the growth of American trade, especially in the Caribbean; complex Far Eastern problems, including the fate of the Philippines, on which Bryan attempted to impose his policy of independence for the Islands; anti-Japanese legislation and attitudes in California, which violated Bryan's sense of rights and his personal liking for the Japanese; and the problems inherent in developing the embryo Chinese republic into a viable independent nation. Increasingly, too, he became involved in the growing indications of an expansionist Japanese policy.

In all of these international problems, many of them of crisis proportions, it is possible to point to weaknesses and inconsistencies in attitudes and solutions presented or developed by the Wilson administration and its secretary and Department of State: they have been called unrealistic, unfair, neo-imperialist, dollar-diplomatic. It is equally clear that they were less than successful. But it is difficult to question the intent of two men of intense moral convictions who at the same time were attempting to construct a stormy balance with national interest. The problem was made infinitely more complex by the chain of events started on 28 June 1914 in Sarajevo, Bosnia, when the administration had little more than a year of experience in attempting to bring a moral order to bear on complex international problems.

V *War*

The war broke out before the State Department had completed its transition from a Republican to a Democratic administration, and the ensuing confusion compounded practical as well as policy problems: the preservation of neutrality, the protection of American interests, and—Bryan's major moral interest—an immediate cessation of hostilities. On 19 September 1914 he proposed a course of action to the President:

The European situation distresses me. The slaughter goes on and each day makes it more apparent that it is to be a prolonged struggle. All parties to the conflict declare that they did not want war, that they were not responsible for it and that they desire peace—and to make their positions more nearly identical they desire a lasting peace.

I cannot but feel that this nation, being the only great nation on friendly terms with all, should urge mediation, since none of the nations engaged are willing to take the initiative. The responsibility for beginning it, and this responsibility, if pressed upon the consideration of the belligerent nations, might lead them to consent to mediation—no nation can afford to refuse. . . . The world looks to us to lead the way, and I know you desire to render every possible assistance. . . .

It is not likely that either side will win so complete a victory as to be able to dictate terms, and if either side does win such a victory it will probably mean preparation for another war. . . .

Would it not be worth while for you to address a note to all combatants reciting the awful horrors of this conflict, and pointing out—

First, that all deny responsibility for the war and that all express a desire for peace;

Second, that responsibility for a continuance of such a war is as undersirable as responsibility for beginning it, and that as such responsibility attaches to this nation as well as to participants, my suggestion is that you earnestly appeal to them to meet together and exchange views as to the terms upon which permanent peace can be insured.

They could be reminded that, while mediation can not be asked or accepted with conditions, the parties are under no compulsion to accept unsatisfactory terms. . . .

. . . there is reason to believe that such an offer would have the satisfaction of knowing that you had rendered an international service almost if not quite without parallel.

I feel so deeply that this is worth trying that I desire to confer with you about it. . . . Even if it fails—and that cannot be known until the offer is made—you will have the consciousness of having made the attempt.[10]

However, the attempt was not made for a variety of reasons until after America's entry into the war, when it may have influenced the development of Wilson's Fourteen Points; but Wilson joined Bryan in the search for a true neutrality through the attempt to prevent loans to the Allies by J. P. Morgan and Co. and others, by attempts to find a truly neutral solution to the problem of arms sales to belligerents, to solve the problem of violations of American freedom of the seas as freely by Britain as by Germany, and, increasingly, to resolve the problem of Americans taking passage on British ships.

Equally serious to Bryan was the nightmare of human suffering, not only in Belgium and France, but, as the result of the British blockade, in Germany also. Attempts to except food for the civilian population from proscription by the British blockade failed, just as did Bryan's attempts to persuade Germany to cancel its proclaimed war zone around the British Isles.

Increasingly, too, in Cabinet deliberations, he found his the only consistent voice of neutrality, supported on occasion by Josephus Daniels, secretary of the navy. Wilson, although an avowed neutral, was an admirer of the British; Robert Lansing and Ambassador Walter Hines Page were strongly pro-Ally; Dudley Field Malone, customs collector in New York, either through carelessness or deliberate conspiracy, accepted false or incomplete bills of lading for British liners; Theodore Roosevelt, from his pulpit in Sagamore Hill, demanded that America go to war as sinkings continued and American lives were lost.

The sinking of the British Cunard liner *Lusitania* on 7 May 1915 provided the incident that forced Bryan's resignation. Torpedoed without warning by the German submarine U-20, the ship sank in less than fifteen minutes, wracked by internal explosions, with the loss of 1,153 passengers, including 128 Americans. British and American investigations blamed German barbarism. But evidence not made public suggested British duplicity, leading Lord Mersey, who conducted the British investigation, to request of the prime minister that "henceforth I be excused from administering His Majesty's Justice" and to confide to his children that "The *Lusitania* case was a damned dirty business." [11]

The German embassy had published warnings to Americans not to sail on British ships, and modern scholarship—in spite of documents concerning the case still classified—has demonstrated that the ship was carrying munitions falsely listed as well as Canadian soldiers in civilian clothing, and that Malone, through negligence or worse, had accepted a false bill of lading. Furthermore, the intense internal explosions have been confirmed by visits to the hulk. But at the time, American public opinion was aroused, and many of the president's advisors suggested the possibility of war. On 10 May Wilson made the famous public remark that was to haunt him: "There is such a thing as a man being too proud to fight."[12]

Drafting an appropriate note to Germany to protest the act fell to Wilson and Bryan, with the assistance and strong influence of Lansing. Bryan cautioned Wilson against haste and seeming belligerency:

> In individual matters friends sometimes find it wise to postpone the settlements of disputes until such differences can be considered calmly and on their merits. So it may be with nations. The United States and Germany, between whom there exists a long standing friendship, may find it advisable to postpone until peace is restored any disputes which do not yield to diplomatic treatment.
>
> Germany has endorsed the principle of investigation embodied in the thirty treaties signed with as many nations. The treaties give a year's time for the investigation and apply to all disputes of every character. From this nation's standpoint, there is no reason why this policy should not control as between the United States and Germany.[13]

Wilson's note, however, was strong; under pressure of Lansing and other cabinet members, he reaffirmed American rights to sail on such ships and demanded repudiation of the act as well as reparation. Bryan signed the note, commenting, "Mr. President, I join in this document with a heavy heart."

Germany's reply was equally strong, insisting that the sinking was a legitimate act of war. It arrived on Memorial Day, while Wilson was speaking at Arlington, a fact which momentarily cheered Bryan. But the response, drafted by Wilson after consulting with Bryan and Lansing, was quick and harsh; while Lansing and Bryan differed sharply over its content, Bryan was troubled. When the completed draft arrived at the State Department on 4 June, Bryan confided to Mary that he could not sign it, and he protested to Wilson. On 8 June, when it was decided to send the note, Bryan submitted his resignation to the president:

> It is with sincere regret that I have reached the conclusion that I should return to you the commission of Secretary of State with which you honored me at the beginning of your administration.

Obedient to your sense of duty and actuated by the highest motives, you have prepared for transmission to the German government a note in which I cannot join without violating what I deem to be an obligation to my country, and the issue involved is of such moment that to remain a member of the Cabinet would be as unfair to you as it would be to the cause which is nearest my heart, namely, the prevention of war.

I, therefore, tender my resignation, to take effect when the note is sent, unless you prefer an earlier hour. Alike desirous of reaching a peaceful solution of the problems arising out of the use of the submarines against merchantmen, we find ourselves differing irreconcilably as to the methods which should be employed.

It falls to your lot to speak for the nation; I consider it to be none the less my duty as a private citizen to promote the end which you have in view by means which you do not feel at liberty to use.

In severing the intimate and pleasant relations which have existed between us during the past two years, permit me to acknowledge the profound satisfaction which it has given me to be associated with you in the important work which has come before the State Department and to thank you for the courtesies extended.[14]

Wilson accepted Bryan's resignation with profound personal regret, and the note was sent. It was, however, qualified by a request for any evidence that the Germans might have which would alter the American position—an addition which Bryan insists was made without his knowledge, while Wilson's supporters insist that he knew; the debate has not yet been resolved.

Determined to continue the campaign for peace, Bryan made public a long statement on 10 June which reaffirmed his specific reason for resigning, that is, to continue the battle for peace as a private citizen, and which defined, with precedents cited, the means by which the source of tension, Americans in the war zone, might be avoided. In a press interview, he was briefer:

The President still hopes for peace and I pray, as earnestly as he, that Germany may do nothing to aggravate further the situation.

Because it is the duty of the patriot to support his government with all his heart in time of war, he has a right in the time of peace to try to prevent war.

I shall live up to a patriot's duty if war comes—until that time I shall do what I can to save my country from its horrors.[15]

Bryan joined the active peace movement quickly; he spoke

widely, opposing Wilson's preparedness program and supporting Henry Ford's peace ship venture (and regretting its failure). He also resumed his old causes, particularly prohibition and women's suffrage. In 1916, he and Mary established a new home in Florida, but his legal residence, his old home, and his political base remained in Nebraska.

Although defeated in his attempt to be a delegate for the Democratic national convention in St. Louis in 1916, he attended as a working journalist, determined to keep a Democrat in the White House. Although the 1912 platform had pledged the candidate to a single term, the convention was tightly controlled by Wilson forces, and Bryan was not scheduled to speak. The press pointed out that he was in no position to make trouble. But he was as active as before, consulting on the platform and directing the convention toward peace. The keynote speaker lauded Wilson—and Bryan—for keeping the peace, and Bryan spoke by demand of the delegates; his theme was simple: "I join the people in thanking God that we have a President who does not want the nation to fight."

Wilson's renomination, the campaign slogan, "He kept us out of war," and Bryan's fall campaign, through nineteen Western states at his usual pace, were foregone conclusions, as was Wilson standing before a joint session of Congress on 2 April 1917, less than a month after his inauguration, asking for a declaration of war. Equally predictable was Bryan's immediate telegram, offering his services, if necessary as a private soldier, for the duration. But his services were restricted to the home front, they were largely politically based, and they were successful.

Bryan's two major wartime campaigns were prohibition—for the first time on a national basis as a war measure to conserve grain—and woman's suffrage, both of which became law at the cost of substantial measures of his traditional political support. His third political war measure, government ownership of railroads, remained a lonely, unsuccessful battle, his political base in Nebraska eroded, and he was eventually to move his legal residence to Florida in a last, desperate, and unsuccessful bid for what he had once had. But as the war came to a close, as he experienced his last major successes in the Eighteenth and Nineteenth Amendments, he experienced two major disappointments: Wilson ignored his bid to serve on the Peace Commission and later refused Bryan's plea that the reservations to the League of Nations be accepted. An imperfect League, Bryan was convinced, was better than no League at all.

VI   *More Transitions*

As 1920 began, Bryan sought a national return to peacetime pursuits, and he attacked profiteers in war and peace with fury, but he found himself for the first time in his life without a major issue. His sixtieth birthday, on 19 March, was an occasion for a good deal of sentimental recognition, but his health had become weak, and Mary was seized with crippling arthritis. Yet he remained optimistic: he had seen most of his reforms enacted into law, and a Democratic convention and campaign were approaching. Further, he had found new—or perhaps regained old—interests; he began to dabble in Florida real estate, and he became active in the church, an activity that was to lead to his last great campaign.

That year saw his last political battle in Nebraska, and he won, largely because of his insistence that women be allowed to vote in the primary. He was elected delegate-at-large to the Democratic national convention. But none of the candidates pleased him— Governor Edwards of New Jersey was not merely wet, he was soaking; Herbert Hoover was too vague; Attorney General Mitchell Palmer was soft on profiteers; William G. McAdoo, Wilson's son-in-law, was untested; James Cox of Ohio was too wet. Against Bryan's advice, Wilson insisted that the platform and the campaign be a referendum on the League.

Bryan came to the convention, he was welcomed, and he fought for a strong prohibition plank; he spoke eloquently, but he was defeated. Cox's nomination displeased him, and for the first time he did not campaign, only announcing on election day that he had voted for his party's candidate in what became the worst defeat for a Democratic candidate in Bryan's memory.

In 1921, largely because of Mary's health, he moved his legal residence to Florida, but he looked forward to 1924. He applauded Harding's Washington Disarmament Conference, but he was disappointed that he was not asked to participate; he began to cultivate Florida politicians, charming some and frightening others, and he began what was to be his last major battle against what became the subject of an often-repeated speech, "The Menace of Darwinism."

VII   *Darwinism and the Scopes Trial*

The factors that instigated Bryan's determination to prevent the dissemination of Darwinian theory in the public schools are debatable; not only had he been attracted by the theory in college, but he had not been hostile to it in his often-repeated lecture, "The Prince of Peace." In his newly published book, *In His Image,* a compendium of ideas and a major lecture that he put together in 1922, however, he saw Darwinism as the source of acceptance of the world as it was, with its "contemptible" money-grubbing, its prejudice, its inequities; it denied his basic conviction that "Belief in God is the basis of brotherhood; we are brothers because we are children of one God," and he demanded that the theory not be taught to children.

As a delegate to the General Assembly of the Presbyterian Church in 1923 he fought modernists in the pulpit with limited success, but in his latest campaign he had, once more, the support of many of his people, and even as he marshaled his forces for what was to be his last Democratic national convention he carried his antievolution fight to campuses and legislators. But he counseled moderation in proposed legislation, moderation that the Tennessee legislature was unwilling to accept. Nevertheless, Bryan determined that he would be heard, and it was to lead to his only ignominious defeat.

In a sense the Democratic national convention of 1924 was prefatory to the Scopes trial the following year. Elected a delegate-at-large to the convention in the home territory of Governor Al Smith of New York, Bryan had a strong platform of opposition to the Harding-Coolidge policies that had produced the revenue actions of Secretary of the Treasury Andrew Mellon, and he deplored the Harding scandals then unfolding as well. But he had no candidate: Smith was a wet; McAdoo was still untested; and John W. Davis was tainted by Wall Street. Reluctantly, he threw in with McAdoo in spite of his Teapot Dome associations; he fought for a dry plank and for restraint in dealing with the Ku Klux Klan, an issue that he feared would destroy the party. He saw Davis nominated and his brother Charles nominated for the vice-presidency as a sop to the still magic name of Bryan. Tempted to join LaFollette's Progressives, Bryan refrained and he saw his party defeated overwhelmingly in November. Still, he wrote to Charlie, there would be 1928. But he was aging rapidly, his diabetes was out of control, and he was tired.

In this context, the Scopes trial was for Bryan a tragedy that should not have been and yet was perhaps inevitable. The events of those unfortunate days of July 1925 in Dayton, Tennessee, have been recreated many times, as has Bryan's fundamental failure to avoid battle on Clarence Darrow's own ground or to demonstrate clearly the dimensions of the cause for which he was fighting. It has been said that he was unprepared as well as ill and tired. He was both ill and tired, but he had prepared carefully. But he had not tried a case in court for many years, and his preparations were for the lecture platform rather than the courtroom. The results of that preparation remain in two documents that he had written for the case but which remained in his briefcase as his tragedy unfolded. The first, of two pages, is an indictment of Scopes; the other, of twenty-six pages, was to have been his closing argument to the jury.

In his indictment Bryan presented an argument that was clear and concise. In keeping with his faith in the people, the issue was clear. The people had made the law because they had the right to control their schools; Scopes, as a teacher, was obligated to obey the law and he had not. That was all there was to the case:

> The Tennessee case is represented by some as an attempt to stifle freedom of conscience and freedom of speech, but the charge is seen to be absurd when the case is analyzed. Professor Scopes, the defendent in the Tennessee case, has a right to think as he pleases—the law does not attempt to regulate his thinking. Professor Scopes can also say anything he pleases—the law does not interfere with his freedom of speech. As an individual, Professor Scopes is perfectly free to think and speak as he likes and the Christians of Tennessee will protect him in the enjoyment of those inalienable rights. But that is not the Tennessee case and has nothing to do with it.
>
> Professor Scopes was not arrested for doing anything as an individual. He was arrested for violating the law as a *representative* of the *state* and as an employee in a school.[16]

The second document was to have been his closing argument in the case: had it been given, it would have been the last speech of his life. However, by mutual agreement, the case went to the jury without final argument, and Bryan died as he was preparing the speech for publication. Where the earlier statement had been as clear and concise as the nature of the case in law, the second is a complex indictment that moves from the case in law to an indictment of evolution itself, not merely as an unproved hypothesis but as a social evil.

Bryan's opening remarks were perhaps what one might expect from him under the circumstances, but in the context of the debate early in the trial over whether or not each day's session should open with prayer, they took on an added dimension:

> Demosthenes, the greatest of ancient orators, in his "Oration on the Crown," the most famous of his speeches, began by supplicating the favor

of all the gods and goddesses of Greece. If, in a case which involved only his own fame and fate, he felt justified in petitioning the heathen gods of his country, surely we, who deal with the momentous issues involved in this case, may well pray to the Ruler of the Universe for wisdom to guide us in the performance of our several parts in this historic trial.[17]

Bryan's second and third introductory paragraphs, directed to the jury, might be dismissed as transparent, self-serving, condescending flattery by another speaker, but Bryan, who had closely identified himself with the townspeople, meant every word:

Let me, in the first place, congratulate our cause that circumstances have committed the trial to a community like this and entrusted the decision to a jury made up largely of the yeomanry of the State. The book in issue in this trial contains on its first page two pictures contrasting the disturbing noises of a great city with the calm serenity of the country. It is a tribute that rural life has fully earned.

I appreciate the sturdy honesty and independence of those who come into daily contact with the earth, who, living near to nature, worship nature's God, and who, dealing with the myriad mysteries of earth and air, seek to learn from revelation about the Bible's wonder-working God. I admire the stern virtues, the vigilance and the patriotism of the class from which the jury is drawn.[18]

But Bryan's flattery or sincere tribute was incidental, as was his analysis of the nature of the crime and its commission by Scopes; to Bryan, the most significant part of the trial, and that to which he addresses his concluding remarks, was the case against the teaching of evolutionary theory. First was his legal definition of evolution:

Evolution—the evolution involved in this case, and the only evolution that is a matter of controversy anywhere—is the evolution taught by the defendant, set forth in the books now prohibited by the new State law, and illustrated in the diagram printed on page 194 of Hunter's Civic Biology. The author estimates the number of species in the animal kingdom at five hundred and eighteen thousand, nine hundred. These are divided into eighteen classes, and each class is indicated on the diagram by a circle. . . . Thirty-five hundred mammals are crowded together in a little circle that is barely higher than the bird circle. *No circle is reserved for man alone. . . .* What shall we say of the intelligence, not to say religion, of those who are so particular to distinguish between fishes and reptiles and birds, but put a man with an immortal soul in the same circle with the wolf, the hyena, and the skunk? What must be the impression made upon children by such a degradation of man?[19]

Bryan answered his question in the five indictments which he raised against the teaching of evolutionary theory, two of them concerned with its relationship to scriptural Christianity and three associated with Bryan's concept of social morality. The first was a simple, literal discrepancy:

Our first indictment against evolution is that it disputes the truth of the Bible account of man's creation and shakes faith in the Bible as the Word of God. . . . It not only contradicts the Mosaic record as to the beginning of human life, but it disputes the Bible doctrine of reproduction according to kind—the greatest scientific principle known.[20]

The second principle, building on the first, was more complex, demanding an array of supporting evidence:

Our second indictment is that the evolutionary hypothesis, carried to its logical conclusion, disputes every vital truth of the Bible. Its tendency, natural, if not inevitable, is to lead those who really accept it, first to agnosticism and then to atheism. Evolutionists attack the truth of the Bible, not openly at first, but by using weazel-words like "poetical," "symbolical" and "allegorical" to suck the meaning out [of] the inspired record of man's creation.[21]

In describing this inevitable sequence of events, Bryan turned to the evidence provided by three individuals: Darwin, who testified to his gradual departure from conventional religious beliefs; James H. Leuba, professor of psychology at Bryn Mawr, who documented such loss through his study of biographies in *American Men of Science* and a student questionnaire; and the most startling of all, the evidence presented by Clarence Darrow himself in his arguments for the defense in the notorious Leopold-Loeb murder case the previous year. Bryan concluded his analysis of Darrow's position as the keystone of his argument and a reaffirmation of his own code of personal responsibility:

Psychologists who build upon the evolutionary hypothesis teach that man is nothing but a bundle of characteristics inherited from brute ancestors. This is the philosophy which Mr. Darrow applied in this celebrated criminal case. "Some remote ancestor"—he does not know how remote—"sent down the seed that corrupted him." You cannot punish the ancestor—he is not only dead but, according to the evolutionists, he was a brute and may have lived a million years ago. And he says that all the biologists agree with him—no wonder so small a per cent of the biologists, according to Leuba, believe in a personal God.[22]

Bryan's last three indictments were imbued with the spirit of reform and the faith in man's ability to control his destiny and improve his lot that had dominated Bryan's political and social beliefs. The third was the simplest of the three indictments, insisting, in essence, that evolution was a political and social red herring:

Our third indictment against evolution is that it diverts attention from pressing problems of great importance to triffling speculation. . . . The science of "How to Live" is the most important of all the sciences. It is *desirable* to know the physical sciences, but it is *necessary* to know how to live.[23]

The fourth indictment was Bryan's objection to the Gospel of Wealth, a doctrine propagated by Andrew Carnegie, Russell Cornwell, and others, and personally and philosophically repugnant to Bryan: "Our fourth indictment against the evolutionary hypothesis is that, by paralyzing the hope of reform, it discourages those who labor for the improvement of man's condition."[24]

Bryan's fifth indictment was that evolution was a denial of what he held to be the ideal relationship among human beings:

Our fifth indictment of the evolutionary hypothesis is that, if taken seriously and made the basis of a philosophy of life, it would eliminate love and carry man back to a struggle of tooth and claw. The Christians who have allowed themselves to be deceived into believing that evolution is a beneficent, or even a rational process, have been associating with those who either do not understand its implications or dare not avow their knowledge of these implications.[25]

Bryan concluded with the evidence of Darwin's decline and with an attack on Nietzsche as Darwin's spokesman. He then pleaded not merely that justice be done in this simple case, but that Christianity, threatened as never before since the crucifixion, be preserved:

Again force and love meet face to face, and the question, "What shall I do with Jesus?" must be answered. A bloody, brutal doctrine—Evolution—demands, as the rabble did nineteen hundred years ago, that He be crucified. That cannot be the answer of this jury, representing a Christian

State and sworn to uphold the laws of Tennessee. Your answer will be heard throughout the world; it is eagerly awaited by a praying multitude. If the law is nullified, there will be rejoicing wherever God is repudiated, the Savior scoffed at and the Bible ridiculed. Every unbeliever of every kind and degree will be happy. If, on the other hand, the law is upheld and the religion of the school children protected, millions of Christians will call you blessed and, with hearts full of gratitude to God, will sing again that grand old song of triumph:

Faith of our fathers, living still. . . .[26]

But the speech was never given, although the jury upheld the law and Scopes was convicted. One can only speculate on the effect of that speech, using techniques that had proved effective on countless platforms in the past, not merely on a rustic jury, but on those who would crucify Bryan and his beliefs. But the speech was not given, then or at any other time. On 25 July he prepared the speech for publication; on the twenty-sixth, he went to church, where he prayed publicly, and then, after lunch, as he had begun to do in recent years, he took a nap. He never awakened. No autopsy was performed, and—perhaps the final ironic contradiction in a life beset by ironies and confused by contradictions—his body was, as he wished, returned to Washington for burial at Arlington National Cemetery, among warriors and statesmen, poltroons and patriots.

CHAPTER 10

The Rhetoric of a Reluctant Revolutionary

B RYAN'S death on 26 July 1925 was not merely the end of a life or a career; in a very profound sense, it marked the end of the nineteenth century in America, just as Jefferson's death a century before had marked the end of the eighteenth. Jefferson's ideas were firmly rooted in the rational tradition of the age into which he had been born, and Bryan's political and personal philosophy in the age of romantic democratic reform into which he had been born. Just as Jefferson became the catalyst for the age of democratic expansion in the nineteenth century, Bryan was the catalyst for pragmatic democratic change in the twentieth. Curiously, however, Jefferson's role led to his near-deification in the following century; Bryan's role has resulted in his condemnation for being other than what he was.

Bryan's political ideology, which took him to the threshold of the White House three times, and his moral ideology, the source of his condemnation by a more sophisticated age, are inseparable in providing insights into the causes he championed, the near-adulation of his millions of followers, the eclipse of his reputation among twentieth-century intellectuals, and his obscurity in the popular mind. Like Jackson, his political mentor, Emerson, who gave intellectual sustenance to the age in which he was born, and the nameless frontier evangelists who guided his spiritual growth, Bryan had an unlimited faith in the perfectability of the common people and in their intrinsic goodness, and an equally unlimited hostility to the institutions that prevented their perfection and inhibited their goodness.

The age that molded Bryan's character and his thinking was that of pre–Civil War America, the age of reform that saw its energies absorbed by abolitionism and war, its voice stilled in the presence of hundreds of thousands of casualties, and its political instruments, the major political parties, captured by alien doctrines. In the one case, capture was effected by those who looked to the past for their justification, and in the other, by those who sought a material salvation in a new industrialism. With their success the country became dominated by those whose scripture was extracted from Adam Smith and Charles Darwin and whose Gospel of Wealth made government the instrument of the will of those who were strong enough to seize it, together with the tools of power and wealth.

The political environment in which Bryan reached his intellectual and legal maturity in an obscure Illinois prairie college was not that of the open Jacksonian frontier society in which his political ideals were rooted, nor was it that promised by the prophets of the machine age. It was the era of a moribund Democratic party unable to find a new identity and purpose in a period it was unable to understand and of a Republican party whose cause and reason for being had been lost in the very victory that it had pursued at its birth. Rural Illinois was itself a backwater, neither of the dynamic frontier that had passed it by nor of the equally dynamic city that had grown up on the lakeshore to the north.

Bryan was one of countless young men who came of age in the rural Midwest in that period that Sherwood Anderson has called a time of waiting, in which America paused, uncertain of its path to the future, whether to the realization of a greater human or a richer material reality. Bryan might have gone on to a modest success, as had his father, as a small-town merchant or farmer or lawyer or all three. Or, as had thousands of his contemporaries, he might have gone to that city on the lake to seek a greater success in the new mode. But he did neither, and the course of history was changed in his time and ours.

That he did neither was the result of the tradition that he accepted, the ideas with which he was imbued, and the talent that he considered God-given, and hence his responsibility to develop, to use, and to share. The tradition was that of the fading frontier, the tradition that took Bryan to the West, to town, to the law, and to politics, the same path that Abraham Lincoln had followed a half-century before and that eventually carried Lincoln from the town to the White House. Whether or not Bryan was consciously influenced by Lincoln is immaterial; it was the one path by which a bright, articulate, ambitious young man might rise in a world moving from frontier chaos to an orderly society in which disputes were solved by the rule of law. It was the path, too, that his generation believed in with a mystic faith, the path of hard work, ambition, dedication, sobriety, and Christian virtue, the path that insured success in an age that accepted the reality of the open society and the natural aristocrat. All his life, Bryan, like Jefferson, believed that both were the essence of democracy.

The ideas with which he was imbued were those that dominated his life to the end: his belief in the spiritual and social perfectability of man, in the role of government as the creation and servant of the people, in the innate wisdom of the people as a political entity, in the reality of love, both human and divine, in an ultimate unity of human and divine morality. Perhaps more than anything else, Bryan believed in himself as a creature of the divine will, and he sought to carry it out as it was made manifest to him.

At the heart of his determination to carry out the divine will was his determination to use to the fullest what he knew was his major talent: his ability to speak in an age in which the human voice was the single most important means of communicating, explaining, and convincing. The last half of the nineteenth century has been called a golden age of oratory, the age that began with Edward Everett, reached its heights with Robert Ingersoll and Bryan himself, and died with the rise of what we have come to call the mass media, those technological means by which the human voice has been made both greater and lesser. Bryan was the last of an age of great orators; he may have been the greatest. But oratory has proved an ephemeral art.

By all accounts, however, when Bryan spoke, whether on the political stump, in Congress, a convention hall, or on the lecture platform, he was superb. His clear voice reached every person in a crowded hall, a humid tent, or an outdoor political gathering; he was enthusiastic, he was lucid, he was interesting, not merely to those to whom his word was gospel truth, but to those who disagreed with every word that he spoke. He was sincere, friendly, and unpretentious; for his people, political supporters or not, he was indeed "the Great Commoner."

Intellectually and morally a product of the first great age of reform that marked the first half of the nineteenth century and that had found its clearest expression in the political and religious faiths into which he was born, Bryan reached his majority at the beginning of the second great age of reform, when rural overproduction and urban industrialization had begun their great clashes over the distribution of the nation's wealth. In 1878, when Bryan was eighteen, the candidates of the Greenback party polled over a million votes, sending a message that was perhaps clearer to Bryan than it was to most of his contemporaries.

But discussion of Bryan's origins does not define what he was or was not, what he accomplished or failed to accomplish, or his place in American intellectual, political, and literary history, however useful those details may be in providing insight into what are at best debatable judgments imposed by the people of one age upon those of another. He may or may not have been a political philosopher, and he may or may not have been a statesman; cases have been made for both and neither, but the definitive interpretation is unimportant, as are attempts to ascribe to him a definitive place in any of the dimensions of American history.

Bryan's place in the evolving course of American life was, in its simplest sense, functional. The product of a rural, agricultural West caught up in the crisis of social and economic change, he was the spokesman and the conscience of that area, and in that sense he was the provincial, the regionalist, that he has often been called. But the importance of his function was that it transcended the region out of which he came and became truly national.

His function was to bring to bear upon the problems of a new, post–Civil War America the idealistic principles of the age in which the country had become a national entity. His heritage, the American heritage, was that of the American past, a heritage compounded of the faith in individual natural rights of the eighteenth century, of the nineteenth century's faith in the worth and dignity of the individual, and a firm faith in progress and perfectability that had been shared by both ages. For all of them he became an eloquent spokesman, at the same time that he became an outspoken critic of ideas, institutions, and people that denied the old truths.

The problems were those inherited from the past—the tariff, the nature and origin of currency, the distribution of goods—all of them made more intense by the new age, but they were also problems uniquely the result of a shrinking rural agricultural society and a growing urban-industrial complex. They were the result, too, of the changing attitude toward the common people as they passed from dignified individual to cannon fodder for a war that lost sight of the greater dignity for which it was fought. The ensuing transition was inevitable: the common people became raw material for the industrialism that the war unleashed. Inevitable too were a consequent sense of a lack of dignity in work; the cashless crisis on the farm and the lack of employment in the cities; the new relationship between

government and the governed as the result of new concentrations of
economic and political power.

The intensification of continued crisis in the cities and on the
farms threatened mindless revolt as well as the inept political action
that had produced Grangers and Greenbackers, Knights of Labor
and anarchists, the Homestead strike and the Haymarket riot. It
was into this breach of confidence and leadership that Bryan moved
in the last decade of the nineteenth century, by 1896 becoming not
only a presidential candidate but, at the age of thirty-six, a
spokesman for an age of frustration and failure.

As the Boy Orator, the Great Commoner, the Peerless Leader,
Bryan, according to his critics, knew little of the forces that had
shaped the world of crises in which he had assumed leadership; he
presumably neither understood nor articulated the post–Civil War,
post-Marxian economics, post-Darwinian evolution, post-Jamesian
psychology, or the pragmatism that grew out of them all. In a
sense—the sense of intellectual perspective—those critics are right.
Bryan was neither well educated nor widely read, although when he
faced a problem such as the tariff he did "read up on it" with
dedication if not discrimination.

But in another sense he had a keen intuitive understanding of all
those forces as they narrowed the scope of the American dream and
excluded his people from its pursuit, and not only did he speak for
them, articulating their demands of government as well as defining
their dreams and values, but in so doing he demonstrated that
intuitive grasp as he clarified issues, defined problems, and laid out
courses of action. His critics among his own contemporaries and
ours notwithstanding, the printed record that is all that remains of
what was to the end a golden voice refutes the two major charges
laid against him. He was not a demagogue and neither did he
exploit his people, using them for his own ends, nor did he incite
revolution other than the only revolution acceptable in a free,
democratic society—that of the ballot box.

Nor was he the simpleton portrayed by those who accept the
lapses of his last years—indeed, his last weeks—as the Bryan reality.
He knew economics, perhaps better than any of his political
contemporaries; he knew that money in the hands of the many is
not only morally better but economically more useful than money
in the hands of the few; and he knew too that artificial barriers,
economic barriers among people and nations, limited their sense of
identity even as they inhibited their economic well-being.

Although he had never read extensively in modern psychology, he knew his people better than any of his contemporaries, and he knew them because he was one of them and he knew himself. The least of these results was the fact that he was always and everywhere a crowd-pleaser, and the greatest was the love and respect which he freely gave and graciously received.

Without having read Darwin he understood evolution, and without having read James he understood pragmatism, and he rejected both because they threatened the only reality it was possible for him to accept: a reality in which reason and morality, hand in hand, gave the people control over their future. The orderly, moral growth of individuals and institutions, guided by God, was the essence of his political and personal philosophy, and actions and doctrines that threatened either or that denied the traditional absolutes of democracy and Christianity were abhorrent to him. Both evolution and pragmatism invited a chaos he could neither accept nor tolerate. He demanded and promised an orderly progress no longer acceptable or possible for the more skeptical age that began with industrialism and materialism.

Few of Bryan's causes were realized under his leadership, and his legal vindication at Dayton was ironic and tragic, yet he championed every significant reform of his day and made their accomplishment possible, contributing to the enhanced reputations of others at the expense of his own. Some of his dreams had to wait a half century for realization. Yet the list of his causes is the history of progressive reform in this century: constitutional amendments resulted in the income tax, the direct election of senators, women's suffrage, and national prohibition, only the last of which was subsequently rejected; Philippine independence, although it had to wait for half a century and another world war; currency reform—carried out to an extent that might even shock him as bimetallism has become nometallism; and a measure of dignity for the common people, for his constituency, beyond the imagination of those of his generation less farsighted or realistic.

In the course of his reform crusade he proclaimed no dogmas that were either new or revolutionary, preferring instead to look to a romantic past rather than a realistic future for his goal and inspiration. Yet the fact of his demand, that the American dream of a new relationship among people and between the people and their government, the people and their God, become real was itself a revolutionary demand, a demand that could only be made by a person such as Bryan, a man of energy, compassion, and above all, faith.

Bryan did, indeed, refurbish a moribund American liberalism and make it a functional reality for the twentieth century, as he insisted with increasing conviction that individual rights were superior to property rights and that the role of government was to protect those individual natural rights, in eighteenth-century fashion, against those forces that would deny them. In so doing he provided the foundation upon which those who later achieved the presidency have built, and he provided the popular impetus that made reform possible. Political success has, perhaps rightly, made household words of the names of Theodore Roosevelt, Woodrow Wilson, and Franklin Delano Roosevelt; but Bryan's is fortunately better known than those of Alton B. Parker, James Cox, and John W. Davis, although too frequently for the wrong reasons.

Some critics have insisted that it was better for America that Bryan had never achieved the presidency—that his absolute faith in the innate wisdom of the people provided an impetus toward the tyranny of an ignorant minority, as in Tennessee; that his suspicion of the Easterner, the intellectual, or the expert, was equally danger-ous to democracy; that his insistence upon the moral basis of political activity was not merely naive but demagogic; that his concern for principles merely marked a neurotic ambition—yet one wonders as one looks at the array of men who have achieved the presidency in Bryan's lifetime, including the long array of Ohio Civil War generals and a lone major; the political functionary; the lone Democrat who had sent a substitute to the Civil War; and the twentieth-century triumvirate of Taft, Harding, and Coolidge.

But Bryan has been remembered, and he will be remembered, not only for the wrong reasons, but also for the right ones. In spite of his shortcomings—and they have been chronicled and dissemi-nated for more than three quarters of a century, as avidly now by some scholars as they had been by some editors in his own lifetime—Bryan contributed perhaps the single most important dimension of discussion to political life in his time and ours: he became the spokesman for issues that he had neither created nor inspired, issues which were in each case highly controversial but which demanded resolution if a viable democratic government was to be durable enough to survive in a nation no longer rural and agrarian. Jefferson had seen urban industrialization as fatal to a viable democratic society. Refusing to accept that conclusion in spite of its source,

Bryan insisted that the two were not incompatible; the results in the form of the reforms of his two great Democratic successors, Woodrow Wilson and Franklin Roosevelt, proved that he was right.

He will be remembered, too, even in an age that finds it difficult to comprehend or appreciate it, for what was his greatest individual talent, without which his determination and his faith would have had little impact. That talent was a reflection of his great courage and part of his great vitality, the only tangible records of which, other than a few scratchy recordings, remain on the printed page in the thousands of copies of his works that survive. In them are reflected not only the substance of his causes and the courage with which he supported them, but the rhetorical magic and the metaphorical eloquence that are as evident after more than half a century, even after the changing fashions that have accrued in the interval, as they were in his lifetime. The words, the images, the remorseless probing, the clear definitions combine to give them a life and a meaning that can still stimulate controversy, evoke a response; they can bring alive a past that was not only vital and dynamic in his day, but relevant in ours if we would know what we are and from whence we came. In his works, people and events, issues and values, still live and speak; they still reveal what America is, and they give life to an image of what it yet may be.

Notes and References

Chapter One

1. For the facts of Bryan's life I am indebted to Paolo E. Coletta, *William Jennings Bryan*, 3 vols. (Lincoln, 1964–1970); Louis W. Koenig, *Bryan* (New York, 1971); William Jennings Bryan, *The First Battle* (Chicago, 1896); and William Jennings Bryan with Mary Baird Bryan, *The Memoirs of William Jennings Bryan* (Philadelphia, 1925). For the interpretation of those facts, I am responsible.

2. Bryan, *Memoirs*, p. 40.

3. William Jennings Bryan, *Speeches* (New York, 1913), 2:373; hereafter cited in the text as *S*.

Chapter Two

1. Quoted in Koenig, *Bryan*, p. 61.

2. Ibid., p. 63.

3. Bryan, *Memoirs*, pp. 248–49.

4. Allan Nevins, *Grover Cleveland* (New York, 1932), pp. 439–40.

Chapter Three

1. Bryan to Charles Brown, 30 June 1890, Bryan Papers.

2. Quoted in Charles Morrow Wilson, *The Commoner* (Garden City, N.Y., 1970), p. 143.

3. Ibid.

4. Ibid.

5. Ibid., pp. 143–44.

6. Ibid.

7. Bryan, *The First Battle*, p. 71.

8. Quoted in Koenig, p. 73.

9. Ibid.

10. Mary Baird Bryan, "Life of William Jennings Bryan," in *The First Battle*, p. 50.

11. Ibid., pp. 52–53.

12. Bryan, *The First Battle*, p. 71.
13. Ibid., p. 72.
14. Quoted in Koenig, p. 84.
15. Mary Bryan, "Life," in *The First Battle*, p. 54.
16. Willa Cather, "The Personal Side of William Jennings Bryan," *Prairie Schooner* 23 (Winter 1949): 337.

Chapter Four

1. Quoted in Wilson, p. 186.
2. Ibid.
3. Quoted in Koenig, p. 126.
4. Quoted in Wilson, pp. 188–89.
5. Ibid., p. 190.
6. Quoted in Koenig, p. 147.

Chapter Five

1. From the text in *The First Battle*, p. 199; hereafter cited in the text as *F*.
2. Bryan, *Memoirs*, p. 114.
3. Ibid., pp. 114–15.
4. Koenig, p. 200.
5. Edgar Lee Masters, *Across Spoon River* (New York, 1969), p. 209.
6. Koenig, p. 232.

Chapter Six

1. Koenig, p. 266.
2. Ibid., p. 263.
3. William Jennings Bryan, *Republic or Empire?* (Chicago, 1899), pp. 9–10.
4. Quoted in Coletta, 1:229.
5. *Republic or Empire?*, p. 13.
6. Ibid., pp. 14–15.
7. Ibid., pp. 15–16.
8. Quoted in Wilson, pp. 262–63.
9. Ibid., p. 262.
10. Bryan, *Memoirs*, p. 123.
11. Ibid., p. 124.
12. Ibid., p. 125.
13. William Jennings Bryan, "The Issue in the Presidential Campaign," *North American Review* 170 (June 1900): 753–71.
14. Ibid.
15. Ibid., p. 761.

16. Ibid., pp. 761–62.
17. Ibid., pp. 760-65.
18. Ibid., pp. 770–71.
19. Bryan, *Memoirs*, p. 125.
20. William Jennings Bryan, "The Election of 1900," *North American Review* 171 (December 1900): 793.
21. Ibid., pp. 794–95.
22. Ibid.
23. Ibid., p. 23.

Chapter Seven

1. *The Commoner*, 23 January 1901, p. 1.
2. Ibid.
3. Bryan, *Memoirs*, p. 283.
4. Ibid., pp. 286–88.
5. Ibid., pp. 288–89.

Chapter Eight

1. Koenig, p. 371.
2. Ibid., p. 389.
3. William Jennings Bryan, *The Old World and Its Ways* (St. Louis, 1907), p. 299.
4. Ibid., p. 305.
5. Ibid., p. 488.
6. Ibid., p. 482.
7. Koenig, p. 449.
8. Ibid., p. 478.
9. William Jennings Bryan, "Individualism vs. Socialism," *Century Magazine* 49 (April 1906): 856.
10. Quoted in Coletta, 1:396.
11. William Jennings Bryan, "My Conception of the Presidency," *Collier's Weekly*, 18 July 1908, p. 173.
12. Ibid.
13. Ibid.
14. Ibid.

Chapter Nine

1. William Jennings Bryan (unsigned), "The Arbitration Treaties," *Outlook*, 12 August 1911, p. 802.
2. William Jennings Bryan (unsigned), "The World Missionary Movement," *Outlook*, 13 August 1910, p. 802.
3. Koenig, p. 477.

4. William Jennings Bryan, "The Reason," *North American Review* 194 (July 1911): p. 10.

5. Ibid., p. 24.

6. Koenig, p. 489.

7. Coletta, 2:69.

8. Coletta, 2:241.

9. Bryan, *Memoirs*, pp. 386–87.

10. Ibid., pp. 388–92.

11. Colin Simpson, *The Lusitania* (Boston, 1972), p. 241.

12. Coletta, 2:315.

13. Bryan, *Memoirs*, p. 400.

14. Ibid., pp. 407–8.

15. Ibid., pp. 412–13.

16. Ibid., pp. 527–28.

17. Ibid., p. 529.

18. Ibid.

19. Ibid., pp. 534–35.

20. Ibid., p. 537.

21. Ibid.

22. Ibid., pp. 546–47.

23. Ibid., p. 547.

24. Ibid., p. 548.

25. Ibid., p. 550.

26. Ibid., pp. 555–56.

Selected Bibliography

PRIMARY SOURCES

1. Books and Pamphlets (in chronological order)

The Money of the People. Chicago: C. H. Sergel, 1895.

The First Battle. Chicago: W. B. Conkey, 1896.

Republic or Empire? The Philippine Question. Chicago: Independence Co., 1896.

Life and Speeches of William Jennings Bryan. Baltimore: R. H. Woodward, 1900.

The Second Battle. Chicago: W. B. Conkey Co., 1900.

Speeches Delivered in Tokyo. New York: Japanese Society, 1906.

British Rule in India. Westminster, England: British Committee of the Indian National Congress, 1906.

Letters to a Chinese Official. New York: McClure, Philips & Co., 1906.

The Old World and Its Ways. St. Louis: Thompson Publishing Co., 1907.

Bryan's Silver and Gold Speeches. New York: Bi-Metalism Association of America, 1907.

Guaranteed Banks. Chicago: M. A. Donohue Co., 1908.

Thou Shall Not Steal. New York: Civic Forum, 1908.

The Prince of Peace. Chicago: Reilly & Britton Co., 1909.

The Speeches of William Jennings Bryan. 2 vols. New York: Funk and Wagnalls Co., 1909.

Speeches of W. B. Cochran and W. J. Bryan at the Chicago Congress on Trusts. Chicago: Civic Federation, 1910.

Bryan on Imperialism. Chicago: Bentley and Co., 1910.

The Fruit of the Tree. London, 1910.

The Forces that Make for Peace: Address at the Mohonk Conferences on International Arbitration, 1910 and 1911. Boston: World Peace Foundation, 1912.

A Tale of Two Conventions. New York: Funk and Wagnalls Co., 1912.

The Speeches of William Jennings Bryan. 2 vols. New York: Funk and Wagnalls Co., 1913.

Remarks of Secretary of State William Jennings Bryan Before the California Legislature of 1913. Sacramento, 1913.

The Making of a Man. New York: Fleming H. Revell Co., 1914.

Man. New York: Funk and Wagnalls Co., 1914.

The Royal Art. New York: Fleming H. Revell Co., 1914.

The Message from Bethlehem. New York: Fleming H. Revell Co., 1914.

The People's Law. Washington, D.C.: Government Printing Office, 1914.

Christ and His Companions: Famous Figures of the New Testament. New York: Fleming H. Revell Co., 1915.

Two Addresses Delivered by William Jennings Bryan at Peace Meetings Held in New York June 19 and 24, 1915. N.p., n.d.

Why Abstain? Address Delivered by Secretary Bryan at Philadelphia, March 15, 1915. N.p., n.d.

Prohibition: Address by Hon. William Jennings Bryan Presenting in Substance the Line of Argumentation by Him in the Sixty Speeches Made in Ohio During the Week of October 25 to 30, 1915. Washington, D.C.: Government Printing Office, 1916.

Citizenship in a Republic. Washington, D.C.: National Education Association, 1916.

Temperance Lecture Delivered Before the 128th General Assembly of the Presbyterian Church at Atlantic City, New Jersey, Sunday, May 21, 1916. Atlantic City: J. J. Hamilton, 1916.

The Causeless War. Lincoln: *The Commoner,* 1915.

War in Europe. Washington, D.C., 1915.

Prohibition. Senate Document No. 254, 64th Congress, 1st Session. Washington: Government Printing Office, 1916.

America and the European War. New York: Emergency Peace Federation, 1917.

The First Commandment. Chicago: Fleming H. Revell Co., 1917.

Heart to Heart Appeals: Speeches Delivered 1890–1916. New York: Fleming H. Revell Co., 1917.

Heart to Heart Appeals: Speeches Delivered 1910–1916. New York: Fleming H. Revell Co., 1917.

World Peace: A Written Debate Between William Howard Taft and William Jennings Bryan. New York, 1917.

Mr. Bryan on Food Conservation. Pittsburgh, 1917.

Address of Hon. William Jennings Bryan to the Fifty-Ninth General Assembly of the State of Missouri, January 24, 1917. Jefferson City: Hugh Stevens Co., 1917.

In His Image. New York: Fleming H. Revell Co., 1922.

Famous Figures of the Old Testament. New York: Fleming H. Revell Co., 1922.

Orthodox Christianity versus Modernism. New York: Fleming H. Revell Co., 1923.

Shall Orthodox Christianity Remain Christian? Seven Questions in Dispute. New York: Fleming H. Revell Co., 1924.

The Dawn of Humanity. Chicago: The Altruist Foundation, 1925.

The Last Message of William Jennings Bryan. New York: Fleming H. Revell Co., 1925.

The Last Message of Mr. Bryan. New York: Fleming H. Revell Co., 1925.

The Memoirs of William Jennings Bryan. Philadelphia: The John C. Winston Co., 1925. With Mary Baird Bryan.

2. Collections of Papers

William Jennings Bryan Papers in the Library of Congress.

William Jennings Bryan Papers in the National Archives.

William Jennings Bryan Papers in the Nebraska State Historical Society.

William Jennings Bryan Papers in the Illinois State Historical Society.

3. Articles

"The Currency Question: A Prophetic Utterance." *Arena* 16 (September 1896): 529–37.

"Has the Election Settled the Money Question?" *North American Review* 163 (December 1896): 703–10.

"The Issue in the Presidential Campaign." *North American Review* 170 (June 1900): 753–71.

"The Election of 1900." *North American Review* 171 (December 1900): 788–801.

"The Next Democratic Nomination." *The Independent* 55 (21 May 1903): 1177–80.

"The Statute for Establishing Religious Freedom." In *The Writings of Thomas Jefferson*, ed. Andrew A. Lipscomb et al. Washington, D.C.: Jefferson Memorial Association, 1903. 8:1–11.

"Farming as an Occupation." *Cosmopolitan* (January 1904): 369–71.

"The Future of the Democratic Party: A Discussion of Moral Issues in the Pending Questions." *Outlook* 77 (19 December 1904): 919–27.

"Has the President the Courage to be a Reformer?" *Public Opinion* 39 (15 April 1905): 557–59.

"A Remedy for Trusts." *Public Opinion* 39 (29 April 1905): 645–48.

"Individualism vs. Socialism." *Century Magazine*, n.s. 49 (April 1906): 856–59.

"Path to Peace." *Independent* 61 (30 August 1906): 483–84.

"How Could the United States, if Necessary, Give Up its Colonies?" *World To-Day* 14 (February 1908): 151–54.

"My Conception of the Presidency." *Collier's Weekly* 41 (18 July 1908): 173.

"Why the Philippines Should be Independent." *Everybody's Magazine* 19 (November 1908): 640d–f.

"The United States and Puerto Rico." *Independent* 69 (7 July 1910): 20–23.

"The World Missionary Movement." *Outlook* 95 (13 August 1910): 823–26.

"The Reason." *North American Review* 194 (July 1911): 10–24.
"The Arbitration Treaties." *Outlook* 98 (12 August 1911): 801–2.
"Taft and Roosevelt." *National Monthly* 4 (December 1912): 164.
"Why I Lecture." *Ladies' Home Journal* 32 (April 1913): 9.
"Our Foreign Policy." *Independent* 76 (9 October 1913): 73–75.
"The Democrats Should Win: A Forecast of the 1916 Election." *Independent* 86 (3 April 1916): 13–14.
"Citizenship in a Republic." *School and Society* 4 (July 1916): 86–88.
"Why I am for Prohibition." *Independent* 137 (17 July 1916): 88–89.
"Prohibition's Progress." *Independent* 40 (19 May 1917): 332.
"Prohibition and the Farmer." *Country Gentleman* 82 (21 July 1917): 1163–64.
"Rights of Residents." *Independent* 98 (5 April 1919): 12–13.
"Democratic Policies at San Francisco." *American Review of Reviews* 62 (July 1920): 42–45.
"God and Evolution." *New York Times*, 26 February 1922, sec. 7, p. 1, col. 6.
"Tampering with the Mainspring." *Presbyterian* 93 (29 June 1922): 8–9.
"Prohibition." *Outlook* 133 (7 February 1923): 262–65.
"Our Responsibility for the Ruhr Invasion." *Current History* 17 (March 1923): 898–99.
"The Fundamentals." *Forum* 70 (July 1923): 1665–80.
"My Brother Charles." *World's Work* 48 (September 1924): 553.

SECONDARY SOURCES

1. Books

Abbot, Willis J. *Watching the World Go By*. Boston: Little, Brown and Co., 1933. A touching memoir by an old friend.
Coletta, Paolo E. *William Jennings Bryan: Political Evangelist, 1860–1908*. Lincoln: University of Nebraska Press, 1964. First volume of the definitive political biography.
———. *William Jennings Bryan: Progressive Political and Moral Statesman*. Lincoln: University of Nebraska Press, 1969. The second volume of the definitive political biography.
———. *William Jennings Bryan: Political Puritan*. Lincoln: University of Nebraska Press, 1969. The third volume of the definitive political biography.
Commager, Henry Steele. *The American Mind*. New Haven: Yale University Press, 1950. Comments perceptively on the trial and Bryan in the context of American tradition.
Durden, Robert F. *The Climax of Populism: The Election of 1896*.

Lexington: University of Kentucky Press, 1965. Sees 1896 as the zenith of agrarian unrest.

GINGER, RAY. *Six Days or Forever? Tennessee v. John Thomas Scopes.* Boston: Beacon Press, 1958. Harsh treatment of Bryan in Dayton that colors Ginger's attitude toward Bryan throughout his life and career.

GLAD, PAUL W. *McKinley, Bryan, and the People.* Philadelphia: J. B. Lippincott, 1964. A perceptive examination of the issues, the candidates, and the electorate in 1896.

————. *The Trumpet Soundeth: William Jennings Bryan and his Democracy, 1896–1912.* Lincoln: University of Nebraska Press, 1960. An examination of Bryan and the campaign for the presidency as an expression of a rural culture.

————. *William Jennings Bryan: A Profile.* New York: Hill and Wang, 1968. A cross-section of scholarly views of Bryan's career and character.

HERRICK, GENEVIEVE, and HERRICK, JOHN D. *The Life of William Jennings Bryan.* Chicago: Grover C. Buxton, 1925. An uncritical posthumous biography.

HIBBEN, PAXTON. *The Peerless Leader: William Jennings Bryan.* New York: Farrar and Rinehart, 1929, completed by C. Hartley Gratten. A harsh biographical interpretation.

HOFSTADER, RICHARD. *The American Political Tradition, and the Men Who Made It.* New York: Alfred A. Knopf, 1948. An examination of Bryan as political and social moralist which gave impetus to revived scholarly interest in Bryan.

JONES, STANLEY L. *The Presidential Election of 1896.* Madison: University of Wisconsin Press, 1968. Examines Bryan's first campaign issues in detail.

KOENIG, LOUIS W. *Bryan.* New York: G. P. Putnam's Sons, 1971. A good, essentially sympathetic one-volume political biography.

LEVINE, LAWRENCE W. *Defender of the Faith: William Jennings Bryan: The Last Decade, 1915–1925.* New York: Oxford University Press, 1965. A generally sympathetic appraisal of Bryan's Fundamentalism.

LIPPMANN, WALTER. *Men of Destiny.* New York: Macmillan, 1927. A perceptive posthumous sketch of Bryan.

LONG, J. C. *Bryan, The Great Commoner.* New York: D. Appleton & Co., 1928. An extremely sympathetic biography.

MASTERS, EDGAR LEE. *Across Spoon River.* New York: Octagon, 1968. Comments on Bryan's nature.

MERRIAM, CHARLES E. *Four American Party Leaders.* New York: Macmillan Co., 1926. Contains an early perceptive sketch.

NEVINS, ALLAN. *Grover Cleveland.* New York: Dodd, Mead & Co., 1932. Comments on Bryan's relationship with Cleveland.

POLLACK, NORMAN. *The Populist Response to Industrial America.* Cambridge: Harvard University Press, 1962. Examines Bryan's relationship to Populist radicalism.

ROSSER, CHARLES MCCANIEL. *The Crusading Commoner: A Close-Up of William Jennings Bryan and his Times.* Dallas: Mathis, Van Nort & Co., 1937. A sympathetic account by an old friend.

SIMPSON, COLIN. *The Lusitania.* Boston: Little, Brown, and Co., 1972. Supports Bryan's view of the *Lusitania* question.

WERNER, M. R. *Bryan.* New York: Harcourt, Brace and Co., 1929. A hostile study.

WHITE, WILLIAM ALLEN. *Masks in a Pageant.* New York: Macmillan Co., 1928. Discusses Bryan in political campaigns.

WILLIAMS, WAYNE C. *William Jennings Bryan.* New York: G. P. Putnam' s Sons, 1936. An early scholarly study.

WILSON, CHARLES MORROW. *The Commoner.* Garden City: Doubleday & Co., 1970. An uncritical, sympathetic biography.

2. Articles

BAILEY, THOMAS A. "Was the Election of 1900 a Mandate on Imperialism?" *Mississippi Valley Historical Review* 24 (June 1937): 43–52. Concludes that it was not.

BARNES, JAMES A. "Myths of the Bryan Campaign." *Mississippi Valley Historical Review* 34 (December 1947): 367–404. One of the early serious scholarly assessments of Bryan's career.

CATHER, WILLA. "The Personal Side of William Jennings Bryan." *Prairie Schooner* 23 (Winter 1949): 331–337. A reprinted early portrait.

CHALLENER, RICHARD. "William Jennings Bryan." In *An Uncertain Tradition*, ed. Norman A. Graebner. New York: McGraw-Hill, 1961: 79–100. A sympathetic assessment of Bryan as secretary of state.

COLETTA, PAOLO E. "Bryan, Cleveland, and the Disputed Democracy, 1890–1896." *Nebraska History* 41 (March 1960): 1–27. Good analysis of the deteriorating relations between the two.

————. "Bryan, McKinley, and the Treaty of Paris." *Pacific Historical Review* 26 (May 1957): 131–146. Examines Bryan's role and concludes it was less than commonly assumed.

————. "Secretary of State William Jennings Bryan and Deserving Democrats." *Mid-America* 48 (April 1966): 75–98. Bryan and patronage under Wilson.

————. "William Jennings Bryan and the Nebraska Senatorial Election of 1893." *Nebraska History* 31 (September 1950): 183–203. Bryan's bid for the Senate.

————. "The Youth of William Jennings Bryan—Beginnings of a Christian Statesman." *Nebraska History* 31 (March 1950): 1–24. A study of early influences.

CURTI, MERLE E. "Bryan and World Peace." *Smith College Studies in History* 16 (1931): 111–258. A perceptive analysis of Bryan and the peace movement.

GARRATY, JOHN A. "Bryan: The Progressive." *American Heritage* 13

(December 1961): 4–11, 108–115. Assessment that points out the unfairness of sophisticated assessments of Bryan.

HORNIG, EDGAR A. "The Religious Issue in the Taft-Bryan Duel of 1908." *Proceedings of the American Philosophical Society* 105 (15 December 1961): 530–537. An examination of this still-debated issue.

HOUSE, BOYCE. "Bryan the Orator." *Journal of the Illinois State Historical Society* 53 (Autumn 1960): 266–282. An interesting analysis of the role of Bryan's oratory.

MAHNKEN, NORBERT R. "William Jennings Bryan in Oklahoma." *Nebraska History* 31 (December 1950): 247–274. Examines Bryan's relationship to a friendly, supportive area.

SCOPES, JOHN T. "The Trial That Rocked the Nation." *Reader's Digest* 78 (March 1961): 136–144. The trial in retrospect from Scopes's point of view.

SMITH, WILLARD H. "William Jennings Bryan and the Social Gospel." *Journal of American History* 53 (June 1966): 41–60. Sees Bryan as having much in common with advocates of the social gospel.

Index